above Beddgelert

A Wider Sky

frontispiece Ceri Ellis drinking maté

KW.

A WIDER SKY

KYFFIN WILLIAMS

First impression—1991

ISBN 0 86383 757 3

This volume is published with the support of the Welsh Arts Council.

Printed by J.D. Lewis & Sons,
Gomer Press, Llandysul, Dyfed.

For Shirley

ACKNOWLEGEMENTS

The most exciting and memorable period of my life was during my brief visit to the Welsh community in Patagonia, an experience that was made possible by the generosity of the Winston Churchill Memorial Trust. I must be one of the many who have benefitted from their enlightened sponsorship.

I must also thank the Headmaster and Governors of Highgate School for allowing me to desert them in order to travel to so distant a part of the world, and my assistant, Andrew Dear, who took over my duties and travelled to London every day from a far away village in Kent.

For seventeen years I have lived as a tenant of the Plas Newydd estate in a charming house on the edge of the Menai Strait. Lord Anglesey rebuilt the house for me and ever since he and Lady Anglesey have been concerned for both my artistic and everyday welfare, providing me with a haven of peace in which I can continue my work as a painter. I will always be very grateful for their kindness.

Miss Eiluned Rees of the National Library of Wales read my manuscript and suggested the title of this book, while the institution itself has always been most helpful to me. The North Wales Arts Association has given me continual support and Mrs Margaret Ungoed Hughes deciphered my eccentric handwriting, made many useful suggestions and patiently created reason out of chaos. To these and many others I owe a considerable debt.

CONTENTS

INTRODUCTION

If I refer to this book as an autobiography I am not being entirely accurate, for in reality it is a selection of stories about different parts of the world and some of the fascinating people I have encountered. Never in this, nor in my previous volume *Across the Straits*, have I ventured to express any views on philosophy, religion or society. Such opinions, even if they might be illuminating, would inevitably introduce an element of seriousness and destroy what is, I hope, just an easy and uncomplicated book. I hope my memory has allowed me to be as accurate as possible and that I have not made too much use of a lively Celtic imagination.

I believe that our minds are like large and capacious buckets into which the memories of all our experiences are thrown. Our earliest fall to the bottom and are stored there for ever, while, towards the end of our lives, so great is the accumulation, that our more recent memories cannot be contained and have an infuriating habit of slipping over the rim to vanish, seldom to be recalled. As I have an unusually vivid memory, I have never felt the need to keep a diary, but from time to time I have committed to paper some of the more amusing and interesting moments of my life.

Even though my life has been enriched by my many friends it has, nevertheless, been a lonely one for, because of my epilepsy, I have always been an observer looking into the real world and sensing that I was not part of it. I had never intended to be a painter but was advised to take up an artistic life on the advice of the medical profession. As an artist I began to train myself to use my eyes, and the more I looked at the world, the more I began to see and perhaps to understand. As a race, the Welsh are obsessed by people and are intrigued by them. I hope that this book will show how I share this obsession.

In *Across the Straits*, I told how my great great great great grandfather, Wmffre ap William ap John ap Rhys, became a wealthy man after finding a crock of gold in his smithy in Anglesey. A knowledgeable local historian told me that it was a good story but one that had been created to account for the fact that my family had suddenly become wealthy, that Wmffre was not a blacksmith and that there never had been a crock of gold. I was disappointed but not convinced that my story was inaccurate until one day, as I was looking through the book of the pedigrees of north Wales families, I saw something that previously I had overlooked. I noted that Wmffre, who was born in 1661, had married, as his first wife, Catherine Meredydd, born in 1593, so if they had been married when he was twenty, his bride would have been eighty-eight years of age. Evidently he had found a crock of gold and had married her, for she came of a wealthy family. She lived for a further ten years and then Wmffre married Margaret Prydderch, and I am descended from that union.

When I wrote *Across the Straits*, I had little idea of the many kindly letters I would receive after it was published. I had written how two elderly cousins, dressed like nuns, used to wander round the back-streets of Shrewsbury after darkness had descended, picking up those whom they believed to be fallen women in an attempt to save them from a terrible fate. I received a letter one day from a very old lady who wrote that one of my cousins had come across her wandering around the streets and had arranged for her to take up domestic service with a kind old couple in the town. She stressed that she had never been a fallen woman but had merely been locked out by her father, a waggoner, who always bolted his door before nine o'clock of an evening. She also wrote that her mother had worked, as a girl, for Lady Eleanor Butler and Miss Sarah Ponsonby, the Ladies of Llangollen.

Agnes Hunt, the orthopaedic pioneer, was a distant relative, and in 1884 she emigrated, with her mother and ten brothers and sisters, to Australia. Their plan was to buy an island on the Great Barrier Reef in order to breed Angora goats. In my book I wrote how they had failed to find anywhere suitable, and how eventually they had been forced to return to Shropshire. One letter I received was from Brisbane, and the writer informed me that it was a pity that they had returned as an 'Angora Billy' had recently been sold for forty-thousand dollars.

The opinions I expressed about my housemaster at Shrewsbury

School were hardly flattering for he lived in a world of his own, inhabited by youthful heroes striving to win games for the honour of their house and housemaster. I heard from a fellow pupil that, as the Eighth Army was locked in combat with the Afrika Korps and as Spitfires and Messerschmidts endeavoured to blast each other out of the skies, a soldier from the Field Post-Office wormed his way across the sand, postcard in mouth. It was from our housemaster and it bore the brief and tragic message:

'Lost second House swimming, but Stevenson was absent.'

It was possible that had this cryptic message fallen into the hands of the enemy, it might have been deciphered in such a way that the whole course of the desert campaign might have been altered.

The attitude of the world of art towards me and my work has been interesting, for art authorities have always looked upon me either as the outsider that I am, or as a maverick on whom they have been unable to place a label. This situation has been entirely beneficial for me as I have been able to stand aside and develop my own work without having to worry about the pressures that are put upon so many artists. In this book I have not written about this extra-ordinary world obsessed with the pursuit of genius, the creation and exploitation of a possible genius, or the financial rewards that await those who are able to persuade the experts that they have indeed discovered a genius. This fascinating and often unpleasant world demands another kind of book from mine.

Apparently, *Across the Straits* brought pleasure to many people. Perhaps this was because our memories tend to be selective, so that the more unpleasant moments become obscured and the happier remain clear. Nevertheless, I failed to mention that, whilst attached to the Headquarters of the Royal Welch Fusiliers in Wrexham in 1939, I came across three unusual and impressive lance-corporals. Their names were Jack Hawkins, Andrew Cruickshank and André Morel. They were older than their fellow recruits and had already established themselves as serious and talented actors, but success in their profession could not have been noticed in their attitude to their comrades for they were always kind, courteous and more than willing to do anything that was asked of them. When off-duty they entertained local people by reading from plays in which they had acted.

At one time, early in 1940, I had attained the dubious distinction of being appointed Temporary Messing Officer in the regimental barracks. Every week a Mess meeting, at which I presided, was held in the dining hall. I was assisted by Staff Sergeant Whalley, the senior non-commissioned officer in charge of the kitchens. He was short and rotund, a man of few words that when uttered were alarmingly comprehensible. One week, as was usual, the several companies sent an elected representative to air whatever grievances had arisen concerning the food. I noticed that Lance-Corporal Cruickshank was representing Number 2 Recruit Company and when his turn came to speak, he addressed us in the well-modulated tones of a professional actor.

'Sir,' he began, 'I have been talking to the lads, and we all feel that we would like to partake of a glass of milk and meringues at eleven o'clock every day.' Out of the corner of my eye I could see that Staff Sergeant Whalley's demeanor was verging on the apoplectic as Lance-Corporal Cruickshank continued,

'Yes, sir, and some fresh fruit would be appreciated.'

I suggested to my Staff Sergeant that they were very reasonable requests but the man of few words was unable to produce any at all. The face of Lance-Corporal Cruickshank wore the most genial of smiles.

There have been unhappy moments in my life but I see no reason for dredging them from the mental congestion in my own personal bucket. When I look back on my life the glories of past summers are more memorable than the storms.

1

I suppose I was half in love with my cousin Gwen. Tall, beautiful, high-spirited, and apparently without fear, she led a wild, outrageous youth, flirting, captivating, ensnaring and often destroying, for as well as being glamorous she could also be ruthless, as many an admirer had learned to his cost. One more dangerous ingredient was added to the complexity of her personality, and that was almost unlimited wealth.

Her father was my cousin Owen, a kind, professional gentleman who had served in the Royal Flying Corps and later in a cavalry regiment. Owen was good-looking and tolerant but, in trying to do the right thing throughout his life, had only succeeded in doing nothing.

The cause of this failure was certainly his wife Brenda, a ponderous, unattractive heiress who believed that everything could be achieved through the spending of money. I suppose she was right, for she bought her husband out of the army, and I came to the conclusion that the only way she could have gained her four children's affection was by paying for it. I remember her as a heavy, lethargic woman, permanently sunk into the depths of a comfortable chair, occasionally plucking, with fingers encased in knuckle-dusters of diamonds, the expensive chocolates that nestled in a large box beneath her ample bosom. Brenda was always demanding food, fun and attention and her husband was always at hand to obey her every wish. Servants were not prepared to tolerate her constant demands, so the long-suffering Owen found that he was expected to cook, to clean and to drive one or other of the Rolls-Royces that graced their garage. One day, he rebelled and drove away to Torquay. Brenda called in the police and he was escorted home.

It could hardly have been a happy home for their children as they were brought up to believe that fun was the most important thing in life and that it could readily be bought. Horses, cruises, yachts, cars and parties dominated their lives, while education, scholarship and any form of culture were ignored. Clothes were bought if they were expensive, while works of art were never bought at all. Consequently, at the age of eighteen, Gwen had very little sense of values. She had already run away from home because of some youthful obsession with a local man and had eventually been discovered by a policeman as she was out riding on the Sussex Downs. She duly horse-whipped him but did not have to appear in court. When this escapade was over, her high spirits made her act as a driver for a gang of men who illegally smuggled sheep from one county to another. They were apprehended and this time she did appear in court; the men were found guilty but Gwen, expensively defended, wept into a small silk handkerchief while putting on such a convincing show of innocence that the jury acquitted her. Little did they know that they had inspired her to embark on a life of romantic and dramatic litigation.

With this undisciplined background, it was surprising that she was allowed to join a part of the government that had established itself at Blenheim Palace, near Oxford, but family connections, and the fact that she had been presented at court, may have told in her favour. Gwen, and the other girls who worked with her, lodged in Keble College and it was there that I first met my fascinating cousin.

It was 1941 and I had just been invalided out of the army with the surprising advice that I should take up art for the good of my health. As most men were in the armed forces I was able to get a place in the famous Slade School of Art that had left London to join the Ruskin School in the Ashmolean Museum, which was only a short walk from where Gwen was lodging. I saw much of her and, like many others, began to be captivated by her very considerable charms; but soon I realised that, to her, I was an endless source of amusement as I related humorous Welsh stories that seemed to give continual entertainment to her friends.

It was not long before I realised that Gwen was becoming some sort of Zukeika Dobson in the scholastic life of Oxford and I found, to my embarrassment, that I was being courted by numerous young Oxford undergraduates who believed, erroneously, that I might ease their way into the heart of their beloved. Not only were the students enamoured of Gwen but also members of the armed forces stationed nearby, and one ardent captain of artillery, whose family made sporting guns, provided me with cartridges which, in wartime, were difficult to obtain. Many were the times that I was invited to meals at the Oxford Union, meals that I consumed with relish, for at the time I was considerably impoverished, yet with guilt as I knew that I was incapable of helping them in their amorous pursuits.

Gwen regularly attended the debates, sitting on the balcony swathed in white furs and apparently nodding to selected members as if to suggest that they had been silent too long. She enjoyed her life in Oxford and I enjoyed her exhilarating company, even the unbelievable stories she told of her life in a world of wealth. She said she had been given her first book of signed blank cheques at the age of eighteen. She related remarkable stories of the strength and bravery of her younger brother David of whom she was immensely proud. Once she told me how, when he was in the navy, his ship had visited Naples. Apparently, he had been attacked by a drunken Italian in a back street; a knife had been sunk up to its hilt in his stomach, but David, holding it there with his left hand, had knocked out his assailant with his right. Years later, while dining in an expensive restaurant, I asked David if this had been true.

'Just like Gwen,' he replied, 'a typically garbled version.'

'What really happened?' I asked.

'Oh, I killed him,' said David.

Suddenly, and without saying goodbye, Gwen disappeared. Soon I was to hear that she was to marry a naval lieutenant who commanded a motor torpedo-boat and who was stationed opposite Gwen's family home at the mouth of the River Dart. I don't remember being invited to the wedding but heard later that it was an unusual occasion; the captain of artillery had burst into the house and locked himself in a bedroom from where he had made his presence known to all by keeping up a loud and continual wailing.

I liked the torpedo-boat lieutenant and always enjoyed seeing him when he and Gwen moved to a large house in Surrey, but after a few years I realised that she was getting bored. I also sensed that the marriage might not last very long. When they moved to a farm in Devonshire I felt that new surroundings might relieve her boredom, and one day I received a letter asking me to stay there. Gwen met me at Newton Abbot station, looking as well as I had ever seen her and told me that she and I would be joining the South Devon Hunt on Dartmoor the next day. She told me what fun it would be and that she would provide me with an excellent hunter. I noticed that she never enquired if I was a competent horseman. At the farm, her husband showed concern for my well-being in the hunting field and tried to persuade me not to risk my neck in such a way. As husband and wife argued, I felt that it would be better to risk death than to be despised by my cousin who, being a beautiful rider herself, was contemptuous of those who were not. One problem was that I had nothing to wear, but this was solved by Owen, a stickler for correct proprieties in the hunting field, who volunteered to lend me bowler hat, breeches, boots and everything that made me appear correct, even if it did make me look an idiot.

The next day it was bitterly cold and sleet blew horizontally across the moors. About thirty brave huntsmen and women met above Totnes, and Gwen, top-hatted and riding side-saddle on a magnificent bay, was the focus of everyone's attention. Only the lieutenant looked in my direction and I discerned an element of pity in his eye. The huntsman blew his horn and soon a fox, that had hidden for sanctuary in a thick carpet of heather, was leading the hounds into the teeth of a bitter north-east wind. My horse was obviously keen on hunting and galloped in pursuit. I soon came to the conclusion that it would be better if he took control and that I merely concerned myself with staying on his back; and this I contrived to do as we charged through farmyards, plunged into valleys, splashed through brooks and avoided the jagged rocks that littered the face of Dartmoor. My bowler was blown away, and occasionally I lost my stirrups, but after a frantic half an hour the hounds checked and I managed to stop my energetic mount. As we waited for the hounds to pick up the line again I saw another bowler nestling in the heather. I dismounted and found that it fitted me even better than Owen's. Respectable again, I galloped after the hounds that picked up the

line in the valley below. The brief halt had given most of the field an opportunity to make their way home, for the sleet had been followed by menacing flurries of snow; but, before me, I could see Gwen and I knew that not yet would I be able to seek the comforts of a village hostelry. Gwen and I, a farmer mounted on a powerful grey, and the hunt servants were the only ones who remained of the thirty riders at the meet. I sat tight and prayed until the fox, tired of the chase and unwilling to expose himself to the fury of the storm, dived into a large earth in a wood above the village of Winchcombe. We left the fox safely underground and, with relief, made our way to an inn about two miles away. In front of me rode Gwen and the farmer, and I gazed with surprise as she brought her horse close enough to him to enable her to put her arm around his back and place her face against his shoulder. As he trotted away up a lane I asked her why she had appeared to be so enamoured of him. She looked at me with incomprehension as she replied with some vigour: 'Good Lord, I don't give a damn for him. I just want to buy his horse.'

In spite of her genial husband, the hunting and the lovely land of Devon, Gwen had become bored, so she left with her children to start life again in a Berkshire village where she had bought an attractive house. Once again I became involved in her affairs as I continually received passionate telephone calls from her admirers. The most ardent were a millionaire owner of a well-known brewery and a naval commander who owned a castle in Austria. It was obvious that both were deeply in love with her and, one day, Gwen asked me which of the two she should marry. I replied that the very fact that she had asked me meant that she did not really care for either. I suppose that the idea of living in an ancient castle above the Inn valley was irresistible, so she chose the Commander.

In the summer of 1953 she met my plane at Innsbrück looking radiant. As we left the airport a huge officer on a motor-cycle ordered us to follow him to the police station. Surprisingly, Gwen did so and soon we were in an office being interrogated by an inspector who asked her why she had ignored the speed limit in every town and village in the Inn valley. Gwen must have decided that her

salvation lay in flirtation, for the inspector was smiling broadly and laughing as she explained that she didn't want to keep her cousin waiting. All seemed to be going favourably until the inspector's voice took on a firmer note when he said he would have to confiscate her car. Immediately, Gwen's manner changed from that of a seductress to that of a virago. Never would she allow such a monstrous imposition and she demanded the presence of her Innsbrück solicitor. A young Austrian appeared; matters were sorted out; there were more smiles and handshakes and we drove out of the town and along the Inn valley. Once again, she must have broken every speed limit in every town through which we passed. Suddenly, I saw in the distance a magnificent castle with a tall Roman tower. Gwen told me that it was her home and it was my first sight of Schloss Wolfstein.

Gwen drove upwards through woods and stopped below the formidable tower. Through a huge door beside it came the tall figure of the Commander, a man of about six foot five inches and weighing fourteen stone. He was accompanied by two Irish wolfhounds. He greeted me as if he was hailing a ship at sea, and he and Gwen took me through the great door to look down to where bridges crossed the two courtyards below. In every corner of the castle were sets of rooms joined together by Gothic cloisters hung with heads of deer and chamois. I was told that a stag with a turnip in its mouth meant that it had been shot on the estate. On the second floor on the north side was the *halle*, a large room where we were served our meals attended by pretty Tyrolean girls dressed in the costumes of the district of Branderberg of which the Commander was the Protector. Through a door at the east end of the *halle* was the chapel and hanging over the altar was a superb figure of Christ on the cross,

carved by Veit Stoss, one of the greatest wood-carvers of Europe. Many times later was I to enter the chapel to wonder at that magnificent work of art, but I doubted whether Gwen had any idea of the spiritual beauty that emanated from it. In one corner was a frame enclosing a faded piece of green cloth on which it was just possible to see the head of a man. Underneath it was an ancient handwritten statement by Pope Gregory to the effect that he believed this to be the original veil of St. Veronica. I was told that it had become an object of veneration and pilgrims came from far and near to gain spiritual strength from it.

The castle gave me the impression that it was a happy place. Gwen was full of good spirits, the Commander boomed with good humour, the pretty maid servants smiled continually, while charming little dark-brown squirrels raced along the passages and hung from the beams in the bedrooms. Nevertheless, I never liked the *halle*, or the tower where I once slept. At the foot of the stairs were portraits of Ignatius Loyola and Francis Xavier but they did little to protect me from the sinister bedroom in which I stayed for two sleepless nights.

Schloss Wolfstein had once been the home of the Emperor Maximillian and many of the stags and chamois adorning the rooms and cloisters had been shot by him in the days of the crossbow. Financial troubles had caused him to hand over the castle to the Fuggers, the powerful banking family, in exchange for a long-standing debt, and it had been the bankers who had removed the Veit Stoss from the church in the nearby town of Schwartz to place it above the altar in the chapel of Schloss Wolfstein.

The Commander gave the impression of being a simple, bluff naval officer but I soon realised that this was an incorrect interpretation of his character, for I found him to be a lover of the visual arts and deeply interested in all the technological and political developments that were occurring in different parts of the world. Consequently, he was never dull and was always eager to expound his thought-provoking theories, many of which I felt he put forward so that I could demolish them. One of his most engaging characteristics was his ability to react immediately to any situation, something he must have inherited from his father, an admiral who commanded the British Naval Forces in Germany at the end of the war. One day, it was reported that a barge laden with dead bodies of Jews had been washed ashore. The Admiral immediately ordered a German field marshal, who was the senior officer in the district, to meet him on the barge, and together they looked down at the reeking cargo.

'Damn you,' roared the Admiral, 'you are responsible for that.'

The Field Marshal stood rigidly to attention, his baton firmly on his hip. Gazing with little interest at the bodies, he turned to remark to the Admiral:

'I don't understand what you are worrying about. They are only Jews.' He had hardly finished speaking before the Commander's father had snatched the baton from the Field Marshal's hand and had brought it down with all his strength onto his Teutonic head. Unconscious, the Field Marshal fell to join the corpses in the depths of that terrible barge.

To react immediately to a problem is not, in my opinion a Welsh characteristic; we tend to let our minds wander through several mental sieves before coming to a conclusion. For this reason we are often thought to be devious, although I believe that the word 'subtle' is more suitable. In the company of the Commander I often wished I had his directness and immediate mental confidence.

In the early 'fifties French forces still occupied the Austrian Tyrol so the Commander felt that it was his duty, as Protector of Branderberg, to invite the senior French officer and his family to lunch at the castle. A cheerful French general, his wife and son, wearing the uniform of the French Air Force duly arrived, but because of the inability of either family fluently to speak the other's language, the verbal exchanges over the lunch-table could hardly have qualified as conversation. In a valiant attempt to break the deadlock, the Commander congratulated the airman on the *Croix de Guerre* that emblazoned his chest and enquired how it had been won. The young man appeared to be embarrassed and attempted to change the conversation. Doggedly the Commander persisted, pointing out that they had all been in the war together and shared the

same enemy. As it was obvious that he demanded an answer, the Frenchman, in halting English, explained that he had been serving in the Lebanon and had been ordered to bomb some British destroyers that were operating off the coast. 'What!' roared the Commander, 'you were in that ruddy little plane that sank me. I didn't know you were going to attack me.' With this broadside he threw himself back in his chair and roared with laughter until tears ran down his cheeks. His guests were horrified with the revelation and totally unable to understand the light-hearted reaction of their host.

Eager that I should take advantage of the magnificent Tyrolean landscape, the Commander decided to act as my guide and chauffeur. Together we drove around the mountains, down the valleys, beside the rivers and lakes, through the villages. He was surprised and rather shocked that the only object I selected to paint was the signal-box beside the station in nearby Jenbach. Although it is undeniably beautiful, the landscape of the Tyrol hardly inspires an artist because the altitude does not create a subtlety of light. The lower slopes of the mountains are covered in an uniform blanket of dull-green conifers, while the rock above has all the dull attraction of an elephant skin. Compared with the hills of my native Wales, the mountains of the Tyrol led me to believe that they had only recently been quarried.

The highest mountain to the north of the valley was the Sonnwendjoch, and the Commander decided that we should climb it and that I should paint the magnificent view from its summit. He knew that my health had been far from good, and so he insisted on carrying my paints, my easel and my canvases; and no amount of argument would deter him. Throughout the long climb through the woods that clothed the lower slopes of the mountain, the Commander bent low under his burden. It was early in the morning and the air was still cool. I wondered how he would feel when the sun had risen from behind the mountains. When finally we reached a hut in the meadows above the trees, he threw himself on the rich green turf and, weary from his exertions, was soon asleep. The sun on his face woke him and together we set off for the summit. I noticed now that he allowed me to carry my canvases. Looking down from the slippery grass slopes and the soft warm rock, I could see, far below me, the silver sheen of the River Inn as it meandered through the valley towards Kufstein. To the south the mountains were mainly fir-clad but to the west the Stubai Alps, hard and bare, ranged themselves in rows towards the Vorarlberg and Switzerland. I could gaze with wonderment at the world around me but the Commander, like a weary pack-horse, could only see the ground as he dragged himself upwards. When we reached the summit, he threw my paints and easel to the ground and collapsed into a rocky garden of alpine asters and forget-me-nots. To the sound of his snores, I put up my easel and painted a very indifferent picture of the mountains of the Winterreis that lay before us, and through which we had to make our way before descending to the valley of the Achensee where Gwen had agreed to meet us in her car. As I finished my work the Commander, with glazed eyes and a crimson complexion, staggered to his feet. Once again we set off, but this time I was carrying my paints, my easel and my canvases, and was fearful that at any

moment I might have to carry the Commander as well. And so we stumbled silently across the wilderness of mountains above the Inn valley, for my companion by this time was inarticulate. Gratefully we began to descend through the trees to where the Achensee lay below us, and there, on the side of the road, the Commander collapsed in a heap murmuring that he was surprised that I still appeared to be so energetic. Tactlessly, I told him that I was used to climbing as I had spent my youth hunting foxes in the mountains of Caernarfon and Meirionnydd. He looked at me with uncomprehending eyes as we waited to be driven back to Schloss Wolfstein. I did not see the Commander the following day and word came from Gwen that he had stayed in bed. She smiled conspiratorially.

The day after he had recovered from his ordeal, he and Gwen attended an Anglo-Austrian ball in Innsbrück which took place yearly in the largest hotel in the town. Gwen must have looked particularly attractive for an Italian Count made numerous attempts to get her onto the dance floor. Eventually she accused him of trying to cadge drinks and suggested that she might partner him when he was sober. The Count immediately left the hotel to ponder on how he might repay the insult. The next day the telephone rang in the castle with a message from the manager of the hotel to say that the Count had purchased his cellar and had instructed him to deliver the contents to Schloss Wolfstein. Horrified, the Commander made a frantic dash to Innsbruck; there was a confrontation; there were apologies and handshakes and, finally, an invitation to stay in a *palazzo* in Milan. Revenge was sweet for the Count who, knowing that the Commander and his wife were no lovers of opera, had booked seats for them every night at La Scala, while he enjoyed himself in the night-clubs of the city.

The fact that I was a painter meant little to Gwen, but what she did appreciate were my stories of Wales and an ability to make reasonable caricatures of people. Consequently, she appointed me to the position of castle jester, begging me to entertain the many guests who came to stay. The arrival of her parents caused me most alarm. Brenda had provided a considerable amount of money to modernise the Schloss, so she felt that it belonged in part to her. She sat heavily in the *wohnzimmer* and bawled for attention, which invariably she received. She demanded that we played games, and the fear of her tantrums if she lost made everyone co-operate in contriving her victories. Once, Owen, stupidly or carelessly, managed to win a game of scrabble. A storm of petulant ferocity struck the castle. Brenda screamed with rage and in spite of her considerable bulk she managed to convey herself with surprising speed to her suite at the north-west corner of the castle, where for twenty-four hours she raged, while the long-suffering Owen provided occasional bulletins on the state of mind of his wilful spouse.

In many ways Gwen resembled her mother. Brenda had managed to end Owen's life as a professional soldier while Gwen had married the Commander on condition that he left the Royal Navy, in which, as the youngest lieutenant-commander, he had prospects of attaining a high rank. Both Brenda and Gwen fell into moods of

depression, but whereas Brenda's moods were initiated from an inability to get her own way, Gwen's defied explanation and were therefore the more dangerous and incomprehensible. It was not long before I concluded that my beautiful cousin suffered from some type of schizophrenia. Her three children accepted her strange behaviour and when Gwen disappeared for a day or two they appealed to me to entertain them with outrageous stories. This I managed to do as I have always had a wild imagination. The favourite story was about a fierce animal known as a Wiener-schnitzel that lived on the top of the Sonnwendjoch. I related how, in the evenings, it came down from the heights and hunted small furry rodents called *himbersaft* and *apfelsaft*. When they began to lose their fear of him I told them that his real name was Cyril and this seemed to increase their affection for him. Sadly, they listened as I related how a Herr Wurst of Vienna made an expedition and, using baited *himbersaft*, contrived to capture the luckless Cyril, so that he could exhibit him in a Viennese menagerie. This tragedy so impressed itself on their youthful minds that when I returned for my yearly visit, there was an immediate demand for the story of Cyril the Wienerschnitzel, and even if I had forgotten any part of that truly fatuous story, they certainly had not.

Life was luxurious at Schloss Wolfstein and all needs were catered for, as Gwen, when she was not in a depression, was a superb hostess. The only thing missing was a swimming pool and this was an omission they had decided to rectify. The site selected was below a memorial to His Apostolic Majesty Franz Joseph and there, amongst the rocks and fir trees, the workmen gathered. Firstly, the *schlagermeisters* came to fell the trees. Cheerfully they threw themselves into their task, talking the while in endearing terms to the mighty conifers, for the ancestors of these men had inhabited the forests for generations and appeared to consider the trees to be almost human. When the *schlagermeisters* had finished their work, it was time for the *sprengmeisters* to follow them. These more professional and less rustic men bored holes in the rock, filled them with powder and caused explosions that rocked the ancient castle. Finally, the pool was excavated and miraculously filled with water that had its source in the hills above. It was a great success for we could hardly have bathed in the muddy pool that lay below the castle walls, where huge pike and carp swam in wary circles.

The guests were indeed curious. I was surprised that a Scottish naval chaplain had agreed to stay as he appeared to have a pathological hatred of all Germans. To be driven by him down the Inn valley was an experience, for every time he saw a car that came from the Fatherland, he put his head out of the window and roared, 'Get out of the road ye dirty stinking Hun.' I believed his thinking to be singularly unchristian but decided to stay silent for fear that he might turn against the Welsh. An American admiral arrived with his wife from the Deep South. They taught me how to shoot craps and explained that negroes were not yet human. One evening they returned to the castle in a fury. They had been held up outside the town of Schwartz by a large American army convoy. The Admiral told us that after blowing his horn ineffectually for about half an hour, a coloured top sergeant had leaned on the window of their car and, jabbing the Admiral's mid-riff with a huge black finger, had said, 'Less of that. We guys is here to protect folks like you.' Never had such insolent words fallen on the ears of this Southern couple and the next morning they had gone. Diplomats, soldiers and barristers, these and many others came to stay at Schloss Wolfstein—also Mr Simpson with a wife who was the successor of the famous Wallis. It was all such fun and, for a brief period, Gwen was happy.

One summer, Gwen wrote to ask me to pick up the children in London and accompany them to the castle. She sent me their tickets for the plane from Heathrow to Zürich, together with other documents for the flight up the valleys and over the mountains to Innsbrück. On arriving at Zürich I was told that the tickets for Innsbrück were invalid and I realised that we would have to con-

tinue our journey by train. I telephoned the Commander and told him what time in the evening he could expect us. It was getting dark when the train drew into Innsbrück station. Gwen was there to meet us. She looked at me with hatred. No word was spoken on the drive to the castle and she disappeared before we had finished our supper. In the morning the Commander regretfully explained that it would be wisest if I left, suggesting some local hostelries that might suit me. I chose the village of Steinach in the Brenner and there I worked without enthusiasm, occasionally telephoning the castle to ask if it might be possible for me to join them. From the sad tone of the Commander's voice I knew that their marriage was far from happy and that he didn't want to inflict any of their unhappiness on me. Gwen had obviously become bored with the Commander, bored with the castle and bored with Austria. Sadly, I returned to London wondering if I would ever see my strange cousin again.

A year later the telephone rang in my lodging in Holland Park and, on answering, I heard Gwen's voice. She had bought a house in Ebury Street and wanted me to see it. I found Gwen looking cheerful, indeed triumphant. She had gone to India with the Commander after receiving an invitation to shoot tigers on the property of a rajah of their acquaintance. She told me that she had bagged the largest tiger to be shot in the Punjab since the war. The Commander, she added, had only shot a small one, and that she had decided to leave him there in order to return to London with an Indian doctor whom she referred to as 'Buddha'. Indeed, as she spoke, a dark and sinister man appeared and placed his arm in a proprietorial way around my cousin's waist. Gwen explained that her companion had been the Minister of Health in the first Government of the Republic of India. He beamed a crooked smile in my direction and I wondered when he had been sacked. As I returned to my spartan lodgings, I came to the conclusion that Gwen was dangerously unbalanced.

The excitement of litigation now filled my cousin's mind as she employed barristers to help her deprive the unfortunate Commander of money equal to that which her mother had expended on the rehabilitation of Schloss Wolfstein. A dramatic appearance in court drove her to a state of ecstacy and she must have performed brilliantly as the judge decided in her favour. Joyfully, she decided to have a party to celebrate but those invited, believing that justice had not been done, contrived to absent themselves. Gwen immediately decided to go privately and expensively into the Gordon Hospital, more, I believe, as a rest cure than because of a serious ailment. As the hospital was close to Victoria station, she decided to change her name to Victoria Gordon, and thereafter the number plate of her car carried the letters V G.

I saw Gwen frequently when she was in London and sometimes went to stay with her in the farmhouse she had bought in Sussex. It was there that she told me that she was divorcing the Commander and that the castle had been sold to an American named Klump. It became obvious that her health, both physically and mentally, was beginning to fail; no longer was there the usual excitement in her eyes and no longer was there a spring in her stride. The possibility of fun continued to absorb her and she never complained of any deterioration in her health; nevertheless, it was with surprise that I received a letter from her saying that she wished me to meet somebody special. The disastrous possibility of a third marriage came into my mind, so I telephoned her and said that she should not contemplate it. She didn't seem to be put out by my criticism of her private life but asked me to join her in Ebury Street so that I could meet her fiancé. When I arrived at her house, I was amazed to see, leaning on the mantelpiece in her drawing-room, the unmistakeable figure of one of the most distinguished of cricketers, a cavalier batsman who still held the record for the fastest century ever recorded in this country. He must have been forty years older than my cousin. He was certainly entertaining and charming but, sorrowfully, I could only think of the tragedy that would follow were they to marry. I felt I had to tell him that she was, in my opinion, schizophrenic, but on learning that her latest fiancé had served in the Royal Flying Corps with Owen, I considered it was her father's duty to give such a warning; but I feared it was a warning that Owen would never give.

The next day I telephoned her and tried to persuade her not to make the great man's life a misery. I asked her to explain why she wanted to marry him. Impatiently she replied, 'Can't you understand? I have never married an old man before.' They did marry and shortly afterwards they were both committed to hospital. Something terrible did happen but I never discovered the nature of the tragedy.

I never saw her again for she just disappeared from my life. One day I was told that she had died. She must only have been about forty-two years of age. I attended her funeral in a soul-less crematorium in one of the more dreary suburbs of south London. Owen was present but Brenda had stayed away, presumably because it would have upset her. Gwen's children were there and so was the great cricketer, but very few others bothered to say farewell to her.

The pursuit of fun had dominated Gwen's life but when, because of her failing health, such a luxury was denied her, she never complained. For many years she had allowed me to join her in an exotic world that was very far removed from the one into which I had been born. I had enjoyed her warmth and her vitality and to me these qualities always outweighed the flaws that contributed to her complex personality.

2

In 1941, as most men were being drafted into the Army, I was being invalided out of it. The medical authorities, after submitting me to numerous tests, had announced that I was abnormal and advised me to become an artist. I don't know which piece of advice worried me more. I did not like the idea of being abnormal and confided my concern to a lovely hospital Sister from County Kerry who, with glorious Irish logic, whispered:

'Ah, don't ye be worrying yerself about that. Ninety per cent of everyone are abnormal.'

I was able to resign myself to the diagnosis that I was slightly odd, but the question of whether I should try to become an artist exercised my mind considerably. Finally, I explained my problem to Professor Randolph Schwabe, the Principal of the Slade School of Fine Art and he, being a benevolent man, allowed me to enrol as a student.

It was not long before I realised that I was out of my depth, as my fellow students appeared so talented and I, in comparison, so pathetically incompetent. I knew that a long struggle lay ahead of me, and in this struggle I often found myself in the company of three students of curious and divergent character.

Tom Griffith was the son of a distinctly bourgeois Welsh father who, in an army hospital in the First World War, had met and married the daughter of a Norfolk squire. Out of the mixture of genes, Tom appeared to be distinctly Welsh and possessed of the sort of mind that has filled our legal system with mercurial Welsh lawyers: youthful and puckish, he deflated pomposity as if armed with a rapier and then, before the final plunge, perversely allowed his victim to escape. He was a talented water-colour painter and would-be *bon viveur*, but his Welsh nonconformist blood held him back so that invariably he was the onlooker and keen observer of the world around him.

Often I accompanied Tom on his visits to the Speakers' Corner at Marble Arch. He loved a verbal skirmish and selected his victims with discrimination. One day we stood before a soap-box on which an aggressive man was propounding the benefits of anarchy. Every time he thought he had made a clever point, Tom countered it with a shrewd and witty retort. I could see that the orator was becoming infuriated as his meagre audience began to cheer his persecutor. Suddenly he leaned forwards towards Tom.

'Shut up, you little squirt,' he hissed. Tom had won another confrontation.

Harold Carter was an unusually reserved student. Silently he slipped into the Ashmolean Museum where we worked and sat diffidently in a corner of the life class producing drawings that we were never allowed to see. There was something mysterious about him, and later I was told that his mother kept a Blackpool boarding-house and that his father was a north-country baronet. This latter bit of information might have been true, for he had a head of great distinction and nobody could have referred to him as ordinary.

The third, and the one who had most influence on me as an artist, was Maurice Wood who was, without exception, the most brilliant student during the three years I spent at the Slade. He had the most impeccable artistic judgement, was a brilliant draughtsman and possessed a remarkable sense of colour. He seemed to have everything and yet what talents he had been given were of little use as his parents were wealthy and Maurice was indolent. Bespectacled and with a head like a pea balanced on top of his lengthy, stooping body, he appeared to fascinate the girls who clung around him, anxious to do his bidding. Coldly he ignored them. Maurice never got up early enough to dash to the Ashmolean by nine o'clock in the morning to draw lots for an easel when a new pose was to be arranged, for he knew that if he turned up two hours later it was certain that there would be a girl only too willing to give him her place. Maurice would accept it as if of right.

I was very jealous of Maurice because of the devotion he inspired, and because of his talent. It was Maurice who opened my eyes to a world of beauty that I hardly knew existed. He made me aware of many things, for he knew the colour of a puddle, of a wet slate-roof or the deep shade of a chestnut tree. His eye was infallible and with Maurice as my mentor I began a long journey into the world of artistic perception. All this information he imparted with generosity, but in other things he turned out to be unusually mean. Once, when refusing to pay for a cup of coffee, he justified his action by telling me that my family had been wealthy in the past while his had not, and now that they too had plenty of money he was determined that they would not lose it.

Later I felt that all his energies had, perhaps, been directed to conserving the family fortunes and there was nothing left for the creation of works of art.

When, in 1946, I found that the urge to paint made it frustrating for me to teach six-days a week, the kindly headmaster of Highgate School suggested that I taught for only three days and asked me to find a friend to preside over the other three. I invited Maurice to join me and this he agreed to do: consequently he took a room in 12 Bisham Gardens where I lodged with Miss Mary Josling. I believe he paid his rent but I do not believe he did so with any good grace. When, one day, Miss Josling asked me to collect the shillings from the gas meter in his room, I found to my astonishment only a single coin in the unlocked tray. I decided not to inform Miss Josling, so when Maurice returned to London I told him to sort the matter out with her. A year later she asked me again to collect the money and yet again I saw the single shilling. I felt I had to tell her. She sat very still for a while and then a huge smile crossed her face.

'Do you know, Mr Williams,' she said, 'that must be the most energetic shilling in London.'

In spite of everything, I suppose the two years that Maurice and I taught together were successful. His lethargy was still enormous and many times I had to go to the school to supervise the first lesson because he had decided to stay in bed. He knew that it was unnecessary for him to teach, so he decided that the least amount of work he did the happier he would be; nevertheless, his influence was beneficial, for those boys who loved painting found in him a kindred soul who was an able guide for their youthful enthusiasm. They hung on his every word and were led happily into that satisfying world of beauty and of art appreciation.

After two years, Maurice had become bored and decided to give up his three days of teaching in order to lead a fuller life. Like all the others at the Slade, he had been encouraged to admire the works of Augustus John, Orpen and Wilson Steer, but naturally his preference was for the more exotic and exciting paintings of Cézanne, Matisse and Bonnard. France was where these artists could be seen at their best, so it was to Paris that Maurice travelled in the autumn of 1949, the address of Harold Carter in his pocket.

Harold was living in the Rue Daunou with a girl called Suzy Froment and it was to their appartment that Maurice made his way. Suzy was a lovely, generous girl from La Flêche in Normandy. Above her strong peasant body was a broad smiling face, two wide-apart eyes, a deliciously *retroussé* nose and a mass of fair undisciplined hair. She was eminently desirable and Maurice arrived to find to his delight that Harold had gone to London to collect the allowance that he received from his father. Every year he cashed his cheque, rolled up his ten-pound notes and forced them into one-pound tubes of Flake White paint, for he knew that, thus contained in lead, the device that detected any smuggled currency was rendered ineffective. Harold was no fool and knew that in this manner he would be able to take out more money from the country than was legally permitted. What he did not know was that in his absence Maurice had replaced him in Suzy's bed. Philosophically, as one who had always been buffetted by fate, he shrugged his shoulders and curled up in the kitchen.

Suzy had made her way to Paris in order to work for her famous aunt, Madame Suzy, who made expensive hats for film stars and the wives of ambassadors, the aristocracy and the consorts of the crowned heads of Europe. Sometimes the famous did not pay for their hats, believing that to be seen wearing a creation of Madame Suzy was payment in itself. Royalty never paid. One day the wife of a British ambassador brought to the salon the wife of Ernest Bevin, our Foreign Secretary. Great attention was paid to her and when her choice was made she opened her purse and, to the astonishment of the Madame and her staff, insisted on paying. Two days later the wife of the ambassador arrived to claim her commission.

After her training with her aunt, Suzy left to open her own business in the Rue Daunou and by the time Maurice had arrived to usurp the rights of his old friend, she had acquired a considerable reputation in France and in England. Maurice was a happy man for he had access to the great art of France, a delightful mistress, and lodgings for which he did not have to pay anything. He did not even have to cook, as Harold did that in exchange for his lodgings. While Suzy made her hats in the front room, Harold concocted extraordinary dishes in a bohemian room that served as both kitchen and wash-room, with a bath that was filled with cooking utensils, and a lavatory seat that was used as a chopping-board. It was in truth *la vie bohéme*. When he needed a rest and possibly a bath, Maurice returned to the room he had kept in Bisham Gardens and occasionally visited his parents in Torquay.

The happy *ménage á trois* would have continued indefinitely had not Suzy discovered that she was pregnant. The news came as a

happy surprise for Suzy, who thought that she was unable to have a child, and as a terrible disaster for Maurice, for he realised that for the first time in his life he was not in control of a situation and that money could not buy his way out of it. Terrified he returned to Torquay where his father agreed to stop his allowance so that Suzy could not benefit from the family wealth. Many were the times Suzy telephoned to me from Paris. Always she wanted to know where she might find Maurice, for it was obvious that she was not making many hats and that the bills were not being paid. Many times she was in tears as she cried into the telephone:

'I hate him, I hate him, but oh, what a lover.'

One day Suzy telephoned from Paris to tell me that she had given birth to a little boy and that she was going to call him Maurice.

I do not believe that I saw Maurice again. I wrote to him several times but never did I receive a reply. I suppose he considered me part of his past, a period of his life that he wished to forget. My last letter ended with the remark that if I did not receive a reply, I could assume death. There was no reply.

The tragic story of Maurice Wood reinforced my belief that talent in itself is a dangerous asset. He had all the ability that would have enabled him to be one of the most important figures in post-war art in Britain; that he was not was due to a tragic weakness in his personality. His talent was so much greater than mine and I was jealous of it, even though I need not have been. He taught me so much and, in spite of everything, I shall always be grateful to him.

Two years later, I, too, went to Paris and sought out Harold and Suzy in the Rue Daunou. They seemed to be happy and welcomed me into their strange dwelling. Harold told me that he wanted to marry Suzy and adopt the small Maurice, but for some reason she preferred to remain single.

I lodged in an unenchanting hotel near the Bastille but was often invited to dine in the Rue Daunou. The meals were eccentric, for whenever I arrived Suzy was sitting in front of a mirror with what looked like a bird's nest on her head. It was, in fact, a curious assemblage of material and pins and was the initial stages in the creation of a hat. Inebriated singing from the kitchen-cum-bathroom meant that food was being prepared. I decided not to investigate too closely. When Suzy felt hungry she shouted to Harold and, with the bird's nest still on her head, took her place at the table. Harold always seemed to emerge as if he was performing some music-hall act for, with a laden tray swaying above his head on his outstretched palm, he performed a delicate *arabesque* before placing our meal in front of us. Harold was a good cook and evidently enjoyed his wine.

One evening, after our meal, a dark, impressive woman came to see Suzy. She was Madame Mijouin. She and her husband lived in the top flat and used it as the headquarters of the Central Communist Cell of Paris. Monsieur Mijouin had spent the war in Dachau concentration camp and his wife had shared the same fate in Ravensbruck. The object of her visit was to invite Suzy and Harold to attend an important meeting. As Harold showed little interest, Madame Mijouin asked me to accompany Suzy. It sounded interesting and five minutes later, after Suzy had removed her bird's nest, I found myself seated at a table in a darkened room lit only by candles. Through a haze of tobacco smoke I was aware of many faces and I noted that they were all kindly. At the head of the table sat Monsieur Mijouin. He was a stocky and serious Paris taxi-driver and on his face were the marks of suffering. He rose from his seat when we entered the room and explained to his fellow members that I was a British artist and hoped that they would make me welcome. There was obviously no need to introduce Suzy. The meeting started and opinions were aired with vigour but without anger until I began to realise that a petition was to be sent to Monsieur Pinay, the French Secretary of the Interior, objecting to the sending of troops to Algeria. I watched with apprehension as a long piece of paper was passed along the table so that each member could sign it and realised that it would, eventually, be placed before me. The man on my right signed and then I saw it, huge and demanding, on the table in front of me. A pen was put into my hand and vague smoke-veiled faces gazed at me almost willing me to sign. I rose uncertainly to my feet and in unpardonable French explained,

'Monsieur Mijouin, mes amis, s'est tout a fair impossible pour me signer cette document. Je ne suis pas politique pour jesis seulement un peintre. Pardonner moi, mais c'est impossible.'

As I sat down I realised everyone in the room was clapping. Cheerfully they passed me a bowl of nuts and a glass of wine. Someone shouted, '*Vive I Angleterre*' as Monsieur Mijouin stood at the head of the table with a large smile on his face that made me wonder if it was inspired by my sentiments or my French. It was with relief that I passed the petition to Suzy.

I enjoyed my visit to Paris. I loved its style, its character and smell that made me aware that I was abroad. It was a smell that was not specifically of France but one that I have noticed elsewhere in Europe. Sometimes I felt that I was able to detect some elements of garlic, Gauloises and drains in the all-pervading aroma, but, whatever the composition might have been, I inhaled it happily as I wandered around the city, luxuriating in its difference. It was autumn and the leaves were falling off the trees on the banks of the

Seine. The lights were reflected in the puddles, and barges passed gently between the strong man-made walls that enclosed the most romantic water in Europe. Superficially, it was similar to the Thames and yet so different. As I walked across the bridges I sensed, for the first time, that I was in the larger world of Europe and was conscious that I came from an off-shore island.

I made drawings along the Seine, in the markets and up in Montmartre. I visited the Louvre and fell under the spell of Rembrandt's 'Bathsheba'. I can still remember the passion of Titian's 'Deposition' and I was deeply impressed by Courbet's 'Funeral at Ornans', but when I stood in front of the 'Mona Lisa' I was unmoved. Perhaps familiarity had bred contempt. In the Orangerie, it was Monet who made the greatest impression, for his work appeared to go beyond the bourgeois element in so much of impressionist work. I like to be moved and I was greatly moved by the paintings of Monet, Cézanne and Van Gogh in a way that I was not by the work of Renoir and Degas. I admired them greatly but I did not think that they would ever make me cry. These were my thoughts in the late 'forties and I do not think they have changed to any marked degree. I found that, compared with the paintings in the Orangerie, those in the Musée d'Art Moderne appeared to be too contrived and lacking in warmth. The world of the new art seemed to be one that searched the complexities of the mind more than the subtleties of nature. I found that I was impressed by Braque but not by Picasso, and that in the work of Marquet there was a continuation of all that was great in French landscape-painting. I hoped that he would not be the last in the great tradition.

Even though I could only afford to eat at the cheaper restaurants, I found Parisian food to be a delight. In one restaurant a waiter asked me if I had been in the war. Fully aware that I had played a less than distinguished part in that conflict, I nevertheless told him that I had served in Les Fusiliers Gallois Royales. At the word 'Gallois' his face became animated.

'*Gallois*. Rugby?' he asked.

'*Certainement*,' I replied, and then there followed a ridiculous swapping of names of those who currently were playing for their respective countries.

'Aha,' said the waiter, 'Cliff Morgan, *formidable*.'

'*Mais oui*,' I replied, 'Jean Prat *aussi formidable*.'

'*Peutêtre*,' went on my new friend, '*mais* Rhys Williams *aussi formidable*,' to which I countered yet again with:

'*Mais oui, et* Pomathios *trés formidable*,' and so we continued this amazing dialogue until we had named every player in both the French and Welsh teams. Eager to continue the conversation, he asked me where I lived. In order to answer him I had to ponder deeply, for in London I lived in Highgate village and I was not sure how I could translate this into French. Consequently, as I felt sure he must have heard of the great football club that had its ground not far from the bottom of Highgate Hill, I told him that I lived '*près* d'Arsenal'. Thinking that I had reverted into English, he cried:

'*Ma foix*; you play for Arsenal?' Excitedly he beckoned to all the waiters and they left their tables to stand admiringly around me.

Once again my waiter launched into a list of the names of the Arsenal players:

'Forbes,' he shouted, 'Forbes *bien formidable*,' but I was out of my depth and ignorant about the heroes of Arsenal. Nevertheless, I had heard of Forbes because he had a reputation for being the hardest man in the game, so with a: 'Forbes *bien, bien, bien formidable*,' I gave up the struggle and let them just admire me, the man who played for Arsenal.

Before I returned to London I had my last meal with Suzy and Harold. In the bedroom little Maurice gurgled contentedly and his mother asked me to send him to sleep with a Welsh lullaby. I cannot recall what I sang but it had the desired effect, or maybe he became unconscious out of self-preservation, for not all Welshmen have good voices. When I left it was with apprehension for the future of that little family.

I believe that the best landscapes have been painted in the countries where the land has been most fertile and, consequently, the most beautiful works have been produced by artists from France, the Low Countries and England. In countries where farmers have had to fight their unresponsive land, few landscapes of great merit have emerged. In Italy, Canaletto, Guardi and Bellotto painted the towns, and in Spain the Cretan El Greco's 'Toledo' must be its greatest landscape.

France is a land much loved by its people. Perhaps it is the loveliest in Europe for it appears to have everything—great rivers, beautiful valleys, extensive forests, magnificent mountains and an exciting coastline, so it is not surprising that its artists have produced such wonderful work. France is a land that has been painted by artists from other countries and I have visited it many times.

I have worked in Celtic Brittany and have painted and drawn the stones of Carnac. Further south in the Dordogne I have painted among the hazel forests and along the banks of the river from which the area has taken its name. South of Bergerac I stayed in the village

of Loubes-Bernac, in the wine-growing region of the Côte Duras. It was the picking season and in the countryside a madness had striken the local men as, with an almost religious zeal, they swarmed over the grey and sticky land dragging cartloads of grapes behind decrepit tractors, and staining the narrow roads with the strong red blood of the vine. Since I have been a total abstainer for fifty years, the whole exercise appeared to be one of obsessive futility, and the accuracy of my judgement was confirmed when I was told that the wine produced was the worst in France. Ten miles away was the land of Montbasillac and I remembered how Suzy, many years before in a Paris restaurant, had leaned across the table and said with a wicked smile, 'Kyffin, if ever you want to have your way with a girl, give her Montbasillac.'

The Pyrenées, the Haute Savoie and the Medoc, all these places I have visited and painted. In Bordeaux I had an introduction to a firm of wine exporters. The son of the chairman drove me around the vineyards in a magnificent Peugeot car. He was a confident young man and as he drove he named the many *chateaux*. In one lived his uncle, Phillipe, in another his sister, Marie, and there were others who were in some way associated with the family. We passed down an avenue of poplars and stopped before yet another *chateau*.

'And this,' he explained with pride, 'is where I live.'

He went inside, soon to emerge with a beautiful riding habit. He told me that it belonged to his mother who was the master of a pack of buck-hounds and asked me if I would deliver it to a tailor in London as it was in need of repair. As we drove away I congratulated him on his motor car.

'Ah, yes,' he explained, 'I married the daughter of Monsieur Peugeot.'

I have always loved the Romanesque and have visited Vezelay, Moissac and Conques. It took me longer to appreciate the Gothic. At Chartres I stumbled into the darkness of the cathedral and imagined that it was filled with huge white cyclamen. As my eyes became accustomed to the light, I saw that what I had thought to be white petals were in truth the head-dresses of a party of nuns.

I have never been excited by the *chateaux* of the Loire, but in one of them a guide pointed to a single fire-dog cast in the image of an old man with a beard and he told us that nobody had ever discovered where the other might be. I could have told him, for it stood outside the front door of our old family home in Anglesey.

Not many members of my family had visited Paris but, in the early years of the nineteenth century, those who had become wealthy through exploiting the copper mines of Anglesey had journeyed there on business, with the result that the bottoms of the French men-of-war were sheathed with Anglesey copper. It is possible that at the Battle of Trafalgar all the ships of the British, French and Spanish fleets sailed proudly with sheathing that had its origin in the earth behind the small Welsh town of Amlwch. Thomas Williams, one of the wealthier members of the family, had visited Paris in 1831, and it was there that he had his portrait painted by Sir George Hayter. It is a magnificent character study of a conceited and sensuous man and it had once been attributed to Delacroix. At one time it hung in my studio in London, and girls who came to have their portraits painted invariably asked me to remove my relative from the wall for they said that they did not like the way he looked at them.

Several of my relatives were artists, and in the 1870s my cousin, Fanny Ramsay, had studied in Paris under the great French teacher Bouguerreau; but in 1949 I was unaware that I was to become a serious painter. I was still conscious that I had been told to take up art for the good of my health and not because I had talent; so I wandered around the streets of Paris in some sort of an artistic limbo, not knowing if anything I produced was of any merit and uncertain of the direction my future might take.

Many other friends and fellow students could not resist the lure of Paris for in the 'fifties it still retained its position as the centre of the world of art; and still boasted a vigorous school of representational painting. Andre Minaux was the accepted master while others, like Rebeyrolle, Guerrier and Ginette Rapp, were popular artists; but the most popular of all was Bernard Buffet. Buffet had immense talent and had wasted it in an apparent desire to make a fortune, and his work, that in his youth was so brilliant, became shallow and facile. Nicholas de Staël, an artist of genius, had only recently killed himself, leaving Manessier as the leader of the abstract painters of France. America was yet to force its way into the leadership of the art world.

Into this fascinating world came Edouardo Paolozzi, an Italian from Leith in Scotland. I met him at the Slade after the school had returned to London, and remember him as a large unsmiling man who seemed not to approve of traditional values, referring disparagingly to those who did as 'greengrocers'. Edouardo had a dominating presence and his work had a distinctive Italian flair. I always believed that if fifty artists were given a lump of clay and told to heave it out of a plane at five hundred feet onto the tarmac runway below, Edouardo's lump would land in the most attractive manner. Success came early to Edouardo, and when Suzy came to London with her creations, Mrs Edouardo Paolozzi was on her list, together with the name of Lady Louis Mountbatten.

Edourardo was a poor boy from Leith, and Raymond Mason, a friend from my days at the Slade, could hardly have had a more

privileged background in Birmingham, where I believe his father was a taxi-driver. Raymond had always suffered from asthma, an illness that caused his departure from the navy. He joined the Royal College of Art in Ambleside whither it had been evacuated at the outbreak of war. I understand that Raymond's brief spell there caused the staff to consider whether it might be wiser to risk the bombs in London, for his excess of good-natured energy shattered the peace of the small Cumbrian town. There was no wickedness in Raymond, only a zest for life, but this was not understood by the Royal College who duly passed him on to the Slade in Oxford. Raymond was a large, well-built man with a strong face and black, wiry hair. Like Edouardo he had a presence and we reckoned that we had a future artist among us. If Raymond had misbehaved in Ambleside, in Oxford, a place more used to youthful exuberance, he conducted himself with propriety, working hard and joining in the student life of the school.

One day he arrived at the school with a tall, bearded and balding Swede and a French girl who smoked a pipe. They were Harry Blomberg and Mimi, and from then onwards the three were inseparable. Here we felt were three true artists, for they dressed like artists and behaved like artists; their work, if immature, was also distinctly artistic. When they left the Slade they exhibited together, advertising themselves with huge posters that they put up all over the West End. Suddenly, they vanished and I heard that they had left for Paris.

I think it must have been Tom Griffith who told me that he had run into Raymond in Montparnasse where he was living with a Chinese girl and enjoying life in a city where, for the first time in his life, he found himself to be free of asthma. Occasionally, Raymond returned to London to hold an exhibition in a well-known gallery. He had become a sculptor, a social commentator and in canalising his energies had become a successful artist. Raymond had found himself and a home, and I doubted if he would ever return to England.

I never returned to Paris but Tom Griffith went there often and always visited Suzy and Harold in the Rue Daunou. I understand that Suzy had given up making hats as she was unable to make and sell enough to keep Maurice, but they still lived together while Suzy studied to become a teacher. One day Tom telephoned to say that she was in hospital with tuberculosis and that Harold had returned to England. Later, however, I heard that she had returned with Maurice to her home in La Flêche and it was there that she died.

3

At Christmas-time in 1949 I returned home to Wales a sick man, for my epilepsy was making life very difficult indeed. I asked my doctor if he could arrange for me to be looked after in a hospital and he found a place for me in an institution in the Midlands. The authorities did what they could and, considerably better, I returned to my lodgings in Highgate with instructions that I should not teach for a year. A holiday in new surroundings was suggested and that is why, in February 1950, I crossed the channel for the first time on my way to Rome.

I travelled as a pilgrim, for it was Holy Year, and in my baggage was a document, known as a *tessera*, that enabled me to travel in Italy and visit their art galleries at a greatly reduced charge. Even though I am not a Roman Catholic, I travelled with no sense of guilt for I was so confident in the business acumen of the Vatican that I believed that they would be making money out of me.

I stayed with friends near the British School in the Via Giulia. The spring had come early and already I was aware of the sweet scent of mimosa. There was blossom on the trees and a different and exotic smell in the air. My senses, accentuated by my illness, devoured the novelty and what was to me a new world. Unfortunately, there was an unavoidable difficulty. The doctors had prescribed a drug that produced as a side-effect a total inability to see anything when the sun was shining on it; consequently, at times, the pavements, the buildings and the river Tiber disappeared into a vivid and disconcerting glare.

I awoke on my first day in Rome to find an overcast sky and thunder in the air. My knowledge of Italian was restricted to the two words *'basta'* and *'troppo'* which meant 'enough' and 'too much', and thus linguistically equipped I set out to cross the Borghese Gardens to discover the delights of the great city.

The sky was blue black and a thunderstorm struck as I was near a small classical chapel. I ran towards the porch to avoid the downpour and noticed that a road-sweeper was already sheltering there. Together we watched the vivid lightning and the torrential rain, and in a break between the deafening claps of thunder he turned to me and asked if I came from England. When I replied that I did his eyes lit up with joyous expectation. '*Mama mia*,' he cried, 'and do you know Ivy Bushell?'

When I disappointed him with my reply he told me that he had been a prisoner of war and had worked in Shropshire for a farmer who had a very beautiful daughter by the name of Ivy. On being repatriated, he had never forgotten her and had tried to get news of her from everybody whom he thought might have come from England. It was as well that he knew some English, for my *troppo* and *basta* would not have helped him much in his search for his beloved. The storm ended and the thunder died away as I bade farewell to the romantic road-sweeper. The sun came out and burst onto the wet roads, the dazzling pavements and into my eyes. Cautiously I felt my way down the Spanish steps into the Via Babouoni and in the darkened sanctuary of a coffee bar, I learned the difference between a *capuchino*, a *cafe grande* and a *cafe late*. Already my vocabulary had increased to five Italian words. I managed to return to the Via Giulia after visiting a barber's shop where *troppo* and *basta* proved to be invaluable.

The next day I visited the British School, a strange institution slumbering under the ill-mannered direction of a Roman archaeologist. It had been founded with funds made available after the Great Exhibition of 1851 in order to give scholars the advantage of working in what, at one time, was the cultural centre of Europe. Young painters, sculptors, engravers, musicians and archaeologists won places in the school for periods of one to three years and there they were supposed to study, but a stupefying aura of lethargy hung over the place and I wondered if I too would have had my creative faculties made blunt had I been able to win a Rome scholarship. At that time I was fully aware of my artistic shortcomings and knew that I would not have stood a chance against the cream of the art schools of Britain. I met many of the scholars. Brian Kneale was

painting brilliant little pictures in the manner of Sickert: Bill Price, from Swansea, drew impressive cartoons with all the skill of a young Russell Flint; and David Smith, the son of a deck-hand on a Lowestoft trawler, painted with amazing vigour and industry. Stephen Dodgson appeared to be the only musical scholar.

It was David Smith whom I came to know best. In his youth he could have become a pianist or an artist, for he was equally talented in both disciplines. He decided to become an artist. When war broke out he joined the Royal Air Force and, confined in the nose of a bomber, made drawings from the air of the devastation of Berlin. While on an air station he had fallen in love with a pretty aircraftswoman, had pursued her on a bicycle from airfield to airfield and finally had married her. When David painted in his studio, his wife taught the children of British diplomats stationed in Rome.

It was with David and Libby Smith and an archaeological student that I visited Orvieto. The town is built on a plateau lying on the top of natural geological walls of pink rock above a green saucer-shaped valley. In time of war it must have been impregnable. We stayed near the magnificent cathedral in a small hotel that was covered with morning glory. In the daytime, when the sun blazed down on the light stonework, the town became invisible, so I stayed inside the cathedral and enjoyed the frescoes of Luca Signorelli. When night came I sat under an archway on the side of the *piazza* and painted the west front by moonlight. We returned to Rome on a Sunday night and when I visited the British School two days later, David's studio was already full of pictures of Orvieto, painted from the many drawings he had made during the short weekend. Even if he was no longer in the Royal Air Force, his motto still appeared to be 'Per Ardua ad Astra'.

I tried to paint the city of Rome from the Janiculum but the brilliance of the light made my task almost impossible. A small Italian boy watched me with a patience that soon ran out. Excitedly, he snatched the brushes from my hands and attacked the painting himself. Further criticism came from Count Barbizetti da Prun, an officer in the Italian Navy. At the end of the war their fleet was so reduced in number that many officers were temporarily put in reserve and had to find other ways of employing their time. The Count made pots in the Via Babouoni and led a happy life in Rome. One day he asked if he could see my pictures, and when I showed them to him he burst out laughing.

'*Un vero Inglese*,' he cried, '*Tutti umbro, tutti umbro*.' They were certainly *umbro*, but I was sure that an Italian would have made a similar criticism of the work of any British artist in Rome.

One day I decided to visit the Vatican galleries. At a counter I handed in my *tessera* and after it had been stamped I crossed a hall to where a lift was about to ascend. Two *carabinieri* with swords blocked my way. I avoided their weapons and pushed my way into the lift where a group of people were waiting patiently to ascend. Pandemonium broke out: the *carabinieri* shouted to the man who had stamped my *tessera*; the bystanders shouted; the people in the lift shouted, and it seemed as if only I was silent. Suddenly, the *carabinieri* shrugged their shoulders and the lift doors closed. As I stepped out into the galleries, an American woman touched me on my shoulder whispering:

'I guess you didn't know what all that was about.' She felt it was her duty to enlighten me. 'Pilgrims walk up the stairs,' she said.

When my friends in the Via Giulia returned to London, I moved into a *pensione* near the Pantheon, owned by two venerable brothers. They attended to their visitors with great benevolence but on Sundays they indulged in their weekly blood-letting. Dressed in heavy military coats, protuberant breeches, huge leather boots and swathed in cartridge belts, they mounted a fragile scooter and, with their guns pointed vertically and with a terrified cross-bred spaniel wedged between their ample bodies, they roared away down the streets of Rome and into the surrounding countryside to bring death to the sparrows, blackbirds and thrushes of the *campagna*. In the evening they returned flushed with success, the tattered bodies of a few small birds in their shooting bag. After dinner they celebrated with a glass of wine and I joined them with my inevitable glass of orange juice. As I understood them to say that on one glorious day they had bagged a snipe, I attempted to tell them that an Anglesey relative had been wagered £365 that he would not shoot three hundred and sixty five snipe in three hundred and sixty five

consecutive shots. I told them how, picking his shots carefully, he had won his bet. Although I had increased my Italian vocabulary, I was still incapable of any normal conversation. Consequently, the two old men came to the conclusion that I myself had performed this memorable feat, so for the rest of my stay I was treated with unwarranted deference. Sometimes my habit of endeavouring to speak more of a language than I could understand resulted in my becoming some sort of a hero.

I drew in Frascati, Nemi, Tivoli and near the Pope's Palace at Castel Gandolfo and painted a picture on the battered sea-front at Anzio. I was beginning to feel that my illness had been a blessing.

When I left Rome it was to go to Venice. At the end of the eighteenth century, my family had made such a large fortune out of the Anglesey copper mines that they had built a mansion on the Thames near Marlow and bought houses in Berkeley Square and in Venice. The Venetian house had long been sold and I never discovered in what part of the city it might have been.

I found a bed in a youth hostel in which I discovered that all the wash-basins and light switches were about two feet off the ground. I was told that in term time it was an infant school. The beds were of a normal size and in them slept a remarkable cross-section of the human race. There were Frenchmen and Yugo-Slavs, an African, who went to bed with a large knife strapped to his pyjamas, a permanently somnolent Guatemalan art historian, several Americans, and an English youth who, every night, shattered the peace of the dormitory by bursting drunkenly through the door, cursing the fact that he couldn't find the light. Roaring 'God, what a bloody fug', he used to stagger between the beds and fling open the windows with such a clatter that even the heaviest sleeper awoke. It said much for international goodwill that nobody threw him out.

A British frigate was anchored off the Giudecca and every morning I awoke to the sound of 'A Life on the Ocean Wave'. Later in the day I watched the sailors as they wandered sadly and impecuniously down the alleys, gazing at unattainable objects in expensive shop windows. They must have felt envious of the seamen from the American cruiser *Baltimore* who strode confidently from shop to shop laden with gifts for their families at home. One day, as I painted near the Salute, I realised I was being watched by a sad-faced mariner. When I asked him if he was enjoying Venice—'Blimey, give me Chatham any day' was the reply.

I was happy in Venice for, even if it was difficult for me to see properly in the strong sunlight, inside the churches and galleries I fell under the spell of Venetian Art. I had always loved its exuberance and lack of inhibition and now I was able to see some of the greatest paintings in the world. Although he may not be greater than Titian, Giorgione or Veronese, Tintoretto appeared to me to be the epitome of the vigour of Venetian Art and I felt certain that his 'Crucifixion' in the Scuola di San Rocco was one of the greatest pictures ever to be painted. His work is so imbued with nervous energy that my own neurotic system seemed to react to it immediately as if electric impulses were passed through me. Carlo Crivelli is another Venetian I love for there is a similar passion in his work, but because he painted before the secret of the oil medium

came to Venice, he, unlike Tintoretto, was unable to indulge in its sensuousness.

I could have stayed longer to enjoy the luxury of great art for in spite of my inability to see in sunlight, I was amazed at the light of Venice when the sky became leaden and the buildings rose silver above the light-grey water. It might not be the average memory of Venice but it is the one I took away with me after this my first visit to what I felt must be the most beautiful of all cities.

I had not driven a car for twenty years but in 1960 I believed that it was time that I did. I knew that my 'grandmal' attacks were controlled by drugs, so I set about the task of persuading the doctors that I was fit to drive. This was not easy and it was only through the intervention of a medical friend that eventually I obtained a licence. A wider world was now open to me and after buying a small Austin van I prepared, once again, to visit Italy.

I crossed to Calais and drove over the northern plain of France to spend my first night at Epinal in the Vosges. I had chosen this route because I wanted to see the Isenheim altar-piece by Grünewald in the town of Colmar. It surpassed all my expectations. The lacerated, blistered, plague-ridden figure of Christ manages to retain its dignity in spite of its putrefaction. This centrepiece, and all the other work that makes up the whole, made me believe that it must be one of the greatest masterpieces in Europe. I had yet to see the 'Night Watch' by Rembrandt. I have never seen Van Eyck's 'Adoration of the Lamb' or El Greco's 'Funeral of Count Orgaz', but I had seen Tintoretto's 'Crucifixion' in Venice and I am sure that the Grünewald is as great as any of these.

I crossed the border to Freiburg, in the Black Forest, and drove along the Bodensee, spending sleepless nights in vineyards bordering the lake. I thought that the war had been forgotten but thumps on the side of my van and cries of '*Schweinenhund Englander*' reminded me that, for some Germans, the memory lingered on. The north shore of the Bodensee is a lovely land with attractive towns, but nevertheless I was glad to cross to Austria to make my way south to Innsbrück, Kitzbuhl and Lienz to the Italian border. I crossed into the land where Titian was born and once again crossed the

causeway into Venice. I stayed near the Academia and every morning, as the sun was rising, I wandered across to Zateree to paint the sun as it rose above San Giorgio. My drugs had been changed so I was now able fully to enjoy the light above the *campanile* and its dancing reflections on the water near the Giudecca. I thought of all the great artists who had worked in Venice but tried not to remember their work. I found that an early start before breakfast was most necessary, for after ten o'clock it is not easy to work along the canals of Venice. I began to imagine that every Venetian father, when his children had reached the age of six, would take them aside and tell them to go away from under his feet, and go out to watch an artist at work. It must have been the advice of countless family men, for every time after the sun had risen high in the sky, I found that I was surrounded by innumerable little boys shouting, pushing, criticising in such a way as to make work impossible.

When I moved to Florence I was allowed to work in comparative peace. After the colour and richness of Venice, it appeared to be a drab, khaki-coloured city and the Arno a poor substitute for the Grand Ganal. I enjoyed the Renaissance architecture and decided that the Uffizi held a greater number of masterpieces than the Academia. I believed the greatest of these to be Boticelli's 'Birth of Venus', for I do not believe that any other work contains more poetry, charm and simple beauty; indeed, its very simplicity and lack of complication adds to its perfection.

One day as I returned to my *pensione* for lunch, the *signora* clutched my arm and with a voice of anguish told me that there was '*Multa, multa piove in Ingleterra.*' I understood that it had been raining in England.

'Oh, yes,' I replied as if I was proud of the fact. '*In Ingliterra in Augusta, multa multa piove.*'

She threw up her hands in horror and disappeared into the lower regions of the *pensione*. A few days later I realised that she had been trying to tell me about the Lynmouth flood disaster.

In the Church of Santa Croce, I watched a group of Americans studying their guidebooks. As I was unable to decide which of the frescoes had been painted by Giotto, I approached one of them and asked him if he could help me. He gave me a grin, prodded a large finger into the middle of his Florentine tourist travel book and whispered, 'These guys don't know nothing. They make up the whole damn thing.' Another church I wanted to visit was San Miniato al Monte. It is a Romanesque church with a complicated black and white façade built high above the wooded left bank of the Arno. I sat on a terrace above the graveyard and attempted to draw the lovely building, but the complexity of its proportions defeated me. Angry with my failure, I screwed my drawing paper into a ball and hurled it into the cemetery below. Immediate feelings of guilt made me follow it and I found it eventually lying on the top of a large flat tomb bearing the name Walter Savage Landor. I had painted on his property in the Llanthony valley without knowing that he was buried so far from home.

In the twelfth and thirteenth centuries northern Italy lived in a permanent state of war as city fought city and *condottieri* made

fortunes leading armies into battle. I always found it confusing as I never knew why states should dislike their neighbours so much. I knew that there were two main warring factions fighting under the banners of the Guelphs and Ghibellines, but I knew little about the reasons for their dislike of each other. I had a vague idea that Florence favoured the Guelphs but I wondered why because Guelph was the name of a German family. I also believed that the neighbouring town of Siena was on the side of the Ghibellines who were originally a German aristocratic party. I also knew that the Pope fitted into the complexity of the situation and I had read that the Holy Father, possibly with divine guidance, was prepared, from time to time, to change his allegiance from one side to the other. I felt that I should not favour the Guelphs alone so I decided to visit the Ghibelline city of Siena where I knew the art to be so different, a difference made all the greater by the animosity between the two cities. In the fourteenth and early fifteenth centuries, when Florentine artists were experimenting with perspective, it was vital for Siena to ignore such exercises, for it was undesirable to have been seen to be influenced by the enemy state. For this reason, the Sienese artists continued to create works that were more spiritual than intellectual.

The appeal of the city was immediate. Pink, brown and yellow buildings clustered together around several little hills that rose out of a plain, and at the highest point stood a magnificent Gothic cathedral with a tower and a distinguished façade, the whole rising in layers of black and white marble above an elaborate, stepped pavement. It was similar to the cathedral in Orvieto but of a more superb conception.

I discovered that I had arrived on the day before the *palio*, an eccentric horse-race that takes place twice a year on the cobbles of the main *piazza* of the city. The object of the race is to decide which department of Siena should have the honour of retaining a banner on which is woven the figure of the Virgin. The city was in a state of hysteria as the *piazza* was being prepared for the race. Straw was being laid over the cobbles and, in the centre, a fence was erected to keep the crowd away from the track. Against the walls of the houses that were built around the *piazza*, they had constructed tiers of wooden benches. These, I was told, were for the Americans.

Each department of the city had selected a horse and had also enrolled an experienced rider who was necessarily a man of courage and strength. It was a race in which no holds were barred; indeed, there was nothing to prevent one rider from striking another or from hitting a horse's head or body as a deterrent. I have always had a passion for horses and horse-racing, so I went to bed in anticipation of the traditional ceremony the following day.

In the morning the horses appeared in the streets and, accompanied by the riders in full armour, were led into the cathedral where they were blessed. Later I realised how much they were in need of a blessing. After the religious ceremony was over, the parade, led by a detachment of mounted *carabinieri*, wound its way through the town to the *piazza* where I had found a place in the huge excited crowd at the point where the race was to start. Into the *piazza* came the *carabinieri* and, behind them, parties of flag throwers representing the many departments of Siena. They were dressed in colourful, mediaeval costume and carried immense banners which

they hurled towards each other, allowing them to cross in the air above their heads before they were caught in their partners' hands. It was done with amazing skill and the higher the banners were thrown, the greater was the applause. Time seemed to be of little importance and the longer the procession took, the greater opportunity the performers had to show off their skills. As they disappeared behind the excited crowds filling the centre of the *piazza*, the armoured riders entered, proudly strutting before their mounts which, covered in exotic coats embellished with the arms of the faction they represented, were beginning to show signs of terror. Before the Palazzo Communale they stopped; the colourful coats were taken off the horses, and their riders, laying aside their mediaeval armour, strapped crash helmets onto their heads. Amidst mounting excitement they rode near to the place where I was standing. Two ropes were drawn tightly across the track, one level with the horses' necks and the other at their knees. As I watched I saw fear in the rolling eyes of the horses and wondered if they had been drugged. A lovely grey appeared to be more terrified than the others and, as I watched him, he reared and fell forward over the ropes, dragging them down and rolling onto the track. Immediately, the other horses fell forward kicking and squealing in a terrifying heap. Some rose to their feet and with or without their riders dashed around the *piazza*, to be caught at the far side by the *carabinieri*. As fights broke out, the injured riders, some unconscious, were lifted into the air, to be carried above the heads of the crowd and into the alleys that led away from the scene of the *mêlée*. Sickened by what I had witnessed I pushed my way through the angry crowd and wandered away to seek refuge in an empty church. Half an hour later, the roar of the crowd indicated that the race had started, but by that time it was of little interest to me.

That evening the supporters of the winning faction boastfully paraded around the city, with the banner of the Virgin above their heads. Shouting and singing, it seemed as if they challenged anyone to take it away from them. I heard the noise of fighting during the night but, when morning came, a gentle peace seemed to descend upon Siena. The *palio* was over for another year.

The ferocity of the horse-race was in marked contrast to the serenity of the paintings in the Pinacoteca. The artists of the Sienese School appear to have been more concerned with the creation of beautiful objects than with attempting to make remarkable illusions: consequently there is a timeless and simple loveliness about their work. As a school they came nearer to a spiritual manifestation of beauty than any other in Italy, but a stubborn refusal to admit any influence from outside eventually sapped its vitality; whereas Florence, alert to the energy of the Renaissance, continued to produce great work long after the School of Siena had passed into decadence. Nevertheless, names like Duccio, Simone Martine, Sassetta, Giovanni di Paolo and Matteo di Giovanni are only a few among those who made the name of Siena synonymous with visual perfection.

I will never be an art historian as I am absorbed with my own work, but as a perpetual student of art history I make my own judgement and if my opinions do not coincide with those of scholars and experts, that does not worry me. Opinions, I believe, are important, even if they can be proved to be wrong. Opinion is healthy; blind acceptance of what is stated to be artistic fact is not.

The nervous chemistry that is in the make-up of every individual makes us react differently to every work of art, so when I am more moved by Carlo Crivelli than by Vittore Carpaccio, and more excited by Tintoretto than by Veronese, that is because of my chemistry and not an assessment of merit. As an artist I am in the happy position of stating my preferences; it is not often that art historians can afford this luxury. Visiting the great centres of art, I make my own judgement: if I am told I am wrong, I am not worried.

The artist to whom I owe most is Piero della Francesca. Over forty years ago, while looking at a book on his work in the library of the Ashmolean Museum in Oxford, I turned to a page that showed a reproduction of his fresco of the 'Resurrection' in Borgo Sansepolchro. As the eyes of the head of Christ burned into my head, I found that I was weeping, and from that moment realised the importance of the spirit in art. I made a resolution that one day I would make a pilgrimage to see that magnificent painting. I drove to Arezzo where Piero had done some of his finest work and I remembered being greatly impressed by it but disconcerted, nevertheless, by the white patches of plaster that showed only too obviously the damaged parts. I believe it is the accepted thinking that such areas should never be restored as another hand would violate the individuality of a fresco. As an artist, my thoughts are of what the painter would think were he to see the marks of such deterioration. I believe such artists would like to see sensitive restoration, but in suggesting this practice I know I am in a minority.

Borgo, when I visited it, was a sleepy provincial market town of no great distinction, and it was with little difficulty that I found the Palazzo Communale, the building for which the fresco had been made. Initially I was disappointed in the work of art that had always meant so much to me and that I had come so far to see, for it was so much paler than I had expected it to be, and cracks that had obviously appeared only recently meandered across the wall. As I continued to look at it, the power that had impressed me years before, moved me once again, and the lack of definition was of little importance.

In Assisi the spiritual and the commercial clash to a greater degree than any other town in Italy. The small shops, laden with pottery, burden the visitor with an oppressive demand that they should be purchased. In the narrow streets, mugs, dishes and pots almost defy you to reach the Church of St. Francis unaccompanied by a newly acquired piece of Deruta ware. Any spiritual elation bestowed by the work of Giotto and Fra Angelico is dampened by a return through those soliciting streets. Venice, Florence, Siena, Arezzo, Borgo and Assisi, I had enjoyed them all, and yet there were many more beautiful cities and towns to visit.

There was a vague sense of autumn in the air, so I turned north towards the border. When a French customs official asked me if I had anything to declare, I told him I had nothing. He looked into the back of my van.

'No woman?' he enquired.

'No,' I said.

He shrugged his shoulders as a look of sadness crossed his face.

'*Quel domage*,' he replied.

4

I had never considered a visit to Greece and its islands but when I read that an Hellenic cruise catered for impecunious schoolmasters, I made further enquiries. I was told that if I was prepared to sleep lower-deck aft, a part of the ship which occupied an area below the kitchens and next to the screw, I would be able to make the voyage for sixty pounds. This seemed too good an opportunity to miss. Even though a classical education at Shrewsbury School had left me with an interest in ancient history, my intention was not to visit archaeological sites with the other passengers but to paint the surrounding landscape. I hoped the voyage would enable me to find an exotic place to which I could return at a later date.

The cruise became even more attractive when a medical friend from Conwy also decided to travel but, as he was to have a well-earned rest from his practice, he had no intention of sleeping in my nautical dungeon. He invited me to share his cabin in a more salubrious part of the ship.

I arrived at Victoria Station in mid April 1957 to find a queue of ancient men and women being organised by an energetic courier. As some of the men wore Panama hats, I decided that these were to be my fellow travellers. I joined the queue with the doctor and we boarded a train. On the journey to Dover I wandered along the corridor the better to assess the amateur archaeologists. A party of excited schoolgirls reduced the average age to about sixty, but most members, I assumed, were aged between seventy and eighty. Some younger men turned out to be either classical masters from Bradfield Grammar School or dons from Cambridge who were going to be our guide lecturers. By the time we boarded a ferry at Dover, I had gained some idea of those with whom I was going to sail away into the eastern Mediterranean. On the journey across France our initial reserve fell away and it was a jolly party that crossed into Italy to reach the port of Genoa as the sun was setting.

The *Acropolis*, a tidy little boat built on the Clyde, belonged to a Greek shipping-line and onto it we poured, eager with anticipation for the delights of the lotus-eating lands that awaited us. The lecturers were given the best cabins and the most comfortable of all was to be occupied by Sir Gerald Kelly and his wife. I felt that a talk by Sir Gerald would be most enlightening. As a young man he had been an artistic prodigy and, urbane and talented, he found himself equally at home in the art world of London and Paris. He became extremely successful as a portrait painter, but respectability and the praise of high society contributed to dampen his artistic energies. Eventually he became a member of the Royal Academy and finally its President. When King George VI and Queen Elizabeth came to the throne, it was natural that Sir Gerald should paint the State portraits. He set up his studio in Windsor Castle and found the royal wine so much to his liking that he decided to take as long as possible over his task.

One day, Sir Kenneth Clark asked if Sir Gerald was still in residence.

'Indeed he is,' replied the King with his gentle stutter, 'K-Kelly for k-keeps we c-call him.'

Finally the pictures were finished and hung in the Royal Academy. On the day of the private view the King and Queen and Sir Gerald stood before the portraits.

'Excuse me, sir,' said Sir Gerald remembering the excellence of the Windsor wine, 'may I please have just a few more sittings?'

'K-Kelly,' replied his monarch, 'I'd rather abdicate.'

I found that my Welsh doctor did not snore and that his cabin met all my needs. It was going to be a memorable odyssey.

By the time the *Acropolis* had tied up against the harbour-side of Naples, most of the voyagers had been introduced, and when the buses arrived to take them away to Herculaneum and Pompeii, they might have known each other for years. There was no sign of Sir Gerald.

From the boat I gazed at the iron-grey shapes of the warships of the American Fifth Fleet and at Vesuvius rising across the bay to the south. Ferries passed each other as they sailed backwards and forwards to Capri and Ischia, and tugs, with large brightly-coloured funnels, were tied up alongside the harbour. I have always loved harbours with their bustle and romance so, collecting my box of panels, my pack containing my paints and my easel, I went ashore to see if I could record the fascinating scene around me. As I was walking along the harbour-side towards some large warehouses, I heard the sound of running behind me and I turned to see a short elderly man pursuing me. Standing in front of me, he said that he would carry my easel. As it was comfortably wedged between my paints and my back, I replied that it would not be necessary. When I refused his offer for the second time, he became very angry indeed. Suddenly, he launched himself at me, snatched the easel from behind my back and, turning towards the warehouses, emitted a piercing whistle. Slowly and purposefully a dozen tall young men emerged from the shadows and advanced across the deserted harbour-side to contain me and my tormentor inside an impregnable circle. Nobody said anything and the young men merely looked down at me with menace. The threat was made all too clear. Finally the little man, brandishing my easel, shouted, 'I easel. You pay for it.' There was little I could say, so I showed them that my pockets were empty. I produced my wallet and showed them that there was no money in it. Finally, I let them see my book of unused travellers' cheques. At this moment I regretted that I had not gone to Herculaneum, Pompeii, Paestum or anywhere other than that threatening harbour-side. The gang were obviously divided as to what should be done to me but, eventually, they decided to accompany me to a *bureau de change* outside the harbour gates. I knew then that I was safe. Assuming that they would not knife me in such a public place, I changed a cheque and pressed a ten-*lire* note into the sweaty hand of the aggressive little man. Before he could recover from the insult, I had retrieved my easel and regained the safety of the *Acropolis*. After this experience I deemed it prudent not to show my face again in the city of Naples.

The next morning I rose early and stood in the bows of our boat. To the south lay the island of Sicily invisible in the morning haze, and, as I looked, a line of shining pink emerged. It was the city of

Palermo. Not wishing to risk a repetition of what happened in Naples, I joined the buses that were waiting for us on the quayside. Away through the streets we went and up into the hills behind to stop outside the cathedral of Monreale. Looking at the mosaics inside, I realised that we had broken through some sort of European barrier and were now in the mysterious south, the world of Greece, of Crete, and even of Constantinople. Great mosaics have always moved me and as I looked at the impressive figure in the apse above the altar, I felt there was a power there similar to that in the head of Christ in Borgo Sansepolchro.

Westwards the buses took us through strange villages of blue and white flat-roofed houses inhabited by swarthy men and cloaked women. This was bandit country and the infamous Guiliano was still at large. Through a gap in the hills I saw a honey-coloured building that appeared incongruous in that landscape. It was the Greek temple of Segesta. While the tourists wandered around it, I drew it from every angle and with urgency, for, so far, I had done little to justify myself as an artist. There were heavy clouds in the sky and as we returned through the mountains the storm struck. Torrential rain beat against the sides of the buses as we drove into a darkened Palermo and the welcoming *Acropolis*.

The ancient Greek city of Syracuse was almost invisible as our boat secured itself against the harbour-side. From under heavy clouds the rain beat down and defied us to visit the ancient sites, but led by our senior lecturer, Francis Kinchen-Smith, we staggered into the amphitheatre, straining our ears as the roll of thunder drowned his gentle voice.

That night the *Acropolis* emerged from the harbour into the teeth of a gale with the intention of reaching the north African port of Derna. All night the wind blew and all night the boat rolled and heaved and groaned, so that when I emerged from my cabin in the morning it was into a passageway that was deep in water. I noticed that out of the party of over a hundred people, only fourteen appeared for breakfast. Across the wild Mediterranean we sailed. There were lectures in the saloon; but all we learned was that we couldn't land at Derna because of the weather, and that we were going to Benghazi instead. We anchored outside the harbour and saw a small tug-boat emerging, forcing its way through the furious sea. At the wheel sat the figure of an African dressed in a magnificent blue uniform with gold epaulettes. He should have been black but had turned to an interesting shade of grey for he was being horribly sick. Around him in the wheel-house were several other impressively-dressed figures, while above, on the roof, as if not wishing to associate himself with those inside, was the figure of a man in a wind-swept raincoat, a flat cap on his head. The tug slowed down as it approached the *Acropolis* and the man in the raincoat produced a megaphone.

'Get oot,' he bawled, in a broad Scottish accent. 'Get oot and turn aboot. Ah will na have ye in ma harbour.' As he shouted, the man at the wheel lost control and his boat leaped towards us and crashed into our side. Pieces of wood fell away as he reversed, moved ahead again, rounded our stern and hit us from the other side. Realising that it would be unsafe to enter the harbour, our captain set out hopefully for Crete; but intercepting a distress signal from a cattle boat that was sinking off Sollum, he changed course and once more made his way through mountainous seas towards the coast of Africa. It became evident that the cattle boat had sunk so, avoiding Crete, the *Acropolis* ploughed through the waves towards the island of Rhodes.

On board the boat everyone was trying to be phlegmatic; the lectures continued and new friendships became firmer in adversity. I went to the bar to fortify myself with a glass of orange juice. The ship gave a gigantic oblique roll, chairs crashed against each other, glasses flew around as everyone was thrown onto the floor. I rose from off a small and crumpled figure. It was Sir Gerald Kelly. Proximity mellowed him, and when the bar had sorted itself out, we talked about the world of art and Paris at the end of the last century.

The next day, under a cloudless sky, the *Acropolis* entered the harbour of Rhodes. Without doubt we were in the Middle East. It may have been the contrast with the weather we had experienced, but Rhodes was an island paradise set in a calm and azure sea; small wonder that the Knights of St. John wished to defend it. Once again

we dived into buses to be driven westwards along winding roads to where the Acropolis of Lindos crowned a cliff above the sea. I asked the driver to stop at the top of the hill above the village and, carrying my paraphernalia, I got out and wandered away across a hillside that had been cracked by earthquakes. I put up my easel and painted the distant Acropolis as hoopoes dug for insects in the soil around me. In the village, I drew the priests and the donkeys and felt that that day in Rhodes had made my cruise memorable.

Piraeus, the port of Athens, was our next objective and in the morning I went with the archaeologists to the Acropolis and wondered why such beautiful buildings should have been succeeded by the architectural chaos I saw below me.

After lunch, I stayed behind whilst my companions departed for Delphi. Hoping that Piraeus would be less dangerous than Naples, I walked around the narrow streets above the harbour, finally to erect my easel in a road that dipped down to the sea. After I had been working for about an hour, a small, untidy and barefooted boy stood beside me.

'Beautiful,' he whispered. Thinking he was referring to my painting, I replied that, on the contrary, it was very bad. Once more and louder I heard the word 'beautiful', and again I made a firm denial.

'Beautiful, beautiful.' He was now shouting and obviously very angry indeed. As I did not reply, he spat and dashed away to enter the door of a house larger than the others in that miserable street. I stopped painting for a moment. I looked up to see him beckoning to several girls who were emerging through the doorway. Eagerly he lined them up in front of me.

'Beautiful,' he cried, and at last I understood. The girls he offered me began to smile and when they started to laugh, all the people in the street also started to laugh. When he saw me laughing, the small boy glowered viciously, spat and ran towards the harbour. As he disappeared a carnival atmosphere descended on that dirty little street.

Rhodes is an island that seems to encourage lethargy, but Crete is different, for it has an energy that seems to come from its tough geological construction; indeed, the names of their towns and villages are almost onomatopoeic and accurately reflect the mood that hangs over the island. Zeus could well preside over Crete from the heights of Mount Ida, but in Rhodes I could only think of Aphrodite. The Minoan civilisation conjures up thoughts of beauty as well as of despair and in Knossos the glory of their art is tempered by a deep and brooding sense of tragedy. Indeed, a tragedy struck our party, for an octogenarian member of the party disappeared into the depths of a Minoan sewer. His cries alerted us to his predicament and willing hands retrieved him.

To most amateurs the reconstruction by Sir Arthur Evans appeared to be totally satisfying but our professional classical lecturers thought otherwise and preferred not to accompany us on our visit. But they did cross the island with us to see the other great and unrestored Palace of Phaestos sleeping peacefully, or so it seemed, among the poppy fields below the blue-black shape of Mount Ida. I did not sense a similar peace at Knossos.

As the *Acropolis* sailed north towards Greece, we realised that Sir Gerald Kelly had not, as yet, given a lecture. He and his wife continued to occupy the best cabin, but no lecture had been delivered and none appeared to be arranged. The organisers were contacted, objections to his lethargy were aired, and we were told that approaches would be made to the great man. Finally, a message was passed around the boat that he would not lecture but would answer questions. We waited at an appointed hour and Sir Gerald entered. Hunched up in a small chair he replied sharply and without humour in a manner so different from the one that he had adopted when he charmed the British public on television. He soon showed signs of boredom and retired to his luxurious cabin. I felt that the stormy journey had been too much for him.

After the *Acropolis* had passed slowly through the Corinth Canal, Francis Kinchen-Smith talked at length and with great enthusiasm about Olympia, as we were on our way to visit the site of the ancient games. We anchored off the village of Katakalo and a

small boat ferried us to the shore. On landing, a large, dark woman stepped forward and spat at me. I presumed that she thought I was a German, for another woman had behaved in a similar way and, possibly, for the same reason in the hill town of Cordes, north of Albi. I had previously been spat at in Belfast and in a small village near Pwllheli, but on both occasions I had been mistaken for an Englishman. Nobody has spat at me for being Welsh.

The organisation was superb, for yet again buses appeared from nowhere to transport us through an Elysian landscape, finally to stop in a glade of ilex trees that shaded the ruins of a temple. The bees buzzed and a honeyed peace seemed to permeate the land.

Francis Kinchen-Smith led us over a land of fallen pillars to an amphitheatre and there, in his gentle voice, told us of the games. As he talked I saw another group of people approaching us, led by a very large blonde lady. Imperiously she marched up to our lecturer.

'*Aus, aus*,' she roared, 'I vant to speak.' And speak she did in a loud, teutonic voice that defied any attempt to stop her. As she bellowed, I saw one of our Greek guides moving stealthily towards our own lecturer with an electric megaphone in his hand. Conspiratorially he passed it to Francis Kinchen-Smith. There was a devastating noise; the German woman reeled backwards, angrily shouting that it was not fair, and then furiously drove her audience before her into the distant groves.

Our cruise was almost at an end. We left the Peleponese and turned northwards towards Venice, passing between the islands of Corfu and Ithaca. It had been decided that the last dinner on board was to be a special occasion during which a poem, written in heroic couplets, was to be declaimed telling of our eventful odyssey. Three classical scholars were sought and Sir John Wolfenden and a master from Bradford Grammar School agreed to help. A third poet was needed and, as it had become known that I had been to Shrewsbury School, I was ordered by the organisation to fill the vacant place. I never had been a scholar; indeed, I had found it difficult to get out from the jungle of the Lower School where I had suffered much magisterial disapproval. My usual punishment was the compulsory copying of hundreds of lines from Pope's 'Odyssey', written in heroic couplets. So often was I forced to write out these lines that I found it easier to make them up rather than copy them from a book. As no master ever read what had been written I had managed to get away with it. Now, as the *Acropolis* sailed up the Adriatic, my classical education came to my aid and I completed my task with considerable ease. When I got up after Sir John Wolfenden, nobody could tell that the verses I recited had been written by a scholastic failure.

Later that evening a farewell concert took place. In the otherwise empty saloon, the archaeological lecturers and the schoolgirls were singing 'Clementine' in Greek and I was trying to accompany them on the piano. At about midnight the doors burst open and in came the pyjama-clad figure of our senior organiser:

'Stop, stop,' he shouted, 'Sir Gerald can't sleep.'

One of the distinguished archaeologists stopped singing. He looked seriously at the angry man. 'Bugger Sir Gerald,' he said.

We berthed in Venice in yet another downpour. The city was awash in a state of *aqua alta*. Disheartened we climbed into a train.

Throughout the night it carried us across Italy and France to the port of Boulogne, there to board the ferry to Dover. At Victoria station we bade farewell to each other muttering unconvincing promises to maintain our friendships formed on that most unusual odyssey.

5

Before I went to Holland I had presumed that the flowering of Dutch Art in the seventeenth century was due to pride in new found nationhood and the wealth of its merchants. A visit in 1965 made me realise that there was another factor, and this was the wonderful light created by the proximity of the North Sea and the canals and lakes that cover so much of the land.

I had crossed from Harwich with a party organised by Godfrey Pilkington, the owner of the Piccadilly Gallery in London, and a member of the wealthy family that made glass at St. Helens in Lancashire. He must have realised that, for him, life as an industrialist would have been immeasurably boring and, consequently, he decided to follow the profession of his mother's family and become an art dealer. I suppose the excitement of discovering works of art and the exhilaration of competition with his fellow professionals appealed to his exuberant nature and made him an excellent companion who often amused me with his stories of the darker side of the art world.

Godfrey, his wife Eve and his sister Elizabeth, had hired two motor cruisers in order to explore the canals, the villages and the towns of Holland, and we arrived at the village of Oud Loostrecht to take over the boats that had been given the unattractive feminine names of *Gratje* and *Gretje*. I was put in the *Gretje* and shared a tiny berth in the stern with a small boy of about eight years of age. The space available for two bodies was made even smaller because of my paints and canvases.

Godfrey, at the wheel of the *Gratje*, led the way across the small lake and entered one of the canals. His sister, who was apparently an expert on launches, followed him in the *Gretje*. It was the beginning of a memorable holiday during which Godfrey was going to mix business with pleasure, and often, on seeing a telephone-box on the tow-path, he would leap ashore to contact New York or Milan in order to make some advantageous deal. It was very exciting and the more so when I had mastered the subtleties of steering a motor cruiser in the congested waters of a Dutch canal.

With little trouble we eventually reached Amsterdam and disembarked to visit the Rijksmuseum and to eat at an exotic East Indian restaurant. This appeared to stimulate Godfrey to such an extent that he insisted on conducting us through the interesting red-light district of the city. But soon, disasters were to befall us.

One small boy fell overboard and the other, who shared my cabin, came out in spots, and chicken-pox was diagnosed. Then Eve, attempting to jump ashore whilst moored against a village tow-path, lost her foothold and disappeared into the dark and foeted water between the *Gratje* and the landing stage. We watched as her dark hair came to the surface, accompanied by a most noxious odour, for we were not far from the out-pouring of the village sewer.

The next misfortune descended upon us as we approached the town of Monikendam, when I was at the wheel of the *Gretje*. Godfrey, in the lead, sounded his hooter to notify an official that we

wished to pass under his massive iron swing-bridge. It opened and the *Gratje* passed through. I was about to do likewise when I saw the great iron structure swinging back to its original position. I put my engine into reverse but to no avail; the canal authorities were pumping out a polder and my boat could not make any movement against the flow of water. When I gave the order to abandon ship, even the small boy with chicken-pox obeyed me, but I, believing that captains were supposed to go down with their ships, stayed in the wheel-house and waited for the inevitable. At the moment of impact I threw myself on the floor as, with a deafening crash, the superstructure was carried away and deposited in the waters of the canal. Covered in glass and splinters, I lay on the deck of the stricken boat as it drifted helplessly under the darkness of the bridge until it emerged into the daylight to bump gently against the tow-path. A crowd gathered and the police were summoned. Eventually, a gigantic policeman pushed his way through the small crowd of curious onlookers. Over his blue shirt he wore a leather cross-belt and a revolver was strapped to his waist, while covering the lower part of his legs was a pair of well-polished jackboots. He was a formidable man.

'What is your name?' he asked in poor English.

'Williams,' I replied.

To my amazement his face became friendly as he said in Welsh: '*Cymro 'dach chi*?' and I replied that indeed I was a Welshman.

'*O ble 'dach chi'n dŵad*?' he continued, and I told him that I lived in the village of Abererch near Pwllheli in Caernarfonshire. I am not sure why I gave him this information because it was not quite true, for I had left there a few years previously to return to Anglesey. However, it was lucky that I did because he became most excited as he told me that he had served in the Royal Dutch Commandos and had been stationed near the village of Abererch during the war. I told him that his commanding officer had lodged with my mother, and when he heard this it became clear that there was nothing that he would not do to help. He instituted an immediate court of inquiry as to the cause of the accident and very soon he had proof that the bridge-keeper was at fault. He helped us to contact the owner of the

Gretje and while we waited for the boat to be repaired, he regaled me with stories of Wales and of the police force in Holland. I asked him if there was much crime in the district.

'Yes, yes,' he replied, 'my chief of police he sleep with a prostitute and when he wake she lies with a knife in her back. How do you say it in English? Is it not "compromising circumstances"?'

When the wheel-house had been fished out of the canal and replaced on the deck, the *Gratje* and the *Gretje* set forth once again, as my friend, the only Welsh-speaking policeman in Holland, waved us farewell.

We moored that night near a pretty village, but as we went to bed we heard the heavy engine of a barge coming nearer and nearer, until with a slight jolt we realised that it had tied up alongside. Its proximity was made the more obvious because of the nauseating odour that emanated from it, and closer inspection revealed that it carried a cargo of liquid manure. There was no way of escape so, stoically, we resigned ourselves to a very long and unpleasant night.

Early in the morning the barge cast-off and with relief we heard the engines fading away into the distance. When we followed after an hour or two, a very different odour enveloped us from over the high banks on either side of the canal, but this time it was a fragrance of unbelievable delicacy for we were passing through invisible fields of hyacinths. I have always loved the scent of flowers and, in a manner that is most un-English, have often been seen to indulge in the joy of smelling them. The memory of those hyacinths has remained with me and, at times, I am able to recreate its perfection.

Having navigated the dangerous North Sea Canal we returned to the lake at Oud Loostrecht, bade farewell to the *Gratje* and the wounded *Gretje* and set off for home. I had done about fifty water-colours and six oil paintings. I had painted on tow-paths, in towns, in the fields, and had wondered at the glory of the light. I liked Holland. I liked its people, and I decided that some day I would return.

6

Few people know that, at one time, Welsh was spoken in Edinburgh or that the earliest known poetry in the language was written there. The heroic poem, known as the 'Gododdin', written by Aneirin, tells of a band of three-hundred warriors who went south to fight the Saxons. In the neighbourhood of Catterick they were almost decimated and only one man returned to Edinburgh to tell the tale. We, the Brythonic Celts, ruled the land from the Straits of Dover to the land between Strathclyde and the Firth of Forth. Civilisation, as we knew it and as we had inherited it from the Romans, ended there, for in the mountains to the north-east lived the wild, mysterious Picts, while to the north-west our Celtic cousins, the Scots, were beginning to form their own kingdom. I had always been told that the only way the Romans were able to differentiate between their Pictish and Scottish prisoners was to throw a few *denarii* amongst them. The Picts never got any.

As a small boy, I had been told the story of my mighty ancestor, Howel ap Gruffydd ap Iorwerth ap Meredydd ap Mathusalem ap Hwfa ap Cynddelw. Since he was born in the twelfth century a similar relationship can be claimed by any Anglesey man, but somehow he appealed to me as one of my great eccentric heroes. His mother had been the foster-mother to the first Prince of Wales, so Howel, a man of tremendous strength, was brought up in the royal household and later, when his foster-brother became king, he travelled with him to the wars in Scotland.

In that wild and mysterious land, the king became a nervous and frightened man and demanded entertainment to distract him from the worries of his campaign. As the mists enveloped the royal army, he roared to his farrier to place before him a dish of one-hundred horseshoes; then he summoned his foster-brother and ordered him to break the shoes in his mighty hands. Two, four, eight, sixteen were snapped by the muscular Howel.

'More,' demanded the king, and soon one-hundred horseshoes lay broken at his feet. Deeply moved by a success that was in marked contrast to the failure of his armies, he ordered Howel to kneel before him to be knighted for the prodigious feat; and to this day he is known as Syr Howel y Pedolau or Sir Howel of the Horseshoes.

So, on my first brief and peripheral visit to Scotland in 1953, I travelled as one proud of his doughty forebear. I had been asked by British European Airways to paint some pictures of the Outer Hebrides so that, if they were suitable, they could use them to publicise the islands. They promised to fly me to Stornoway without charge so long as a spare seat was available on one of their planes.

From Northolt Airport I flew to Renfrew, where I spent a sleepless night in the pilot's quarters. In the morning I waited again for a seat whilst a loudspeaker asked one Mary McFarlane, a passenger to Stornoway, to report to the desk. As I knew, from the number of people who were waiting, that the plane would be full, I prayed that Miss McFarlane had overslept, missed her bus or that she had lost her memory. The time of departure arrived and I was able to fill the

seat of the missing passenger. Over the Clyde we flew, a happy bunch of Scots with carrier bags, fishing rods and bottles of whisky, and one Welshman laden with paints and canvases. Over the Minch the view was magnificent. To the east, the highlands of Scotland seemed to spread range after range, while to the west was a broken and irregular line of islands. We stopped at the islands of Tiree, Benbecula and North Uist; then, skirting the bare mass of Harris, landed on the airfield of Stornoway. A company vehicle took me into the town, from where a primitive bus loaded with Gaelic-speaking men and women began the journey south; it was a long, tortuous and bumpy expedition. The bus skirted sinuous sea-lochs, crossed a river that flowed with the dark brown of Guinness, stopping occasionally at small, undistinguished groups of houses, and eventually arriving outside my destination, Mr Cameron's Hotel, in the village of Tarbert. It was a Saturday and I only had two days to paint my pictures before returning to London to begin a new term at the school in which I taught.

I had already discovered that this, the larger island in the Outer Hebrides, was divided into a northern part that was populated by Norsemen, and a southern part that was Gaelic, and so great was the disunity that they were unable to meet jointly to govern the island; consequently, one part was organised and controlled by Ross and Cromarty and the other by Inverness. I arrived at my hotel to find it full of officials from the mainland but I failed to find out the county from which they came. From what I heard of their conversation over dinner they were to examine the local schools, and as they were required to start work early on the Monday they had to travel on the Saturday, for on the Sabbath day no transport was permitted.

Sunday morning dampened my spirits. The wind blew a gale from the Atlantic and the mountains were obscured by sheets of rain. Not wishing to offend the religious feelings of the people of Tarbert, my only course was to brave the elements and climb, with all my paraphernalia, to a place where I could not be seen. Upwards I climbed with the rain beating into my face and soaking me before I could even start my work. I found what I believed to be a sheltered

spot and had started to work when a violent blast caught my canvas and lifted it into the turbulent air. I watched it as it was borne away like an inebriated seagull to crash into the heather fifty feet below. At my feet my easel lay flat and contorted. I noticed that one of its legs was broken. I poured the rain out of my paint box, picked up my shattered easel and retrieved the remains of what I had hoped would be a picture. Angry and disheartened I stumbled down to the sanctuary of Mr Cameron's Hotel where, dripping with Hebridean rain, I entered the parlour. Seated in front of the fire was a small official, his arms stretched in front of him the better to warm his hands. He had a long, red nose and watery eyes that turned towards me. He enquired how I fared. I told him how I had not wanted the locals to see me working and how my efforts had come to nothing. As I luxuriated in self-pity, I heard the Scottish voice whining:

'Ah, weel, maybe the people of Tarbet did na see ye, but the Lord did.'

Pools of water followed me as I climbed the stairs to my bedroom where, damp and miserable, I attempted to mend my broken easel.

In the evening it began to clear, so when I felt that the inhabitants of Tarbet, wearied from their devotions, had retired to their homes for the night, I, still wet from the morning's disaster, crept out to a point to the east of the village to paint the houses against the setting sun.

The morning of my second and last day dawned fair. After the rain, the air was clear and I could see the Isle of Skye and the mountains beyond. The colour was so much stronger than around my home in Wales. The sea was a deep ultramarine and, beyond it, the hills were a softer blue broken by vivid splashes of ochre; it was very exciting and I managed to paint one picture in the morning and another in the afternoon. Before it was dark, I made some drawings around an old whaling station away to the west of the village. At least I had done something.

The next morning the same ancient yet energetic bus took me to Stornoway, and on the Thursday morning I had a staff meeting at my school in London. My visit to the islands of the Hebrides had been hopelessly brief and I wondered when I would be able to return to Scotland.

In the late 'fifties I was due to have an exhibition in the Leicester Galleries in London and had decided that, were it to be a success, I would spend my Christmas in Amsterdam; but if it turned out to be a financial disaster, I felt I might have just enough money to make my second visit to Scotland.

A week before the exhibition opened my telephone rang and I heard the familiar voice of my old friend, Sandy Livingstone-Learmouth. Sandy was a Scot who had married locally in north Wales and had become deeply attached to its people, believing fervently in some sort of pan-Celtic brotherhood. He asked where I had been on the previous Tuesday and I told him that I had been staying in the monastery at Downside, for I had gone there to give a lecture. He did not seem to be surprised and proceeded to tell me an unusual story.

As he was irrevocably immersed in a world of extra-sensory

perception, he had visited his favourite guru, a northern Irishman by the name of King, in order to seek his advice on the subject of his daughter, a brilliant pianist and a Batchelor of Music at Cambridge University, who had departed for the island of Ibiza in the company of an undesirable and impecunious painter. Mr King told him not to worry about her as she was old enough to look after herself; and then to Sandy's surprise, begged him to transfer his concern to me.

'At the moment,' he said, 'he is in the company of monks and that is a good sign.'

Then relapsing into a psychic trance he cried repeatedly:

'Kyffin, Kyffin, wake up or you will miss the bus.'

I had certainly been in the company of monks and remembered that after lunch in the monastery a priest had asked me to accompany him to Wells Cathedral. We had intended to catch a bus but it had already left, so we returned to the monastery with the intention of catching a later one. We missed that one as well so the priest, with arms wide apart, stopped a car and, as hitch-hikers, we journeyed into Wells. It all seemed to be improbable but Mr King in Hereford Square, London, had some supernatural knowledge of the fact that I had missed not one bus, but two in far-away Somerset.

Sandy was not impressed by my information, believing that Mr King's concern was aimed at deeper and less trivial matters, and insisted that I made an appointment to see his guru who was concerned that many others were also worried about me. I told Sandy that I had no such worries but to pacify him I telephoned his psychic friend. A dull and disinterested voice told me at the other end of the telephone to be with him at twelve o'clock on the following Wednesday. I offered to give him my name but the voice said that names were of no importance. I rang the bell of a house in Hereford Square and it was answered by an unnaturally clean and tidy man with the pale, unhealthy face of one who habitually shuns the light of day. He had a big head and his eyes were unusually pale and watery. He looked at me briefly before speaking, then firmly but softly said: 'You are going to Scotland.' His words were ominous and I resigned myself to failure.

'Come in, Kyffin,' he said.

'How did you know my name?' I asked.

'Oh, the person who came with you told me that,' and as he spoke I automatically turned round. There was nobody there.

He showed me into his living-room. I took in the bare, slightly oriental décor and noticed a dog, a large boxer, lying in front of the fire. It got to its feet and staggered towards me and I, slightly shaken, made much of it, fearing that it might have been Mr King's psychic familiar.

We sat down and he asked me for something that I carried about with me. I gave him my watch. Holding it in his hand, he sat back in an easy chair, shut his eyes and made some rather ordinary remarks that might have been expressed by a gypsy fortune-teller. He said that I was creative but did not know in what direction my creativity lay; that I was not recognised at the moment but would be later, and that never at any time would I have to worry about money. The last remark was gratifying for at the time I was only just financially solvent. Then, suddenly, he was telling me that the room was full of people; that they were all worried about me and that one of them, a distinguished man in uniform, was especially concerned. I have never concluded whom he might possibly have been. In the throes of his concern for me, Mr King rose from his chair, fixed his pale blue eyes on me and uttered with solemnity, 'You must promise never to see anyone like me again.' I asked him why I should not and he told me that although I might not know it, I was extremely psychic.

'You are like I was once,' he went on. 'I continued with it and it has made my life miserable. I don't want yours to be the same.' Slightly worried, I left this strange man and proceeded to make plans to go to Scotland.

I arrived in Edinburgh at Christmas-time in a cold Caledonian drizzle. I felt lonely and, after Mr King's insistence that I should go to Scotland, apprehensive at what might happen to me. I booked into a small hotel and wandered aimlessly back to the station where a fair was being held. Among the side-shows was a booth where an old man and his wife were telling fortunes. They were obviously palmists, for behind them, painted onto sheets of linoleum, were

some huge and sinister hands. I gazed at those of Heini Schmultz, the Brooklyn strangler; they were huge and shaped like spades with corkscrew lines interweaving across them, while those of Gringo Paletti were mean and narrow. Forgetting the warning of Mr King, I paid a shilling and laid my hand upon the counter.

The old Scot picked it up. 'Laddie, ye're grand,' he whispered confidentially. 'Ye have a couple of lifelines and one of them goes on for ever. Och,' he cried, 'I think ye'll be immortal.' This was the sort of thing I wanted to hear but when he came back to look at the lines that foretold the number of my children, he rather enigmatically announced that I would have one and a half. He must have decided that he should find me a wife to mother them, for he produced a piece of paper with the words 'blonde, redhead, auburn, brown and black' upon it. He drew his pencil through four and left me with the brown. It was then that I remembered the warning of Mr King not to consult clairvoyants, so with a small feeling of guilt I stepped once more into the drizzle to see if I could find the office of my accountant, the capable and motherly Dorothea Vaughan.

Ten years before, I found that income tax demands were dropping through my letter-box with alarming frequency. They came from Crouch End, Camden Town and Willesden, and they perplexed me because my total annual income at that time was between £200 and £300. Believing that they were clerical errors, I tore them up and put them in the waste-paper basket. They were followed by other more sinister demands ordering me to appear in court. Nevertheless, these too went into the waste-paper basket. One day, while having tea with an old friend who worked in the Victoria and Albert Museum, I told of these endless demands, more, I believe, to make conversation than from any serious concern; but concerned he was and he gave me the address of Dorothea Vaughan who had just left London and had opened an office in Edinburgh. He said she was a financial genius and had a passion for sorting out the monetary affairs of unworldly artists and monoglot Chinese restauranteurs. He insisted that I should throw myself on her mercy.

Dorothea Vaughan was married to the remarkable Dr Magnus Pyke who, on being appointed as Scientific Adviser to the Distillers Company, had opened his laboratories in Menstrie in the county of Clackmannan. They lived not far away in the village of Cambus.

Many times, and successfully, did Dorothea Vaughan appear in court for me to persuade the Inland Revenue that I did not owe them anything, only for me to receive more and more demands to explain my financial position. For all this work she charged me nothing. Indeed, she bought my work and so did her husband. So it was as one who owed much to her philanthropy that I went to see her that wet December evening. It was eight o'clock and she was still working, probably attempting to sort out the financial affairs of some inadequate person who, like me, suffered from monetary dyslexia. She seemed delighted to see me, invited me to spend Christmas Day with her family in Cambus and departed to make her hour-long journey back to Cambus.

Christmas Day in Scotland has an air of sadness about it, for the festive season does not start until a week later at the time of

Hogmanay, so when I arrived by train at Cambus, Magnus was still working in his laboratories at Menstrie. I was shown round the house, and everywhere hung pictures given to Dorothea by artistic clients. There were paintings by Vivian Pitchforth, Ceri Richards, Gertrude Hermes, Raymond Coxon, John Bratby and many other well-known painters. It was a collection based on gratitude.

At one o'clock Magnus burst into the house. His legs and his arms seemed to be everywhere and so did the legs and wings of the chicken which he dismembered with clinical ferocity. We ate our meal at speed before Magnus leaped into his car and drove away again.

Around the house, whisky was stored in gigantic warehouses like aircraft hangers, and to prevent any of the millions of bottles from being stolen, sinister-looking uniformed men accompanied by guard-dogs paced the concrete pathways. To one side was the distillery, an ugly conglomeration of tanks, boilers and pipes. Steam came from various places but it seemed as if the smell came from everywhere, a nauseating noxious odour that permeated the whole village and crept into every corner of my accountant's home. As if with resignation she said that it was possible to ignore it. Christmas Day with Dorothea, Magnus and their daughter Bessie was unusual and, in many ways, hilarious. It was certainly unforgettable. Two days later I returned to London.

I had gone to Scotland at the urgent wish of Mr King, but nothing really had happened. There had been no dramatic event, no artistic conversion and no new and exciting romance. I could only presume that had I stayed in London a ghastly fate might have befallen me. It was strange but if I had done nothing else I had made contact with the Pyke family, and Cambus was to become a base for me for future artistic forays into the wonderful land of the Highlands that lay to the north and west.

I returned to Scotland the following year as Dorothea had asked me to paint a portrait of her daughter Bessie. Because of the advice and financial assistance of my accountant I had been able to become independently mobile, so, in my new Austin van, I drove proudly northwards. Just north of Gretna Green an untidy figure raised a thumb and pointed in the direction I was going. I stopped and the man climbed in uttering some incomprehensible information as to his destination. After about a quarter of an hour of silence I ventured to suggest that, from his accent, he came from the Glasgow area.

'Ach, ah doo,' was the answer. There was another even longer silence and then I tried, once again, to start some sort of conversation.

'From where in Scotland do the people who have soft, complaining voices come from?' I enquired trying to immitate a particular accent.

The man beside me snapped, 'Fra off the bloody stage.'

I made no further attempt, and about an hour later I heard him say,

'And I'll be oot.' I stopped and he got out and shambled away.

I drove into the alcoholic stench of Cambus and viewed my model. She must have been about ten-years old and had large intelligent eyes. She was a witty little girl whose attraction was increased, oddly enough, by a broken nose of which Bessie Pyke was extremely proud.

Next morning I put up my easel in the dining-room and she sat in her school uniform, her satchel on her back. She was a good model and the only words she spoke were those enquiring if I had made her nose 'squiffy' enough. I must have done so because she seemed to be pleased with the result. The next year I was asked to paint Magnus. Unfortunately, my doctor had decided to change the anti-convulsent drug that I had been taking and had prescribed a new one without telling me that it reduced the number of my red blood corpuscles. To make things worse I had not been given a vitamin to counteract the deficiency. Consequently, I felt unbearably weak and the thought of painting a portrait of the dynamic Magnus caused me a considerable amount of worry. On the day set aside for the painting, I was almost immobile with lethargy, and when Magnus drove off for a brief visit to his laboratories I secretly hoped that he would not return. At about ten o'clock a human cyclone hit the house and Magnus burst into the dining-room. He placed his angular body on a chair, crossing his arms and letting his expressive hands dangle either side of his legs: 'How's that?' he said. It could not have been better, but it was with little confidence and no enthusiasm that I started to draw him in. That initial process completed, I started to fill in with colour the figure that I had placed upon the canvas. It was automatic work with none of the so-called inspiration that artists are supposed to possess; but, amazingly, it turned out to be one of my best portraits, conveying an interpretation of energy in my sitter that was in contrast to the debilitating lassitude of the artist.

I left the portrait at Cambus and drove north into the Highlands. Crianlarich and Rannoch were names with a rich Celtic ring to them; and I knew that I was going to feel at home. Glencoe was a disappointment as it appeared to be too green, and too civilised, and nowhere in the great valley did I sense the tragedy of the well-known massacre. I decided that the rock-strewn valley of Nant Peris, dividing Crib Goch from the Glyder, in the mountains of Snowdonia, was infinitely more impressive. The colour of the Highlands and the west coast amazed me and made my own land of Wales seem drab in contrast. In the evenings the grass became orange, the shadows on the mountains were more full of colour than any I had seen in Wales, and the sea attained a depth and richness of

blue that I had never seen before. I noticed that it became more intense the further north I travelled, but in spite of the beauty of the landscape, I felt there was a sadness. The houses were unattractive and, apart from the castles, were comparatively new and hardly pre-dated the Victorian era. Perhaps before that time, if MacGregor built a house, MacTavish would certainly have burnt it down; but then MacGregor would do the same to MacRae and MacRae to MacDonald, and, if I am to believe the Scots, the Campbells would have destroyed them all. I came to the conclusion that the lack of architectural charm derived from a past when true peace was something to be hoped for but seldom found. I thought of the charm of Wales, of the stone cottages, of the ancient farmhouses deep in the wooded valleys; I remembered the comforting security of the strong, stone farm buildings seemingly tied in place by sinuous walls that wound around the hills and dived down into the fields below. I might have been prejudiced when my mind dwelt on the subject of charm, but I had to concede that the beauty of the Highlands was incomparable and that no more beautiful landscape existed in the whole of Europe.

I found that the lack of charm in the landscape was equalled by that of its dour inhabitants. I had decided to spend my nights in houses that advertised a bed and breakfast. Many were the Scottish doors on which I knocked but often was I turned away because I only wanted a single room. When I offered to pay for a double, they looked at me with aggressive incredulity. Sometimes I had to sleep in my van and wash in the burn. In the village of Poolewe in Wester Ross, I found the reason for their hostility. It was there that Mary MacKenzie told me to try Jessie MacCallum who, tight-lipped, suggested that I tried Maggie MacRae who gave me a hard look and sent me on to Jenny MacKay. With apprehension I knocked on a door and a tall, angular woman opened it and, once again, I asked for a bed. There was a silence as she looked me over. She looked at my cap, my jacket and my moustache, and after another silence made up her mind.

'All right, I'll have ye,' she snapped. I followed her into a small hall. 'And ye'll be signing the book,' came an order, and as I finished writing my very Welsh name and address, I heard a very different and warmer voice saying, 'And ye are a Welshman, and I was after thinking you were an English military gentleman.'

From Poolewe I drove north again to Ullapool, to Lochinver, past the mountains of Suilven, Canisp, Stack Polly and Quinag, and over the Kylesqu ferry to a wild Sutherland landscape of dark pools and yet narrower roads that hugged and skirted huge heather-clad rocks around which frustrated holiday-makers drove cars and caravans, and shouted, cursed, blasphemed and vied with each other to gain the sanctuary of a passing place. I decided that it would be wiser to turn south again to stay with the Grisewood family on the Strathnairn estate to the south of Inverness. I arrived on the eleventh of August and was told that I would be shooting grouse the next day. My host, the estate factor, told me that the main moor had been let to a party of Welshmen led by Sir David Evans-Bevan, a south Wales brewery magnate, but he had retained a small piece of land where we were to shoot. We collected a few grouse and, from time to time, the factor would stop in order to listen for the sound of gunshot, but there was an ominous silence from the larger part of the moor. In the evening, MacCallum, the keeper, arrived to report on the proceedings:

'It was no so good,' he said, but then, as a great smile crossed his bearded face, he added, 'but the Welshmen were real gentlemen.' He tapped his pocket significantly.

The next day I started my journey back to Cambus. As I crossed a bleak and heather-clad landscape, I saw distant figures with white flags advancing over the skyline; occasionally a burst of gunshot broke the silence of the moor. As I slowed down to watch the proceedings, I saw on the lonely road in front of me the body of a grouse. I stopped to pick up the bird thinking that I might present it to the friends with whom I was to stay near Braemar. As I was smoothing out its feathers before putting it in my pocket, I became aware that I was not alone. I turned to see, towering above me, an immense ghillie. His face was bearded and weather-beaten; his nose was like a hammer and there was authority in his voice:

'I'll be having it,' he said. Deprived of my present, I drove on to a small house called Claybokie, the home of Callum McFarlane-Barrow, the factor of the Mar estate, a few miles from the royal town of Braemar. I found that it was Callum's duty to provide sport for parties of continentals who descended on the lodge eager to attempt the triple achievement of killing a deer, a grouse and a salmon in the space of a week. When I was staying on the estate, a group of exuberant Frenchmen, led by an energetic Monsieur Brandyballes, was in residence, and Callum was working hard to provide them with their needs.

Probably more stags have been slaughtered on the Mar Estate than anywhere else in Scotland. A large room in the lodge commemorated the fact, and many hundreds of antlered skulls hung in such proximity that it was impossible to see the walls. When he was not attending to the needs of the Frenchmen, Callum drove me up newly-made tracks far into the distant Cairngorms. At the height of three-thousand feet I painted Ben McDhui as it rose like a blue-black whale to the west. The ground was a vivid orange, the rocks pink in the evening sun, and young ptarmigan flew around me as I worked. In the valley below a herd of deer was grazing. I felt very far from Wales.

When I returned to Cambus I found that Magnus was having a short holiday. He suggested that we should have a game of golf and, with borrowed clubs, I joined him at a club nearby where, with immense vigour, he assaulted the ball and light-heartedly chased it in all directions, not always towards the hole. Nevertheless, he beat me and, flushed with confidence, challenged me to a game of tennis on his court beside the house. If he was an exhilarating sight on a golf course, on a tennis court he resembled a dervish, for he appeared to me to have the distinct advantage of having at least three arms and four legs. Once again I was beaten but because of the pleasure of his enthusiastic company, I felt anything but humiliated. Energetically, and artistically fulfilled, I returned to London with Magnus's portrait and exhibited it in the next Summer Exhibition in Burlington House. The following year, 1970, I was elected an Associate of the Royal Academy.

I had always hoped that one day I might become a member of the Academy, for in the nineteenth century my family maintained tenuous relations with Mr George Jones, the acting President in the first half of the century. He was a family friend and visits to London from Anglesey were never complete without a visit to Trafalgar Square to see him at work. George Jones, a good painter and a very handsome man, was often mistaken for the Duke of Wellington who, when told of this, is reputed to have exclaimed, 'How very singular. Nobody mistakes me for Mr Jones.' Another family connection was with the antiquary, Sir Robert Harry Inglis, my great-grandfather's closest friend. My great uncle was christened Inglis and so were both my father and my brother; so, for reasons of nostalgia, I never shared the hostility of other artists towards the institution.

The first time I exhibited was in 1946, but although I submitted year after year, few of my pictures found their way onto the walls of Burlington House; indeed, in order to cheer myself every time I received a rejection slip I resorted to the purchase of a new tie. Eventually my collection of neck-wear became so large I had to discontinue the practice for economic reasons. As soon as I did so, I found, to my great satisfaction, that many more of my pictures were accepted than rejected, until everything I submitted found its place in the Summer Exhibition. I concluded that the Selection Committee had begun to recognise my work and had accepted them for reasons of philanthropy.

One day, I met a well-known Academician who asked me at what art school I taught. When I told him that I taught at a boys' public school in north London, he remarked with great sadness and pity that the Royal Academy had never elected a schoolmaster and would never do so. I saw no reason to leave my job so was surprised when, in 1969, I received an invitation to attend the Annual Banquet. Vivian Pitchforth, a distinguished water-colour painter and a senior member who, after his experiences in the First World War, had become totally deaf, met me in the vestibule which appeared to be crowded with distinguished men from every walk of life. The Archbishop of Canterbury, swathed in purple and red,

merged colourfully into the vermillion arms of the Cardinal Archbishop of Westminster. Ambassadors and diplomats, resplendent with exotic orders and decorations, gazed at each other warily as admirals, generals, and air marshalls looked at anything but the pictures on the walls. Suddenly, Pitch, who was never aware of the strength of his own voice, touched me on the arm and bawled:

'Kyffin, I tried to get one member interested in your work this year.'

His broad Yorkshire accent stopped the conversation as the diplomats, the warriors and the men of God lowered their glasses and gazed in our direction. Pitch was oblivious to their eyes:

'I showed him your pictures. "Kyffin Williams," he said, "I 'ate 'im. Every time I look at 'is work, I feel I've been kicked in the stomach by a pair of 'obnailed boots".'

Stunned into silence, everyone in the vestibule stared at us until slowly they turned away to sip their drinks and continue their conversations.

Even though I had been exhibiting at the Royal Academy for over twenty years, it was apparent that this did not qualify me for a teaching post in an art school. I had applied many times but always my application had been turned down. The fact that I also taught in a secondary school made art officials believe that I did so because I was not qualified to teach in further education.

One day, I heard that there was a post vacant in the painting school at St. Martins School of Art. I decided to make one more application. I climbed the almost vertical stairs from St. Martins Lane and introduced myself to the porter who sat behind a desk on the top floor of the building. He was a solid, heavy and ponderous man. I concluded that he was not a very imaginative man. I asked him if I could see the principal as I wanted to apply for the post. He eased his weight off his chair and padded slowly into a nearby office. I listened to incoherent murmuring before he returned with a piece of paper and pencil and asked me to write down my qualifications. I cannot recall what I wrote but after handing it to him he, once more, entered the office that was apparently the domain of the principal. I waited and soon the porter returned.

'Sorry, mate,' he said. 'Qualifications inadequate.'

A few months later I became the first schoolmaster to be elected to the Royal Academy and was appointed to the position of a Governor of St. Martins School of Art.

When I attended my first private dinner in Burlington House, the President, Sir Thomas Monnington, was in the chair and I was seated between Pitch and an elderly, paralysed member in a wheelchair; opposite me sat the silent figure of A.R. Thomson. Pitch was in his usual good spirits, occasionally asking me a question and passing me a small white pad and pencil so that I could write the answer. Suddenly, loud above the murmur of conversation, I heard his voice:

''Ere, Kyffin, d'ye see yon Tommy Thomson opposite. He's what they call a deaf mute. Can't hear or say a bloody thing and the girls love him. Been married three times has Tommy Thomson.' Oblivious of our conversation, A.R. Thomson, R.A., consumed his whitebait. Coffee was served and the President rose to speak. A minute later his voice was drowned by that of Pitch:

'Kyffin, what's old Tom talking about?'

On his pad I unwisely wrote the words: 'Hot air'. I passed it to him and after studying my writing, he announced in a voice that could be heard by the whole room:

'What's this, Kyffin, old Tom talking 'ot air, is 'e? Aye, 'e always talks a lot of 'ot air does old Tom.'

The President looked at me and the members looked at me, and I thought that I would be asked to resign. Pitch sat back contentedly and enjoyed his coffee.

When I became a member of the Selection Committee, I found that the process of selection was conducted in an atmosphere of amazing generosity. However bad, pretentious or incompetent the work put before it might have been, never once did I hear a critical remark; even when an object six inches high was unfolded to attain a length of over sixty feet, it was folded again and without comment a cross was placed against it.

I was asked to hang the small South Room. Jim Fitton, Chairman of the Hanging Committee, told me that he wanted the walls covered almost up to the ceiling with small and close-hung pictures. I asked two Academy technicians in green-baize aprons to carry out the instructions and seemingly in no time the work was completed. The President arrived and looked at the room with disapproval. He asked me what I thought I had been doing. I replied that I had been carrying out the instructions of the Chairman.

'Take them all down and hang them properly,' he ordered.

I looked at the technicians with pity, but they were professionals and did what they were told to do. Soon the pictures had all been taken down and I had re-hung the room. No longer did they reach to the ceiling and no longer were the frames in uncomfortable proximity. Jim Fitton returned and wanted to know why I had not carried out his instructions. I explained, and he told me in a kindly way, that the President could not countermand the orders of the Chairman of the Hanging Committee. Once again, he told me to pack the walls. I looked at the long-suffering technicians, and they looked at me with resignation before repeating the original hanging. Once again, the President appeared and murmured that I had not obeyed his instructions. Once again, I gazed at the technicians as, impassively, they looked back at me. I had to make a decision, so I asked them if, just for a change, they would hang the room as I wanted it to be hung. They smiled and, as if entering into a conspiracy, the room was re-hung according to my instructions.

I don't think I ever really enjoyed the annual dinner for, almost inevitably, I found myself seated next to ancient men who appeared to be more interested in their food than in conversation. After one particularly boring encounter, I went to see the assistant secretary and asked if I could be seated the following year next to an attractive lady. This he did but he was not to know that she would arrive in an advanced state of inebriation. I spoke to her but she did not reply. Another member who sat on the other side of her also tried, but not a word did she speak as she drank and ate and allowed the ash from her cigarette to fall into her food. But when Sir Hugh Casson, the President, rose to speak, it was with amazement that I saw her leap to her feet shouting, 'Hoorah, hoorah.' Her energy thus expended she resumed her seat and no further word did she utter.

I duly remonstrated with the assistant secretary and he promised me that the following year he would make amends, so it was with anticipation that I found myself placed next to a female artistic guru well-known in the media. Opposite her was a member who, that year, had won a prize for the most distinguished work in the Academy. I soon found that her conversation was directed entirely to him and that hardly a word of mine received a reply. Suddenly, the prize-winner waved his hand in the direction of one of my paintings that hung behind him and remarked loudly:

'Isn't that a most ghastly painting?'

Eagerly the lady agreed as together they demolished my picture as energetically as they had been consuming their food. Wounded and temporarily inarticulate, I turned to speak to another guest who sat beside me, a man who was a well-known figure in the world of art, but he too was engrossed in conversation. I gazed across the table to where the editor of an authoritative daily paper was resting his head against the shoulder of one of the more attractive of our lady academicians. Once again, luck was against me, so I decided that it was to be my last Royal Academy dinner.

I found the elections were interesting and in many ways bizarre. After an excellent lunch, the members enter a gallery and sit before a table on top of which stands a sinister wooden box with a hollow and cavernous protuberance. Behind the table sits the President, with the Treasurer and the Keeper on his right. Beside him on his left sits the Secretary, the only salaried man in the room.

A month before the elections, the names of the candidates are circulated and lobbying takes place, so that disparate groups have already decided to champion favoured candidates. Often there is a Royal College group, a Slade group and an independent group, all sitting impassively and eyeing each other competitively. The voting begins and any candidate with four or more votes has his or her name written on a blackboard by the Secretary. Papers are passed round again until two candidates are left in contention. It is then that their names are placed on the box on either side of the hollow protuberance, and members, presented with a ball by the President, are invited to insert their hands and drop it hopefully into the invisible compartment of their choice. One year, two names, that could have been Smith and Jones, were placed on the box and members proceeded to vote until a certain member, who had tried to place his ball in favour of Jones found the compartment blocked by a piece of crumpled newspaper cunningly placed in such a way that all the Jones votes rolled into the compartment of his opponent. We behaved in a truly British manner. The paper was removed and, without comment, we voted again.

The Royal Academy is financially and artistically independent, for it is run entirely by artists and no cultural pressure-groups bring pressure to bear upon it. It is an institution in which a difference of opinion is expected, tolerated and appreciated. There is a democratic warmth about the place that is increased by the courteous assistance of the officers and servants.

In 1972 I was asked to supervise students from art schools throughout Britain who had won David Murray Scholarships to paint the landscape of their choice. I received a list of their names and the addresses at which I would find them. As the artistic venues stretched from the Scillies to the Isles of Orkney, I realised that it would be impossible to visit everyone. I drew a line from Cardigan Bay to the Wash and decided, partly because of my love of Scotland, to visit the students who travelled north.

After sending postcards to all the students warning them of my arrival, I set off for Scotland and spent a night at Cambus. The next morning I made my way to the outskirts of Glasgow to visit two of the addresses. I found one of them in a bleak tenement building, and after knocking on the door, a bewildered and aggressive woman told me in an almost imcomprehensible dialect that she didn't know what I was talking about. The other address also appeared to have been fictitious. I pressed on north to visit my next student in Oban. In a cafe near Crianlarich I sat down at a table beside a tall blonde girl with a sketch book. She told me that she was on a scholarship

organised by the Royal Academy in London and was somewhat surprised when I asked her why she was in Crianlarich when she should have been in Oban. After looking at her drawings, I drove northwards to stay with friends near Balachuilish and from their house telephoned the owner of a nearby castle to see if a David McDonald was staying there. The owner told me that he was not expected and would not be welcome as he had sixty-eight guests arriving the next day: nevertheless, he told me that I could stay if I so wished.

Donald Ross, the next student I had to visit, gave his address as 'care of Mrs Brown of the Bank of Scotland in Stromness on the Islands of Orkney'. I spent a night in my van at Scrabster near Thurso and on the next day I crossed a stormy Pentland Firth, polluted by plastic cans and bottles. It appeared as if all the rubbish of Europe was passing that way. Eventually, out of the mist, I saw the tall, russet-coloured shape of the Old Man of Hoy, and soon the boat had tied up in the harbour of Stromness. I made my way along a cobbled street of good strong buildings and found the Bank of Scotland House. Mrs Brown answered the door to tell me that Donald Ross had gone to the Outer Hebrides. I asked her where I could stay. She was helpful.

'Ah, yes,' she said, 'try the bicycle shop at the end of the street and Mrs Brown might be able to put you up. If she can't have you, try number 97 and Mrs Brown might have a room to spare, and if she can't take you, try the house with the yellow door for Mrs Brown might help you there, and if you can't get in anywhere, you had better come back here.' I concluded that almost everybody in the Orkneys went by the name of 'Brown'. Having failed to find a bed, I returned to the Bank of Scotland House where Mrs Brown put me in Donald Ross' room and invited me to have a cup of tea. We were talking about the Islands of Orkney when the door opened and in burst Alistair, her husband.

'Have ye locked the door of the bank,' she asked.

'Ach no,' he replied, as she turned to me and said with affection that he was a 'terrible thoughtless man'. Alistair, meanwhile, had opened a bottle of whisky and was having a few drams until, once again, he was on his feet announcing that he was off to the golf club. When he had gone, Mrs Brown told me that Alistair's brother was the well-known writer George McKay Brown and that she was a cousin of Eric Linklater. In that well-built and comfortable house in the far north of Britain, I learnt much of the history of the Orkneys, of the Orcadians, of the Norwegians and of the men from Hamburg who had settled there. At about ten o'clock Alistair burst in once again. I presumed he had consumed a few more drams at the golf club, as he was in a cheerful mood, and when his wife retired to bed Alistair opened yet another bottle and, lying back in his chair, told me that the men of Anglesey and those from the Orkneys were blood brothers with the same Viking lineage. He spoke as if he was a close relative. I warmed to Alistair and understood the frustration of a man with Viking blood when incarcerated in an Orcadian bank.

It was to an unattractive cafe on the harbour-side that I went for my food. Sad tourists waited patiently and in silence for someone to take their orders from a sparse and uninviting menu, and before every meal a wiry, aggressive man burst into the dining-room and, in a voice that defied any argument, roared:

'And it will be fish . . .' and fish it was.

I enjoyed the Orkneys. An impenetrable sea mist covered the islands, and the ancient sites became more mysterious because of it. It crept like a moving carpet across the green fields and over the farms. Tall standing-stones appeared and just as quickly vanished. The sea was everywhere; one minute it was on my left and then on my right, arms of the sea that wound sinuously in amongst the large rich meadows. I tried to draw but what I did was superficial and it did not interpret the mood of that northern land. Had I been on holiday I would have liked to have stayed, for the Orkneys are a magical group of islands, and I enjoyed the hospitality of the Browns; but I realised that I had to continue my search for the wayward students. So far, I had only seen one and I had stumbled upon her by chance.

Back across the Pentland Firth I sailed; a gale blew from the west and the boat, on leaving the shelter of Stromness harbour, plunged and rolled and shuddered and heaved until I wondered if I would be alive to finish my search for the students. Stoically I sat on a hard, wooden seat and tried to convince myself that I was a Viking.

Mercifully, the boat reached the harbour of Scrabster in the county of Caithness and from there I started a long drive down the whole length of Scotland, hopefully to find a student in the Northumberland town of Morpeth. I knocked on a door that was opened by a fragile girl. I introduced myself and asked if I could see her work. Faced with her examiner she contrived to look even more fragile as she explained that she had not done any painting because of an attack of arthritis. She offered me a cup of tea which she poured out with difficulty. Disappointed yet again, I bade her farewell, and it was with little confidence that I drove south in order to visit yet another student in the Yorkshire village of Hutton in the Hole; and, yet again, there was no student at the address I had been given. Although it was frustrating, I was enjoying the varied landscape, and Wensleydale in high summer made me forget briefly the

Academy and its scholarship. There was yet another address to be visited somewhere among those rolling hills and stone walls. I did not believe that I might be successful but the jovial young man who opened the door of an ancient and remote farmhouse was indeed expecting me. He had been working hard and well and was eager to show me what he had done. At last I had achieved some sort of success so, with my confidence restored, I crossed the Pennines to visit a student in the town of Blackburn. Once again, no answer came from a dreary, red-brick house in which there was little sign of habitation.

Weary of my search for the students, I set my car in the direction of Anglesey and it was there, in a Holyhead ice-cream shop, that my travels ended. Vittorio Cirefice, the son of the Italian owner, had been to the local comprehensive school and from there he had gone to study in London. He showed me his detailed drawings of ducks and geese and told me that he knew Charles Tunnicliffe. In the corner of his work-room lay the stinking, decomposing body of a Canada goose, but the student appeared to be unaware of the all-pervading smell. It didn't upset me either for, somehow, in that small room above the ice-cream bar, I had ended my long and tortuous journey with a measure of success.

I wrote to all the scholars asking them to present their work in the Royal Academy. One bleak November day I was greeted by an assembly of cheerful students. As I looked at their work I could see that, even if it had little connection with the many fictitious addresses I had received, it was very impressive. I decided that the 'David Murray' was a worthwhile scholarship after all.

7

A strange relationship has always existed between Anglesey and Ireland. Under the Romans we had grown secure in the knowledge that they would repulse any foolhardy invaders, so when they departed in the fifth century, the Irish saw their chance. Boatloads of wild and ferocious warriors landed on our shores and made such a nuisance of themselves that today, if we want to insult anybody, we call him '*yr hen Wyddel*', an old Irishman. We found our champion in a Strathclyde Welshman called Cunedda and it was he who rode south with his three sons and drove the Irishmen into the sea. Not all the Irish invaders were unwelcome, for some came as holy men and women to join the other saints who came to the island from Scotland, Cornwall and even Britanny.

Nevertheless, our relationship with Ireland remained uneasy and we stayed apart, geographically and socially, until the nineteenth century, a time when the local squirearchy began to look upon Dublin as the unofficial capital of Anglesey. They crossed the Irish Sea regularly in search of wives and to hunt foxes. Many of my kinsmen spent happy times in Ireland where puritan values had seldom existed. One relative in Anglesey, indulging the extravagance of a wild Irish wife, went bankrupt, while another left her teeth in a tree in County Kildare as she relentlessly pursued a fox in the early years of the century. I have a feeling that the annual gathering of the Anglesey Agricultural Society took second place to the Dublin Horse Show.

At a preparatory school on the cliffs at Trearddur Bay I was always conscious that across the sea lay the mysterious land of Ireland. Several Irish boys became my school friends. There was a Patrick Jameson of the whiskey family; Mungo Park, a descendant of the murdered explorer, and two indistinguishable brothers named Birkett. One of them had a glass eye that he removed at night, and it appeared to wink at us from within a glass tumbler, and the other became famous for discovering a cure for a cancer that afflicted the natives of the east African rift-valley. The cure was duly named 'Birkett's Lymphoma'. The Irish element was strong, and early in my life I was determined to visit the island.

From my grandfather's parish of Llanrhuddlad I had often seen the mail boats leaving Holyhead, swinging in a great arc before increasing speed to become a tiny shape far away towards the horizon. I always felt that there was something romantic about the boats of the Irish Mail. In the harbour I had often admired the *Cambria*, the *Scotia* and the *Hibernia* and I knew one of their Welsh captains. I remember him telling me that on one crossing, when nearing Dun Laoghaire, there was a cry of 'Man overboard'. He reduced his speed and brought his boat in a great circle to the spot where, in the water, he could see the figure of a man. When he was aboard again, the captain asked a sailor to bring him onto the bridge. A wet, drunk and untidy Irishman appeared and the captain asked him why he had jumped overboard:

'To be sure, sorr,' he said, 'yesterday I was in Mooney's bar in the Charing Cross Road and I was told that when I saw the hills of Dublin I was to shout "Hooray for old Ireland" and jump overboard.' The Irish are a charming if irrational people.

In the evenings, from near the Rectory, I have watched the sun go down in the west. The red ball dropped slowly until, just before it disappeared, an Irish mountain became silhouetted before the emerald flash that heralded the coming night.

One day, I visited the tough old relative who had left her teeth in a tree while hunting in County Kildare. In the darkness of a shed I could see her pushing a thermometer into a cow's backside.

'Still painting your bloody black mountains?' she shouted. 'Give it up and go to Ireland,' she said, as she removed the thermometer from the rear end of the sick cow.

'It's green and a different life. Don't hang around here. Get over there,' she repeated.

The next week, a letter arrived from a friend in Ireland enclosing a return ticket by air to Dublin and a request that I should go over to stay with him and paint his portrait.

Dermot met me at the airport. He had a beautiful girl on his arm. He explained that she was married to an Irish artist but at the moment she was living with him, and we were going to a great party in the Sherman Hotel and the whole of Ireland would be there, and that he had got a girl for me. I began to understand why my relatives made forays across the Irish Sea.

Outside the hotel I was introduced to my partner. She resembled a large pink marsh-mallow and appeared to be encased in furs. Her name was Gladys. The noise that emanated from the hotel was deafening and it became almost intolerable as we entered a large and smoky room where bodies heaved and swayed and rollicked and roared. I found that the Irish voice, confined and inebriated, produced a painful and incomprehensible wail, that made me think that I had joined a convocation of banshees. Because of my epilepsy it was unwise for me to touch alcohol, so in the midst of this wild, alien and bacchanalian orgy, I felt very lonely indeed. Dermot and his Eileen were shouting and roistering; Gladys, entangled in the arms of a man who looked as if he might have played in the scrum for Ireland, was squeaking and sweating, for, in spite of the heat

engendered by the multitude of bodies, she was still wrapped in her voluminous furs. Bored, I wandered away and watched from the cool safety of the hall.

My host must have remembered that I was in a foreign land and, in the company of Eileen and Gladys, he came bursting and reeling from the party shouting that we were going out to dinner. It was ten o'clock and I was hungry. We piled into his small, open car and plunged through the traffic to stop, after a few minutes of frantic driving, outside the Royal Hibernian Hotel. Dermot was obviously a *bon viveur* and selected his food and wine with flair and with relish and, when the food arrived, consumed them with uninhibited satisfaction. Soberly, I wondered how I could contribute to the conversation. I felt it would be unwise to mention a boy with whom I had been at school, who had lived in Dublin and had murdered his mother. He had put her body in a baby Austin in order to dump it into the sea at Howth, but had run out of petrol in the centre of Dublin. My sobriety inhibited me, and I merely asked if they knew of another school friend by the name of Michael Fanshawe. My host staggered to his feet, a wine glass in his shaking hand. He pointed a finger at me and roared: 'God, he knows Michael Fanshawe.' He turned round and, knocking over a few chairs, disappeared in the direction of the hotel lavatories. Embarrassed, I asked Eileen if I had been indiscreet.

'Well, maybe,' she replied thoughtfully, 'you see, I had a child by him before I met Dermot.'

There was a long and heavy silence as we picked our food, and then Dermot appeared once more, shouting that he wanted to show me the mountains of Dublin. It was half past twelve, and outside an impenetrable darkness covered the land of Ireland; but Dermot had recovered from his shock and had entered the happy state of advanced intoxication. Nobody argued, so once again we squeezed into the car and swayed away through streets, along winding lanes and over bumpy mountain roads, but nothing could I see except the gigantic bulk of Gladys that seemed to hang over me in the back seat of that regrettable car. I had no coat, the car had no roof, and my body had in no way benefitted from the consumption of alcohol. If the others didn't feel the cold, I did, and consequently, I showed little interest as Dermot pointed out the invisible beauties of the mountains of Dublin. At about two o'clock in the morning we managed to stop outside their house near Dun Laoghaire. I found, to my amazement, that Gladys had disappeared. I could not remember if the car had stopped so I presumed that she had fallen out. Somehow, I didn't worry, and felt sure that her bones would have been protected by those dreadful furs. I was put to bed and not surprisingly awoke with a heavy cold.

All morning I waited for something to happen, but not a sound could be heard until after mid-day when the figure of my host appeared announcing that we were to return to the Royal Hibernian for lunch. The car lurched away and soon Dermot was busily occupied at the bar of the hotel. Lunch was taken at two o'clock, after which my host returned home for a siesta that lasted until about seven o'clock, when the whole process of drinks and food started all over again. I found this was the pattern of their life and knew that there would never be any time for me to paint a portrait.

Dermot had asked me to bring some pictures with me and on seeing them he had immediately bought one. He suggested that I took it, with others, to a gallery where it could be framed. The owner was Victor Waddington who had been brought up in Dublin with little money, with a great love of art and with much ability with his fists. In Glasgow, I was told, he had earned enough in the boxing booths to enable him to open his gallery in Dublin and it had been he who, almost on his own, had created a whole school of Irish painting. Victor Waddington was a magnificent figure of a man, tall and straight with a distinguished head covered by a mass of wavy white hair. One half-closed eye appeared to me to be the legacy of his days in the boxing booths. His friend Jack Yeats had left him the contents of his studio in his will, and with all these pictures in his possession he was able to leave Ireland and open a successful gallery in London. I liked Victor Waddington and we became good friends.

Meanwhile, as Dermot ate, drank and slept, I, with my developing cold, staggered round Dublin, sometimes on my own and sometimes in the pleasant company of Eileen. Dublin, I decided, was a city hardly conducive to the creation of works of art. After five fruitless and baffling days, I got on a plane and returned to London.

The following year I received yet another letter from Ireland and another ticket to Dublin. This time it was from a wealthy Welsh businessman who lived in a stately home in County Wicklow, with his own airfield in front of his house and the mountains behind. A car met me at Dublin Airport and I was driven south to Killoughter, the house I had been commissioned to paint. An eighteenth-century building, it stood magnificently in a parkland of palm and eucalyptus trees, with a flight of steps leading to an imposing entrance on the first floor. It was a luxurious country house staffed by a butler called Seamus and several pretty Irish maids. My hostess was tall and elegant and had once been a top model. In contrast to the habitation and mode of living of the wayward Dermot, life at Killoughter was efficient and her husband organised business interests in Cardiff and Wicklow. Luxury, I have always found, does not stimulate my artistic faculties and I knew that I would never be able to work in that lovely place. When, over dinner one night, I said that I would have to go somewhere else to work, I was told not to worry, only to choose somewhere to go and they would pay the bill in exchange for the first refusal on anything I produced.

I decided to stay in Glendalough, a tiny place in the Wicklow mountains. Secure in a ring of mountains, peel towers rose among the ancient churches and on the hillside above the lake was St. Kevin's cell. Up in these hills the sun shone, the bees buzzed, monks contemplated and the land seemed to be embued with an air of holiness. I knew that I could work there.

After a few days, my hostess arrived with her children to take me back to Killoughter. We walked to a wishing well. I wished, the children wished and then I asked their mother if she wanted to. She gave me a smile and replied that there was little point in doing so as she had everything she wanted. Very few people, I thought, would not have asked for more.

I painted a picture on the bridge in Wicklow. Men were leaving a rope-works. They crowded round me in an attempt to see what I was doing. A Welsh accent broke through the clamour of Irish voices and I heard the gentle yet authoritative order: 'Give him some air, boys.' Through the throng of Irishmen came the unmistakable figure of Cliff Morgan, one of the greatest Welsh fly-halves of all time. I saw him often afterwards for he managed the rope-works that was owned by my host.

When I was being driven back to London Airport, I asked the chauffeur to stop at Victor Waddington's Gallery so that I could pick up the pictures he had been unable to sell. Back in London I opened the package to find, among the other oils, the one that had been bought by Dermot. Dedicated as he was to the all absorbing business of eating and drinking, he had not had time to remember that he had purchased a picture.

It must have been about ten years later that I decided that I should cross to Ireland once again, this time without the restrictions of any sort of commission. I decided to go to County Clare and stay in an hotel in the small town of Ennistymon. I crossed by boat from Holyhead, stayed for a night in Dublin and the next day travelled

westwards. As I was waiting on Limerick station to catch the train to Ennistymon, an Irishman hailed me, as Irishmen do, and asked me where I was going. I told him.

'Ennistymon,' he cried, 'well, that is a dreadful place to be going to. Why don't ye go to Kilkee?'

I said that I had booked into an hotel. 'Well, that's a damn fool thing to do when ye can go to Kilkee.'

He was persuasive, so I decided that if Ennistymon had few prospects I would journey on to the obviously desirable town of Kilkee.

The Falls Hotel in Ennistymon had been the home of the Macnamara family from whom had sprung three girls, Caitlin, Nicolette and Bridget. Their father, a feckless and impoverished Irish squire, had been irresponsible enough to leave his daughters in the care of Augustus John. Caitlin duly married Dylan Thomas; Nicolette, the painter Anthony Devas, but I do not know what happened to Bridget. After a night in Ennistymon, I understood why Father Macnamara left for England and why the Limerick Irishman had given me such a warning. I decided that I would take the Ennis-Kilkee train and follow his advice.

The Ennis-Kilkee line was infamous as the trains never ran to time; it also had its own eccentricity in that there were first, second and third classes although all the carriages were the same. The difference only became apparent when, on the first stretch of rising ground, the train came to a halt.

'Second and third classes get out,' shouted the guard. 'First class remain seated.' When the passengers thus summoned were standing on the line, another order came. 'Second class stay where ye are. Third class into the peatbog and dig.' Re-fuelled, the train would get up steam, passengers would get aboard once more, and the train eventually reached its destination. One day, a Kilkee literary man wrote a wicked poem warning people of the unpunctuality of the Ennis-Kilkee railway. The company decided to sue him and it was announced that the case would be heard in the county town of Ennis. The court assembled but there was no sign of the poet. Enquiries were made and it was learned that the train on which the poet was travelling from Kilkee was two hours late. The case was dismissed.

On the way to Kilkee the train stopped at Lahinch and I got out in order to have a game of golf on the links built by the famous Scottish regiment, the Black Watch, whilst stationed in Ireland. It was a very fierce links indeed with the greens placed maliciously in the depths of huge valleys in the gigantic sandhills. I impoverished myself by losing a regrettable number of balls. Humiliated, I boarded a later train and arrived at my small west-coast destination. I enquired about the local hotels and decided to try one that I reckoned would be modestly comfortable.

As I left the station with my baggage and painter's paraphernalia, I saw a small, scraggy brown and white terrier sitting in the road. He barked at me. 'Hi, Clancy,' I said. His right ear cocked, a canine smile crossed his face and he barked again. I felt his name must have been Clancy for, after licking my hands, he dashed off down the road, occasionally stopping to see if I was following. It was obvious that he had adopted me and after I had entered my small hotel he remained faithfully outside.

He was there the next morning and on seeing me, dashed around in ecstatic circles and happily joined me as I explored the small town. Architecturally, Kilkee did not impress me, but in front of the undistinguished houses was a rocky bay almost closed by a reef over which huge Atlantic waves were breaking. The rocks on the southern side appeared to be perforated, for the sea, as if from geysers, burst upwards in a violence of spume and spray. Curraghs, like long, black, canvas slugs, lay on the beach while others, manned by hardy fishermen, braved the turbulence of the reef. It was certainly a lovely place and I was grateful for the persistence of the man in Limerick. The shore was littered with driftwood, a sight that so stimulated Clancy that he picked up piece after piece, threw them in the air, caught them, barked at them and finally insisted that I should join him in his glorious and energetic game. I could hardly do otherwise.

Since my arrival in Dublin I had tried to find an Irishman with a moustache, as I had a theory that such growths marked the tribal

difference between the Goidelic and Brythonic Celts. We Brythons seemed to have them and they did not. Perhaps, in the past, this was the only way they could tell which side they were on when in battle. I saw men with beards and moustaches combined, but nowhere did I see them with a completely unshaven upper lip until, in Kilkee, I saw a dark man with a very heavy moustache. In the hotel I told the publican of my search and how, finally, my theory had been disproved.

'And where did ye see the gentleman?' asked my host.

'He was wearing a white coat and going into the chemist's shop,' I said.

'Ah, yes,' came the reply, 'that is Mr Williams from Caerphilly. He married the chemist's daughter.'

I don't think I saw any other moustaches, but that was in 1960. My theory seems to have evaporated into the Irish mists, for today half the Irish rugby team seem to wear them.

Every day, accompanied by Clancy, I set out along the cliffs, my pack on my back and carrying a box in which I kept my panels. As I painted that wild and exhilarating sea, breaking with a terrible violence on the rocky coast, Clancy energetically chased the seagulls, barking furiously in frustration at being unable to catch them. When he got tired of his failure he lay panting beside me, waiting to accompany me on my way back to the hotel. I never found out who owned him or indeed where he found his food but, while I was in Kilkee, he certainly looked upon me as his master.

One day, as I returned to the hotel with my box of panels, the publican gave me a broad and knowing smile. He left his bar, put his arm around my shoulders, and whispered into my ear that they all knew what I was after in Kilkee and how I was going to make them all rich.

'Ye good health, sorr,' he said as he raised his glass, and everyone in the bar, let into a secret that was beyond my comprehension, joined him happily. Bewildered, I asked my host to tell me his secret. He roared with laughter and said I was playing a canny game.

'Ah, yes, sorr,' he said again, 'and ye will be bringing prosperity to Kilkee.'

After dinner, when he was in an early and lucid state of inebriation, he became more expansive.

'Ah, yes,' he confided, 'we all know how ye go along the cliffs with your little box and your surveying sticks. Gathering samples ye are, aren't ye?'

'Of what?' I asked. 'Samples of rock,' he roared, 'samples of bloody rock, rich bloody rock. Yer after oil, aren't yer? Oh, yes ye are, and ye can't bloody deny it.'

I felt it would be wiser to say nothing in case a denial might bring disappointment and consequent anger. I gave a wink.

It was in that pub in Kilkee that I first became aware of the drinking habits of the Irish. One evening, before dinner, I saw a maid taking a large tray laden with Guinness into a bedroom from which there came a low murmur of voices. A few hours later I saw her again carry a larger tray and I noted that whiskey had joined the bottles of Guinness. In the morning, a graveyard of bottles littered the landing, and strange moaning seemed to come from that bedroom. All throughout the day more bottles were delivered, and the pile of empties got larger and larger as the noise in the room got louder. All through the second night they must have consumed their liquor until they had drunk themselves into an alcoholic coma. On the second morning no sound came from that bacchanalian bedroom, and in the evening the publican was once again behind his bar. Perhaps they had been celebrating their future as the beneficiaries of a massive oil boom.

Next day I paid my bill, gave my host another wink and made my way to the station. Clancy trotted beside me, no longer the bouncing, barking little dog that had adopted me on my arrival, but a sad dispirited figure pathetically aware that his new found friend was deserting him. As the train left Kilkee behind I could see a small patch of dirty white—immobile on a deserted platform.

Many years later I received a letter from someone unknown to me. He lived in Liverpool and wrote to tell me that his daughter was in intensive care in Addenbrookes Hospital in Cambridge. It was with fear and apprehension that he travelled to see her and always, as he waited outside the unit, he found himself looking at a picture that hung on the wall. On it was a plaque with the title 'A Rough Sea, Kilkee' and the name of the artist was Kyffin Williams. He wrote to thank me for the pleasure it had given him at a very sad moment in his life. If only for that, my visit to Ireland had been worthwhile.

8

There is something about the word 'Patagonia'. It makes a happy sound and slips easily off the tongue. People smile when they hear it, for it conjures up an image of an exotic land; very few people seem to know where it is, and those who do, assume that only the Welsh would be mad enough to settle there. In truth, all the plateau-land to the east of the Andes, which forms a natural boundary, belongs to Argentina while one third of the whole, a land of mountains, forests and rivers is owned by Chile.

It was undoubtedly eccentric of the Welsh to form a colony in this god-forsaken land but in the mid-nineteenth century the social conditions in Wales were such that many people believed that the language and the cultural life of the nation were endangered by the actions of insensitive landowners and English exploitation. Worthy Welshmen gathered together and decided that they must find a place in the world where Welsh men and women could go in order to establish a new nation in a land uncontaminated by alien habits. They settled in Ohio and Pennsylvania and even in Vancouver, but Dutch, Poles, Swedes, English and people from many other nations arrived to threaten their way of life. Frustrated, some of them moved south to Brazil and Uruguay, but always they were pursued. The barren, inhospitable land of Patagonia seemed to be the answer.

Somehow, the committee formed to encourage this emigration discovered the diary of a Mr Wickham, the first-lieutenant of H.M.S. *Beagle*, a ship commanded by the interesting Captain Fitzroy. They read that he had navigated the Patagonian River Chubut that flowed into the Atlantic about five-hundred miles south of Buenos Aires and five-hundred miles north of the Straits of Magellan, and that he had noted the presence of trees and cattle. With wild enthusiasm they envisaged some kind of a paradise, with lowing kine wandering through meadows bordering a gentle tree-lined river. Their Celtic imagination was so great that they asked Captain Love Jones-Parry, the adventurous squire of Madryn in Llŷn, and Lewis Jones, a printer from Holyhead, to seek out this wondrous place and to report on its suitability as a new home for the Welsh nation. The two men could hardly have been more different. The Captain, descendant of an ancient family, lived in style in Madryn Castle and pursued women with vigour and often with disastrous results. One year, with his mother as chaperon, he escorted a young lady to Gibraltar. As he rode with her across the border to indulge in some fox-hunting, a Spanish sentry leaped from his post and caught hold of the bridle of her horse. Captain Jones-Parry, an officer and a gentleman, knew instinctively what to do. He horse-whipped the man, whose cries awoke the guard. Out from their post they poured; the Captain was dragged from his horse and locked in a small and malodorous cell. The lady trotted back to Gibraltar.

In no time the Spanish authorities convened a special court that condemned the prisoner to death. Before the sentence was carried out, the British Consul sent a message to London enquiring if any Spaniard in England was in a similar position to that of the Captain. Indeed there was. An exchange was arranged and Love Jones-Parry returned to Gibraltar.

The Captain lived in feudal state in Madryn and exercised an hereditary *droit de seigneur*. It is told in Llŷn that on one hot summer's day, after he had returned from Patagonia, he chased Mary Jones, the milkmaid, into a field of wheat and, having dallied with her, fell asleep. As he slept his farm-men, in line abreast, with their scythes flashing in the summer sun, began to reap the golden corn. This gentle sight of rural simplicity was shattered by a fearful cry as the Captain rose from the field and then fell back in a pool of blood. Not only had the corn been cut but Jones-Parry's leg as well. A local doctor completed the amputation.

Five years later Queen Victoria visited Caernarfon and the local squirarchy was summoned to attend on her. As they lined up, their names were called out and, one after the other, they were presented.

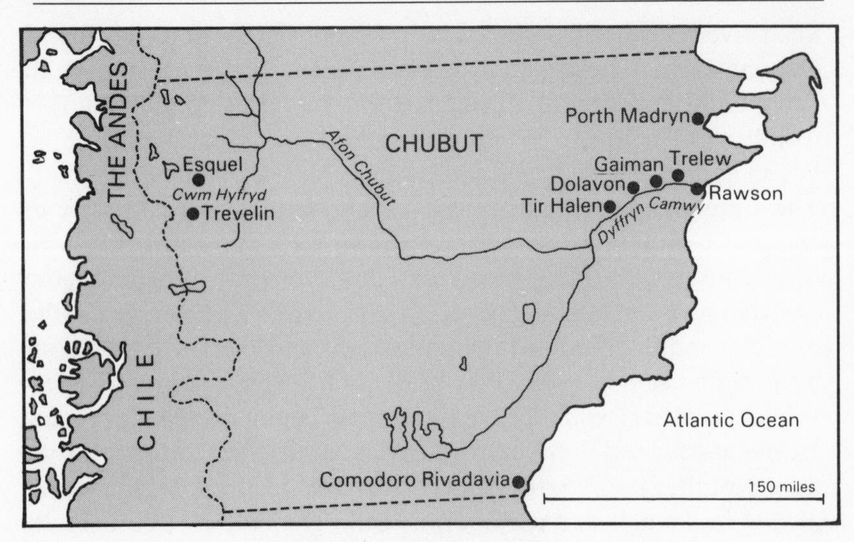
THE ANDES
CHILE
Esquel
Cwm Hyfryd
Trevelin
Afon Chubut
CHUBUT
Porth Madryn
Gaiman
Trelew
Dolavon
Rawson
Tir Halen
Dyffryn Camwy
Atlantic Ocean
Comodoro Rivadavia
150 miles

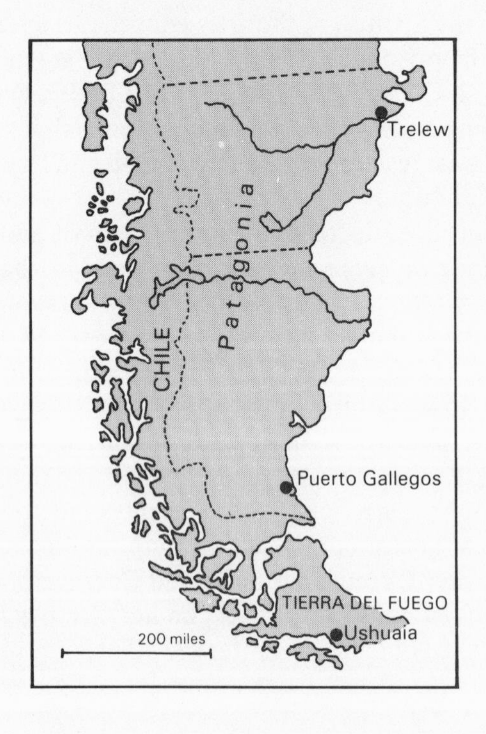
Trelew
Patagonia
CHILE
Puerto Gallegos
TIERRA DEL FUEGO
Ushuaia
200 miles

'Captain Jones-Parry,' cried an equerry, and the squire of Madryn hobbled forward on his wooden leg.

'Captain Jones-Parry,' enquired the Queen, 'and how did you lose your leg?'

'In the field,' replied the Captain.

'Ah,' cried Her Majesty, 'such gallantry must be rewarded. Equerry, a sword, a sword. Kneel, Captain Jones-Parry,' she ordered. The Queen tapped him on his shoulder:

'Arise, Sir Love,' she cried.

Sir Love Jones-Parry had no legitimate children, but one of his natural sons became a Member of Parliament, and a grandson was created a Baronet.

As Lewis Jones was only a printer from Holyhead, social etiquette decreed that it would have been difficult for him to travel in the same boat as the Captain, so it was arranged that they should meet in South America. Together they visited Senor Rawson, the Minister for the Interior of the Province of Buenos Aires, a government that held the distant, disinterested jurisdiction over Patagonia. The province had waged a long and inconclusive war against the Indians until, weary of the slaughter, the soldiers returned to Buenos Aires. The idea that the Welsh might succeed where they had failed appealed to the Minister, so he made it clear that if the Welsh did indeed settle in that inhospitable land, it would only be as subjects of his government. Disheartened, but not defeated, the Welshmen hired a boat with a convict crew and sailed south past Bahia Blanca and along the coast of Patagonia to where the Chubut flows into the South Atlantic. For twenty miles they navigated the river. The land was bare and arid, the only trees they could see were sad *criollo* willows, and there was no sign of any wild cattle. The utopia envisaged by the committee in Wales was, in truth, little better than a desert.

On their return, Jones-Parry and Lewis Jones wrote their reports, neither of which was favourable. Nevertheless, the committee was delighted to learn that no other European settlers had been seen in the sparse undergrowth. Here was a land untainted by foreign culture; a land of purity suitable for the development of a new nation. Energetically they started an advertising campaign for volunteers to sail to the promised land.

In April 1865 the clipper *Mimosa* sailed from Liverpool with 150 very ordinary Welsh men and women on board. Had they been in any way successful, they would never have undertaken an ocean voyage to an unknown land so very far from their homeland. Those ordinary, unskilled people had little knowledge of agriculture and carried with them but a single gun; nevertheless, they had a large stock of prayer-books and Bibles. No expedition to colonise a foreign land had ever been so ill-prepared. In July, in the cold mid-winter of Patagonia, they landed on a bleak wind-swept shore. There was no river mouth and no valley, only a harsh scrub growing on a stony plateau and across this barren landscape a party of men set out to find the land on which they were to settle. As the wind blowing from the Atlantic tore at their clothes, the settlers hacked away at the soft, white rock to make holes in which to shelter. It was a miserable place but they named it 'Madryn' after the gallant Captain.

After the men had discovered the Chubut valley a few miles to the south, the settlers sailed on and then up-river to a place where they decided to form a settlement. They were to name it Caer Antur or Fort Adventure. Their new land they called Y Wladfa, the Colony.

They set to their task of building shelters to live in and in which to worship, for they were a devout Nonconformist community. One day, as they sang their hymns in a rough shack, a group of Indians, interested by such a curious noise, surrounded the settlement. Charmed by what they heard and by the obvious friendliness of the people, they realised that, although white, they were very different from the aggressive Spaniards. From that moment, a warm understanding brought the two groups together, a friendship that has existed for over a hundred years. The Indians taught the Welsh to hunt for their food. Great herds of Patagonian llama or guanaco roamed the desert, together with the ostrich-like flightless bird known as a rhea. These they chased on horseback and they brought them down with the bolo, a weapon of three smooth stones covered

in a casing of skin at the end of a leather thong. In exchange for their help, the Welsh taught the Indians how to bake bread.

When the government in Buenos Aires heard of the success of the settlement, a naval party was despatched, the Argentinian flag was raised above the few houses of mud and stone, and all hopes of a new and independent Wales vanished for ever. No potentially-hostile country had ever been colonised without any violence and the Government of Buenos Aires recognised their success by providing the settlers with all that was necessary for starting an agricultural community.

The Chubut river, that rose nearly five-hundred miles away in the Andes, had cut its way through the soft plateau to form a broad valley forty miles long and about four miles wide. The whole area was saturated with salt, for after the last ice-age, as the ice melted away, so the land rose from the sea. Any water on this land caused the salt to rise and poison the soil. Consequently, a flood ruined the first crops sown by the Welsh, and the following year their agricultural efforts were destroyed by the sun. They realised that gentle

irrigation was the answer to their problems, and it was then that the very ordinary people became extra-ordinary, for with shovels and boundless energy they dug the canals, which eventually brought water from the river to the whole of their land. The valley was divided into districts, each with its truly Welsh chapel and, after twenty years of prodigious labour, the colony was secure.

The Indians told them of a lovely land four-hundred miles to the west at the foot of the Andes. There, they said, the rivers flowed freely into a lovely green valley where there was no need of irrigation. It was decided that an expedition should be undertaken to cross the desert to find this desirable place. Under the Spanish Governor, General Fontana, they rode westward; on reaching some rising ground they saw below them a lovely valley with the snow-topped cordillera rising above it.

'*Dyma gwm hyfryd*,' exclaimed an emotional Welshman, and from that moment it has been known as Cwm Hyfryd or Delightful Valley. Here, at last, was the sort of land envisaged by the committee in Wales and to it the Welsh brought their families and their stock. The colonisation of Chubut was complete.

The last years of the nineteenth century witnessed the success of the colony. Towns and villages were built and a boat sailed from Madryn to Buenos Aires and to Liverpool, returning with sewing machines, the newest fashions, as well as provisions for what had become a successful community. Soon, however, the people of Wales forgot their only colony and turned their thoughts to their preachers, their male-voice choirs and to rugby football. In 1911 the last group of people left to join their fellow-countrymen at the other end of the world.

My father's cousin Ralph had passed that way in 1874 on his way to the Straits of Magellan, where he lived with the nomadic Teuelche Indians. I remember Ralph Williams as a huge and formidable man in a broad-check suit, a *sombrero* on his head and a large drooping moustache. His father, the Rector of Aber, had sent him to Australia to get rid of him but he returned, and with another small financial blessing, went to Patagonia. It would have been difficult in those days for a member of a church family to consort with Nonconformists, so Ralph never visited the settlers in the Chubut valley. After adventures in Punta Arenas he returned to Anglesey where he heard of the discovery by Selous of the Victoria Falls. Fired by his spirit of adventure, he left his wife and small son in our old home and set out for South Africa, determined to visit this new wonder of the world. In Port Elizabeth he bought a sixteen-ox wagon and sent a cable asking his family to join him. When they arrived he hired some native servants and set off on a thousand-mile trek to the falls. Out in the veldt they were surrounded by a Zulu impi. One of the servants enraged a warrior, who advanced upon him with the obvious intention of running him through with his assegai. Bravely, Ralph's wife, Jessie, threw herself between them, so that the assegai intended for her servant was pressed against her own throat. There was a long and terrifying silence and then, slowly, the spear was lowered. On their arrival at the falls, a message arrived to say that a tribe, that had been made aware of Jessie Williams' bravery, was about to cross the Zambezi in order to capture her. They presumed that only Queen Victoria could act in such a gallant way and, as they had recently lost their chief, they had decided that the great white Queen would make an excellent substitute. Ralph decided that it would be wise to retreat and, after a few more adventures, they returned to the safety of Kimberley.

At the end of the last century two of my uncles had left the safety of my grandfather's rectory in north-west Anglesey in order to cross to South America to fight for the revolutionaries in Chile. One stayed to join the Chilean Navy while the other returned with a South American horse to receive a reprimand from his father, who asked what was wrong with the Welsh breed.

These adventurous contacts with such exotic lands gave me an urge to follow the example of Ralph and my two uncles, so when I read that the Winston Churchill Trust was offering a Fellowship in Art for someone who wanted to travel abroad I immediately sent in an application, and was duly asked to attend an interview. The committee was chaired by Sir Trenchard Cox, who had only recently retired as Director of the Victoria and Albert Museum, and before him lay my project to visit my fellow-countrymen in Patagonia in order to make a pictorial record of them and their land, and the birds, animals and flowers of the country. He gave me a kindly smile and said that he didn't really believe that there were Welshmen in Patagonia. Lady Alexander of Tunis also seemed to be sceptical, but Lady Parry-Williams, the wife of one of Wales' greatest poets of the twentieth century, not only assured her colleagues that I was correct about her fellow-countrymen in South America but also stated that it was an excellent idea for me to visit them. I was then asked for details, and I put before them my hopes of hiring a horse in the lower valley and then riding it across the four-hundred miles of desert to Cwm Hyfryd at the foot of the Andes. The idea appealed to the committee, so they duly awarded me a Fellowship. I then began to make my plans.

As I believed that I would be travelling on horseback, I knew that I would have to carry the minimum of paraphernalia, so I restricted my painting equipment to water-colour and a large stock of paper and sketch books. In the past I had only taken a few photographs with a box Brownie, but I felt it would be perverse to travel to such an exotic land and not make a photographic record. I asked advice and bought an excellent Polish camera and an exposure meter which

I had great difficulty in understanding. Machines invariably have a crippling effect on my powers of concentration. As I was on an official expedition, I made contact with Kodak and they agreed to provide me with films at a reduced rate so long as I was prepared to accept them when the boat on which I was travelling was outside British territorial waters. My Celtic extra-sensory perception told me that there was something unsatisfactory about this scheme and I warned the firm of my misgivings. They insisted that it was a usual way for explorers to receive their films, so unassured, I agreed to their plan.

For contacts, I wrote to Mrs Valmai Jones of Caergwrle who had been born in Patagonia and who had two sisters still living in the small village of Gaiman in the Chubut valley. With great energy she made plans for me and provided me with a long list of contacts.

I assumed that my very basic Welsh might allow me to communicate, but of Spanish I knew nothing: consequently, to improve my knowledge of the language, I booked a berth on an Argentine boat that sailed regularly between London and Buenos Aires. On 16 October 1968 I arrived at the Victoria Docks where the *Asunción* was berthed. She had a squat, yellow funnel and her hull gleamed in a tropical white. She looked a tidy ship. Carrying my bags, I walked along the quayside to where I saw a tall man standing at the bottom of the gangway. He told me that he was from Kodak and that he had to tell me that my films had been mislaid. He appeared amazed at my gift of second sight and added that he believed my films had been put on the wrong boat. I was also assured that he had been in touch with Vigo, the *Asunción*'s first port of call, and that arrangements had been made for their delivery to the ship on arrival. Unconvinced I went on board.

I found I had to share a cabin with three others. Ricardo Valdes was a civilised lecturer in English at the University of Buenos Aires. He was a great admirer of everything English and bred smooth-coated fox terriers. He agreed to teach me Spanish. Genaro Bastos was a pastry cook from Montevideo and had spent the summer as a waiter in a Torquay hotel. He told me with pride that on the dinner menu on his last night, the hotel had included an ice-cream called '*Bombe* Genaro Bastos'.

As the boat was about to sail there was a commotion on the quayside as a huge square man, surrounded by shouting and weeping women, made a dash for the gangway. It was my third companion, Luis Gonzales. He burst into the cabin like a wild boar. I noticed that his immense hands were encompassed by a thumb and five large fingers. He threw his cases onto the bunk above the one occupied by Genaro Bastos, leaned against the door and surveyed

us. I felt he would have made a devastating prop forward were he to play rugby for Argentina. His head was huge and his hair was thin: either side of a strong, hooked nose were two small and penetrating eyes and, above a mouth like a trap-door, was a small moustache.

'Too many a bloody womans,' he said.

Later, in the saloon, he told me that he was a gaucho and had been delivering polo ponies to an agent in London.

The engines rumbled and the cabin shook as the *Asunción* slipped slowly out of the dock into the river and out to the darkness of the open sea. I was on my way to Patagonia.

In the Bay of Biscay, as the *Asunción* rolled and pitched, I lay miserably on my bunk and wished that I was back in Anglesey. Gonzalez decided to comfort me. 'Ah, ah, ah,' he said. Later I found that all his utterances were prefixed in a similar manner.

'Ah, ah, ah, you no like sea?' he asked.

'No,' I groaned.

'Ah, ah, ah, you no like boat ?'

I wanted to tell him that I hated the beastly boat but just replied with a single negative.

'Ah, ah, ah, you no like food?' After this question he realised that I was about to be sick, so he changed the conversation.

'Ah, ah, ah, I play polo at Cowdray. I play polo with Prince Philip. He try to ride me off. "Out of the way you dirty bugger," he shout. "Don't you bugger me, you dirty bugger," I say.'

Gonzales gave a great sigh of admiration.

'Ah, ah, ah, Prince Philip a very great gentleman.'

Close to the north coast of Spain, the sea became calmer and I felt less sick, and by the time the *Asunción* had moved into the harbour of Vigo I had recovered. I had informed a purser that I expected a parcel, so I waited with him at the top of the gangway that was shaking under the weight of pushing, shouting and gesticulating Gallegos trying to force their way onto the boat. The men and women were dressed in black with black caps and black shawls. Some of the girls, more daring than their parents, wore scarves of muted colour. I gathered that they were emigrating from northern Spain to join many of their fellow-countrymen in Argentina. I waited patiently until about half an hour before the *Asunción* was due to sail but since there was still no sign of any parcel being delivered, I told the purser that I was going ashore and that he was not to sail without me. I ran down the gangway and into the Customs' sheds; an armed sentry blocked my way, then, for some reason, let me pass. I threw myself at a pile of baggages like a scrum-half extracting a ball from a heap of bodies. Eventually I found a small parcel bearing my name and also the name of some boat destined for the Far East! In triumph, I pushed my way through the weeping relatives of the emigrating Gallegos and sought the refuge of my cabin.

After leaving Vigo, the *Asunción* became a different ship, for the officers put away their dark-blue uniforms and appeared in white with brass buttons and epaulettes. As the weather became warmer, Gonzales became a happier man and I noticed how, as the sun rose, he left his bunk and disappeared into the ship's kitchens. There he drank quantities of Argentinian wine, to emerge at breakfast time crowing with high spirits before proceeding to chase the Gallego women around the boat. Up in the saloon, Ricardo tried to teach me Spanish and, down in the cabin, Genaro slept the sleep of an uncomplicated man.

The food became more inedible as the weather became hotter, and more and more often were we served with squid. Nobody complained and no officer was ever seen in the dining-rooms. I began to dislike the *Asunción*. At meal-times I sat at a table with Gonzales, Ricardo and a diabetic Argentinian naval officer by the name of Caba. Invariably Gonzales was the last person to take his seat. His arrival was heralded by the familiar crowing and into the room he came swaying between the tables and pinching the girls, before taking his seat to survey his audience. If someone was the Captain of the *Asunción*, Gonzales was the King. His appetite was enormous and not only did he devour our unfinished portions but also what had been left over on plates of neighbouring tables, and in between his consumption of octopus he related stories of life on the pampas. My companions were always convulsed with laughter but when Ricardo repeated the stories in English I could only assume that they had lost much in translation.

As the *Asunción* left Las Palmas in the Canaries, the cooling system in our cabin broke down, and a single jet of air shot out in one direction only and that was towards my bunk. I suggested that my companions should occupy my bed on a rota system but, generously, they refused to consider my offer.

One day, it was announced that there was to be a 'Miss Equator Beauty Contest' and everyone on board was allowed to vote. But it was hardly a fair contest because the Gallegos on board outnumbered the rest by three to one, and therefore it was certain that one of them would win. It was also apparent that all the girls were extremely plain and, under normal conditions, they would not stand any chance against the South Americans. The most beautiful girl on board was certainly Hermitte, a honey blonde from Brazil, and the English contingent agreed to vote for her. The day of the contest arrived and we voted. In the evening we packed into the saloon where the results were to be announced in reverse order. A purser appeared on the stage to announce that Hermitte had received third prize. It was then that the British behaved very badly. They booed, they banged on their tables with their shoes, and even invaded the stage to show their displeasure. Chaos reigned and tempers were at breaking point. Only Hermitte smiled.

When peace had been restored, the purser read out the name of the winner of the second prize. A huge pink girl with long black hair stood up. The Gallegos cheered while the British booed and whistled, but her reception was as nothing when the name of the winner was read out and a mountainous girl in a blue velvet gown was ushered on to the stage. The boos were followed by hysterical laughter that bewildered the contingent from north-west Spain. The Argentinians sided with the English and a chaotic, inebriated evening ended with two drunken hippies falling into the swimming pool. Later that night I came across one of them casually throwing the handles for lowering the boats into the depths of the ocean.

In the South Atlantic the clear blue of the sky was darkened by the clouds of black smoke that belched from the *Asunción*'s funnel.

Flying fish now leaped from the sea on either side of the boat as the passengers were engulfed in communal lethargy, and I was able to observe the varied behaviour of the different nationalities. The pure Argentinians appeared in shorts and bikinis, and lay prostrate on the deck. The Germans strode briskly and purposefully around the boat, while the Anglo-Argentinians, conscious of their origins, paced backwards and forwards in a straight line as if measuring a cricket pitch.

As the sun got even hotter, so Gonzales's crowing got louder and his pursuit of the Gallegos more ardent. It was lucky he did not possess a bolo to throw at them as they fled before him like frightened ostriches. With great patience Ricardo Valdes continued in his attempt to teach me Spanish, while Genaro Bastos just grinned and slept.

The *Asunción* entered the port of Santos, passing an architecturally international sea-front that gleamed like a set of broken dentures; but in the area of the port there was decay and squalor. I went ashore in a scalding drizzle that burnt my skin. The soil of the surrounding hills was red and the faces of the people were a similar colour. It was a nasty, sweaty place and I was glad to return to the dubious sanctuary of the *Asunción* and leave the port of Santos behind me.

As the boat slowed down to navigate the shoals and channels at the mouth of the river Plate, an air of expectancy was noticeable. The wash-house became fuller and the women started to put their hair into curlers. Now that the voyage was nearly over I decided that I would be the first ashore, once the ship had tied up alongside the harbour in Buenos Aires.

The *Asunción* arrived to the cheers of hundreds of excited Argentinians. As flags waved, whistles blew and bugles sounded, I presumed that it was out of relief that the boat had arrived at all. On the harbour-side many beautiful and excited girls were waving to somebody on the boat. I glanced along the deck and saw a huge figure leaping up and down, blowing kisses and crowing. It was Gonzales.

First off the boat and first through Customs, I made my way, laden with baggage, towards the dock gates and the crowd of cheering Argentinians who were pressed against the railings. I knew I was to be met, but where and by whom, I knew not. Suddenly, I heard a voice from amongst the crowd and it came from the level of my midriff.

'Kyffin Williams, Kyffin Williams,' it cried. I looked down among the flowered dresses and the jeans and saw a small man in a neat blue suit. Under a large trilby hat was a round, bespectacled face.

'Dan Lewis,' said the owner of the voice. 'President of the St. David's Society of Buenos Aires. Welcome to Argentina.'

He put me into a taxi that drove us to his flat in the Calle Peru and there I met people who were so obviously Welsh that I remarked on the fact. Dan Lewis only observed that he had never seen anyone look less Welsh than I did. As his wife, Letitia, prepared a meal, I was told that Mrs Valmai Jones had organised everything and that I was to be taken to the airport the next day in order to catch a plane for the town of Trelew, the capital of Welsh Patagonia.

One of the people at Letitia Lewis' lunch party was Delyth Jones, one of the best-looking women I was to see in Argentina. She had been invited as she was the only artist from Welsh Patagonia, and she was to be a great help to me later when I was in need of the painting materials that I was unable to find in the far south.

The next morning, Dan Lewis and Delyth Jones arrived at my hotel and escorted me to the city airport. In the plane I felt that I was in some sort of an aerial Welsh bus as I sat alongside my fellow-countrymen.

From the air, Patagonia looked as if it had died far back in the geological past, and I remember the observation of Darwin when he wrote: 'the curse of sterility is on the land'. Hundreds of miles of desert scrub passed below the plane and only seldom did there appear to be any tracks or signs of habitation. When we landed on an arid field outside Trelew, I had somehow failed to notice the valley and the meandering Chubut. I felt immeasurably depressed.

I got out of the plane and stepped into a bitter wind that seemed to blow dust from every quarter. I carried my bags to join some men who were sheltering behind a shack that served as an airport building. Again, from somewhere I heard the enquiry, 'Kyffin Williams?', and a serious-looking man pushed forward, introducing himself as Glyn Ceiriog Hughes. He picked up my bags and heaved them into the back of a small white car and drove me away down a dirt road at great speed. Clouds of dust were thrown up on either side but, when he slowed down, I could see a miserable conglomeration of shacks from which dark Indian faces peered inscrutably, and amongst them ill-clad children threw stones at dogs that scavenged among piles of dirty cans and paper. Dust like grey sand blew in clouds, so it was only when the track dipped down towards some more substantial buildings that I realised that I was in Trelew, the town named after Lewis Jones.

The car stopped outside the Restaurante Patagonicos. Glyn Ceiriog led me through a bar, where men were playing cards, and into a dining-room. A powerfully built man came forward and he was introduced to me as Sturdee Rogers. When I said that his name suited his figure he explained that his father had been very patriotic and had christened him after the victor of the Battle of the Falkland Islands. 'Damn,' he said, 'and I had two uncles, Inkerman and Sebastopol, and two aunties, Alma and Balaclava.' After an excellent steak, Glyn Ceiriog led me back to the car and drove me along some rough streets bordered by some modern and undistinguished buildings and out into a flat valley of mud, scrub and salt pools where here and there, without any obvious signs of planning, stood bleak isolated houses. I saw a forest of telegraph poles, and entangled in the wires were pieces of paper that flew around in the persistent wind. As we drove for about a mile, to where a bridge crossed a green and silent river, I counted the bodies of three dead dogs and two cows.

On a piece of rough and tired land beside the river, that the Welsh call Afon Camwy, stood an undistinguished building. It was Capel Moriah, the Westminster Abbey of the valley. It was built of pink brick and around the doors and windows had been painted broad bands of white. Iron rods had been driven through the walls, and without them I imagine that the building would have collapsed onto that cracked and desolate piece of land.

Plover wailed and the wind blew strongly amongst the poplars, weeping willows and tamarisk hedges as we walked past the chapel to where the floods had almost destroyed the cemetery. The rough ground of scrub and stones resembled a battlefield, for few of the tombstones remained vertical and those that did resembled the survivors of a beaten army. Yet there were still people who cared, for placed reverently at the foot of several graves were posies of apricot-coloured shells. The inscriptions, cut in Bangor on Bethesda slate, recorded the resting place of the heroes of the *Mimosa*. I read the names of Lewis Jones, John Williams of Dolwyddelan and Captain Jones of Porthmadog, and wondered if they had all died of broken hearts. A weeping willow, so common on stones in Welsh graveyards, had also been carved on many monuments in the cemetery of Capel Moriah, and, appropriately enough, similar trees were growing on the river-bank nearby. As I made my first drawings in Patagonia, the wind blew more strongly and grey dust was swept across those slabs of slate. The plover wailed as if to tell me to go away and leave the pioneers in peace.

I followed Glyn to his car and we returned silently to Trelew, that sad, unimaginative town of fourteen thousand people that is the capital of Y Wladfa. Only a dreamy, contemplative people, more concerned with words and music than with visual elegance, could have created such a place.

The hotel, where I found a room, gave the impression that it was waiting patiently for prosperity to come to the town. The road outside was made of dirt and stones and the pavement was unfinished. I decided that it would be a long wait.

I lay on my bed and considered my situation. I was in the Province of Chubut in Argentinian Patagonia and I was in the heart of the Welsh community about which I had dreamed for so long, and yet I felt unbearably depressed. I was yet to discover the valley and its people.

Wherever I went in Dyffryn Camwy I was aware that above and beyond the creamy cliffs that bordered it lay the desert, or *meseta*, and these were the walls that contained the community and gave the people a feeling of security. The valley was almost entirely flat and divided up by roads and irrigation ditches into a chequer board of small areas of farmland surrounded by wind breaks of poplars, that protected the small houses, and by hedges of tamarisk that sucked the salt out of the land. Along the edges of the *ffos* or irrigation ditch grew some of the most magnificent weeping willows I had ever seen. The leaves of the trees were hardly ever still as the winds of the Atlantic and Pacific took turns to blast the land of Patagonia. Above the valley an immense sky created a feeling of insignificance.

Today, the land bordering the Chubut river gives the impression of an organised, if impoverished, place and I only became aware of its beauty when I visited the small farms that, surrounded by ramparts of trees, were welcoming oases in that wind-swept land. The oldest had been built of stone but, later, mud blocks were used to create small homes which, if lacking in distinction when seen

from the outside, were cool and charming within. The floors were covered with tiles and the windows with a close zinc mesh to repulse invading armies of ubiquitous flies. Originally, the buildings were thatched but today even the home of the Governor of the Province has a corrugated-iron roof.

I remember Dyffryn Camwy as a yellow land. Both the scrub bush and the cactus that grew in the desert had a small yellow flower, and the birds in the orchards and gardens made flashes of yellow as they flew from treee to tree. The parched land on which no grass could grow was yellow ochre, and the cliffs to the north and south a uniform cream. From the desert I looked at a land below me that had been created by the energy and industry of the early settlers. It appeared to be a rich valley and the patches that were of the most vivid green were fields of alfalfa, the main crop that is harvested in December, February and April.

Because of the laws of gavelkind the land has been equally divided among sons and daughters, so that today many farms are larger than market gardens but not big enough to cater for any stock. Many of the farmers own large areas of the desert and over this arid land graze huge flocks of merino sheep. The Welsh produce the wool, the Germans buy it and the French, in Trelew, turn it into flannel. Peace is preserved and Dyffryn Camwy appears to be a contented land carved out of a cruel desert.

The initial depression that overcame me when first I arrived in Patagonia soon fell away as I began to meet the Welsh people. Mrs Valmai Jones had organised a group who had agreed to pass me from house-to-house and from farm-to-farm, and everywhere I went I found hospitality that verged on curiosity, for visitors from Wales were rare and a Welsh painter had never been seen before.

Glyn Ceiriog was an indefatigable guide. His name was to me nostalgic, for he had been christened after the gentle tree-clad valley that wanders down from the Berwyn Hills to the English border. As a boy, I had lain on the banks of the river Ceiriog to watch kingfishers and had walked through the bluebell woods in the valley. Such a place was very different and a far cry from the bleak land of Patagonia. Glyn told me how his father, who had been born in Patagonia, had returned from his only visit to Wales. Eagerly they had asked him his impressions of the Old Country.

'Well,' he replied solemnly, 'it is a funny little place and everywhere I went I was knocking my nose.'

Glyn decided that the first person I should visit was Senor Luis Feldman, the Jewish and pro-Welsh proprietor of the *Jornada*, the local Chubut newspaper. I was placed in a chair in his office and photographed so that everyone would know what I looked like. Unfortunately, the photograph that was printed gave the impression that I was a desperate and wanted man, and it must have caused the good people of Y Wladfa to question the wisdom of their offers of hospitality.

The two languages spoken in the valley were Welsh and Spanish. From Ricardo Valdes I had learnt little Spanish, even though he tried hard to teach me, and I have never been able to master the language of my forefathers, so when I was asked to broadcast over Chubut Radio I had certain misgivings. Senora Tegai Roberts, a descendant of Lewis Jones, had driven from the village of Gaiman to interview me on her weekly programme. She and Glyn rehearsed me patiently, but when I came 'on the air' I had a distinct feeling that I was letting them down. Few people appeared to speak English, so by the time I returned to London my Welsh had improved immensely.

Physically, I found the men and women of Y Wladfa to be mostly fair and well-built and far removed from the short dark type that the average Englishman believes to be typical. A hundred years of intermarriage in a small community had resulted in a dominant characteristic of gentleness. Indeed, their gentleness and honesty create a demand for their services in Buenos Aires. Many girls leave to nurse in the capital's British Hospital, and there are always places vacant for Welshmen in the city's banks and in other large towns of Argentina. After a month in the valley I became convinced that the people might benefit from marrying the more aggressive Spanish and Italian stock. I was given to understand that if a Spanish girl married a Welshman she invariably prayed that none of her children would have freckles which, to a Spaniard, are physical blemishes. Unfortunately, her prayers are never answered.

Many people in Wales who had been suffering from tuberculosis had been sent to the dry air of Patagonia as a last hope, and many had been cured. Today, the people appear to be healthy and live beyond their three-score years and ten; nevertheless, the sun, the wind and the dust batter their skin so that many look older than those of the same age in Wales.

The names of the Welsh in Patagonia gave me constant delight. Because of a law decreeing that no Argentinian child could be christened with any name other than a Spanish one, the younger men bore names that could easily be abbreviated satisfactorily. Hence, I met many Robertos, Ricardos and Evanos as well as a small Diego who was always known as Iago, the Welsh for James. The names of the women were the more fascinating and mellifluous for, on marriage, the word 'de' was placed between the maiden name of a girl and that of her husband. I had the pleasure of staying with Senoras Albina Jones de Zampini, Luned Roberts de Gonzales, Valeria Jones de Puw and Gwenonwy Berwyn de Jones. Some christian names were gloriously inventive, for when the arrival of a small Jones girl coincided with the flight of the first aeroplane over the valley, she immediately became 'Aviona' and a little 'Aluminada' celebrated the arrival of electricity.

I began to think about hiring a horse to take me across the desert to Cwm Hyfryd but my enquiries were met with disbelief and even horror. I was told that nobody would accompany me on such a foolhardy journey and if I went alone I would certainly get lost and die of thirst. I soon realised the impossibility of my project; indeed, had I embarked upon it, most of my time in Patagonia would have been spent in the saddle in an unpopulated landscape of unvaried scrub and stones. Despite feeling that I had received my Fellowship under false pretences, I decided to abandon my enterprise and allow myself to be guided by the eager and energetic Glyn Ceiriog Hughes. With an immense sense of purpose he set about his task of introducing me to Dyffryn Camwy. Amidst clouds of dust and under the vast Patagonian sky we visited every strangely named *ardal* or district, at the centre of each was a distinctly Welsh chapel. He took me to Tair Helygen, near the sea, and then to Bryn Gwyn, Bryn Crwn, Treorcki, Bethesda and Drofa Dulog, which, he told me, referred to the armadillo that lived in the valley. As he drove me through Gaiman and Dolavon, he told me that soon I would be staying in both villages. Many times he took me to small and sheltered farms, and in the high, cool rooms we talked of Wales and the places from where their families had emigrated. Often a native girl would bring tea and I would be introduced to her. I found that a very warm relationship existed between the Welsh and the descendants of the Tehuelche and Araucano Indians who, at one time, had ruled the land. The Tehuelche were tall and with a gentleness that is common to people of great height. When the Spaniards had landed on the coast, they had seen their huge footprints and had given the land the name of 'Patagonia' or 'the land of the people with big feet'. It was lucky that the settlers had made their homes in an area populated by these nomadic hunters and great horsemen. The singing of the Welsh people had pleased the Tehuelche but would not have impressed the Araucano, the small aggressive and warlike Indians who lived further north.

It was not long before I had forgotten my early depression, for the warmth of the people in their small farms reminded me so much of the people in Anglesey. Gradually, I began to understand the valley and I realised that the dead animals lay in the fields because the ground was too hard for a grave to be dug. Their bodies lay under the hot sun until the carcasses collapsed and disintegrated, finally joining the clouds of dust that blew over the valley.

At a place named Lle Cul, the Chubut River and the main irrigation ditch flowed side by side below the cliffs at the northern side of the valley. The soft cream-coloured rock had been carved by the incessant wind into great blocks and pillars and in places resembled the ruins of an ancient temple. Holes and crevices provided homes for colonies of screaming parrots. Screes of small stones, shining like mica, emerged from under the cliffs to fall to the edge of the dusty track below. One hot November day, as Glyn and I watched the parrots flying from the cliffs to plunder the fields, I heard a barking sheep-dog on the farm below being admonished by a Welsh voice. We walked down to where a small house, built of mud blocks, sheltered under a magnificent weeping willow. Glyn clapped his hands, as is the custom when visiting, and a young man with a red moustache appeared. He was wearing a beret, voluminous baggy trousers billowed from his waist and, on his feet, he wore the light blue rope-soled slippers that were used by all farmers in Dyffryn Camwy. He greeted us in Welsh as his father and mother carried rough wooden chairs from the darkness of their house. The *ffos*

flowed slowly past us as we sat on the hard-beaten soil below the great tree that hung with ropes of shimmering leaves. Beyond the ditch, and benefitting from it, the small fields were rich and green. We talked of Wales and drank *maté*, the drink that is the sign of hospitality in Argentina. Green Paraguayan tea is put into an empty gourd, which is known as the *maté*, and hot water poured onto it. After allowing it to stew, it is then passed around and the liquid is drawn into the mouth through a metal pipe or *bombilla*. When a host or a guest has drunk through the *bombilla*, it is a breach of etiquette to wipe it, however unhealthy a neighbour might appear to be.

As I enjoyed the unusual taste, we talked of Cardiganshire, the county from which the family had emigrated a century before, and of Wales, a land they had never seen. Tattered photographs were produced showing small stone-built farms nestling against hillsides near Tregaron and Llanddewibrefi. They had photographs of Welsh chapels, of relatives, and of one old man who had been a famous tenor and who had won prizes at many eisteddfodau.

'Didn't you know him? No? Well, well, very strange, very strange,' and so we talked as two fine horses stood in a rough corral below the desert cliff and cattle grazed beyond the *ffos*.

Near Lle Cul we visited the farm of Ceri Ellis. I took a photograph of him standing like a Welsh Gauguin on the river bank, and later I drew him harvesting the alfalfa, which he threw onto a sledge drawn by two dark, bay horses. I looked across the field to see the cream cliffs through a screen of waving poplars and realised there was no better land beyond the hill. This was something the Welsh had known when they settled and they had become content, as indeed I felt that Ceri Ellis was content merely to make a living in the manner their fathers and grandfathers had done before them.

On the dirt road at Lle Cul I drew Lias Garmon Owens. The wind ruffled his white hair and so distracted me that the smiling figure that stood in front of me appeared on paper to be a sad and worried man. Lias was a short man in his seventies and had, as a boy, left the little Denbighshire village of Capel Garmon to join an uncle who owned land in Y Wladfa. He had done well but the simplicity of his

house gave no indication that he was a wealthy man, for his Non-conformist background would not have allowed any ostentation.

Kylsant, the largest house in Lle Cul, had been the home of Benbow Philipps who had tried to form a Welsh colony in Brazil. Finding that it was doomed to failure, he moved south to Chubut where soon he was to play an important role in the affairs of the valley. General Roca, the President of the Republic, had decreed that every Sunday the men of Argentina were to carry out military training. This edict went against the natural inclinations of the Nonconformist Welsh who met and decided that Benbow Philipps should sail to Buenos Aires, there to put forward their objections to the President, General Roca. He was a fierce man who had gained notoriety during the wars against the Indians, but so eloquently did Benbow Philipps plead his case that the Welsh alone, of all the nations that made up the Republic, received official dispensation to carry on the sabbatical way of life as their forefathers had done in Wales.

I soon found the type of paper that was most suitable, and what manner of drawing was appropriate for making quick drawings of the valley and its people. Coloured ink I found to be too harsh, so I developed a style using pencil and water-colour, adding to the paper many notes that would help me when, in my studio in London, I came to paint my oils. The longer I stayed in Y Wladfa, the more often these notes were written in Welsh. Sometimes I drew in black ink but I found that its darkness did not truly interpret the clarity of the light. I tried to draw everything, the landscape, the buildings, the people and the natural history of the valley. I made hurried drawings of the birds that flew from under my feet, for they are unusually fearless in Patagonia. I tried to draw the spurred plover, or *teru teru* but, screaming loudly, these fierce little birds dived at me, extending a spur from their wing-bone as they flashed past my head. I drew the green and yellow *ouraka*, that screeched like jays as they raided the orchards, and also the *benta veo*, a thin and predatory bird that resembled a shrike. In the fields I saw flocks of *bandurria*, large birds with grey backs, yellow chests and with a long, curved red beak. This curious and comical bird was also known as a *gylfinir*, which is the Welsh word for a curlew, although their cry was so different from the bird we know in Wales, for on rising, they emitted an unattractive 'honk honk'. Many ducks swam in the pools and fed in the irrigated fields, but nobody shot them and I could draw them with ease. Pigeon congregated in the thick dust on the many roads and small wood owls gazed at me without fear as I drew them sitting on the fence posts around the farms. I saw blue and red hawks and, invariably, the *chimango*, a dark brown bird of prey about the size of a buzzard, that scavanged the bodies in the fields.

One day, as I drew on the banks of the *ffos*, a Welsh farmer passed me with a parrot in his arms. It was green with a bright red spot on its yellow chest and a dash of red and yellow on its wing. In its eye it had the worried look of a bird with indigestion.

'Poor old parrot,' he said, 'he has eaten too much of my corn. I am going to look after him until he is better.' And that he did, finally to let him go to eat more of his corn. The Welsh in Patagonia do not like destroying the wildlife around them but, in spite of this gentle approach, they appeared to be amazingly ignorant about the names of many birds that flew around the valley. The one bird they all knew was the *robin goch*, or red robin, but this was the size of a thrush and its chest was more orange than the small red-breasted birds we see in Britain.

There were many wild animals in the valley but I did not see many of them. There were hares that resembled those we see in Europe but the Patagonian variety was a tail-less crouching animal that ran like an apprehensive dog. There was a charming and alert little rodent called a *tucu tucu* that lived in holes in the ground and had the useful ability to run backwards as fast as it ran forwards. I presumed that it had mastered this skill in order to avoid the grey and red foxes that came down from the desert to hunt. Once, I saw a dead armadillo but never did I see one alive. Dyffryn Camwy is not noted for its flora and apart from the pink and white convolvulus that covered the banks of the irrigation ditches there were few wild flowers of beauty.

One day, Glyn drove me to Gaiman, the most Welsh of all the settlements, and a village of which I became very fond. Tegai Roberts, the curator of the Welsh Museum, showed me uninspiring pieces of memorabilia, but there was no record there of any artistic creativity and I assumed that the task of cultivating the valley left them with little time to indulge in such luxuries. We went to the Plas y Coed tea-rooms and met the owner, Senora Dilys Owen de Jones. She was a small plump woman with spectacles and a large smile, and she leant heavily on two sticks for she was crippled with rheumatism. She had been born in Rhiwlas, a village above Bangor, and her home was hung with pictures of Snowdon, Caernarfon Castle and the Menai Strait. There was a warmth about her as she welcomed us to her tea-rooms in the middle of a flower garden, and she was obviously delighted to see someone who had come from near the place where she had been born. I made her a promise that I would return.

I never really cared for Trelew, a town seemingly built for no geographical reason and within which there was not a single building that showed any architectural distinction. The Chubut River was a mile away and the *ffos*, that gave so much character to the valley, was piped underground before its waters reached the town. With a little imagination the river could have been an amenity for, bounded by broad-walks of poplars and weeping willows, it could have flowed with advantage through the centre of the town. So Trelew, drab and unattractive, acts as a market town for the farmers of the valley, and as a centre from which produce is carried north to Bahia Blanca and south to the oil town of Comodoro Rivadavia. Around the town, in shacks made out of beaten oil drums lived the Indians, pathetically content to stay as second-class citizens. Everywhere in Trelew there is dust and in the streets, waste paper in abundance. The method of disposal must be unique. From the confined area of the town, it is collected and deposited on an even more confined piece of exposed ground to the west of the town from where the gusting winds disperse it over an even larger area than that from which it had been collected. To Trelew the paper returns, whirling over the houses, to flatten against the fences and railings. It is blown, dirty and discoloured, down the dusty streets and even across the valley to settle irreverently in the graveyard of Capel Moriah, turning that melancholy site into one of disorder. My only sorrow on leaving Trelew was parting with Glyn Ceiriog, my indefatigable guide.

In contrast to Trelew, Gaiman is a place of charm. A broad tree-lined street divides a pink and honey-coloured village that was squeezed between the desert and Afon Camwy. Among the trees on the other side of the river stands an unmistakable building. Capel Bethel is the architectural soul of the community.

I stayed in a large house above the village. It was the home of Senora Mair ap Iwan de Roberts, the grand-daughter of the pioneer, Lewis Jones. In the house lived her daughter, Tegai Roberts, who had encouraged me to broadcast to the people of Chubut, and had shown me her museum. She was tall, fair and distinguished, as befitted the historian of Y Wladfa. Her sister, Senora Luned

Roberts de Gonzales also lived in Plas y Graig with her husband and two small, energetic boys. Luned was dark and cheerful and was the capable headmistress of the Welsh School. In Gaiman I began to understand how completely my fellow-countrymen had colonised the land, for many of the shopkeepers were as Welsh as the farmers in the valley. The two large stores in the village were both owned by men of the same name but with the addition of the christian names of their wives. I never met Bob Jones Matilda but enjoyed my visits to Bob Jones Martha. He was a tall, distinguished-looking man who had emigrated from the village of Dolwyddelan in 1911. He bore a striking resemblance to Sir Clough Williams-Ellis. In a garden behind his *roperia*, he showed me his magnificent roses and talked about the Lledr valley without any *hiraeth*. In his shop I tried to draw him against a backgound of pots and pans, but failed to do him justice.

I returned to Plas y Coed tea-rooms and in a cool back room I found Dilys Owen de Jones feeding her cardinal finches. She made me tea and told me of her life and how she came to Patagonia:

'There we were, landing at Madryn and nothing, nothing, nothing but desert. Well, I sat down in the dust and tears rolled down my cheeks. Whatever were we doing in this dreadful place; and there was typhus and dead animals and dust and wind, and the more I looked the more the tears came, and it was all because of my brother, who was sick, that my father brought us here. My brother had tried to lift a heavy weight, and bang went a blood vessel in his chest, so my father sold everything and out we came, and after a year my brother went back and got married . . . and I suppose we just got used to the place. And, oh, it was much hotter then, oh, much, much hotter and there weren't so many trees, and it is funny how the weather has changed. And the floods were dreadful years ago and the house was under ten foot of water and I was wet, wet, wet, and that is why I have rheumatism and have to walk with two sticks.' In that small parlour with her cardinal finches she told me the whole story of Y Wladfa as she knew it. She dragged herself through her rose garden to say goodbye at her gate and made me promise to return.

One Sunday, Tegai and Luned drove me across the dusty valley to an area of cracked and sour land in the middle of which stood an ugly red-brick building. It was Capel Bryn Crwn, and towards it cars and pony-traps were converging for we were to attend a *cymanfa ganu*, a religious singing festival, so dear to the Welsh hearts. When we left Plas y Graig it had been in the warmth of a November evening, but by the time we had reached the chapel the wind had changed and was blowing an icy blast from the sea. Men, sheltering from it, stood flattened against the building like flies on a fly-paper. I stumbled for warmth and shelter through the crude porch and into a charmless hall. The bareness was horrifying yet typical of a people whose emotions only seem to be stirred by thought and by sound. The women alone filled the pews; the men, observing an ancient custom, stood shivering outside.

When the silence was broken by a wheeze from the harmonium, the men, red-eyed and with their hats clutched in their hands, crept into the building. Unobtrusively they sidled into their seats until no room was left in the pews, so that many of those who had appeared to prop up the walls from the outside, now did so from within. A large ginger-haired man filled a seat and a half beside me and gave me a friendly wink. The festival was about to begin.

A man with the face of a Roman senator mounted a low platform and announced the first hymn to be sung to the tune of 'Glan Geirionydd', and at the sound of that name I was back in Wales on the edge of a sheltered lake that shimmers under the mass of the Carneddau. The girl began to encourage the harmonium. It wheezed and wavered and then, as the senator raised his arms, it responded and the congregation burst into song. Rich Welsh voices echoed around that dreary shed and I, my vocal chords frozen by the wind, could only listen in amazement, much as the Indians had listened in Caer Antur a hundred years before.

The hymn ended. A man offered a prayer in Spanish and then they sang 'O Deuwch Ffyddloniaid' and this, the Welsh 'Adeste Fideles', reminded me that Christmas was not far away. A venerable lady rose to address us and I felt that there was admonition in her voice. Gerallt Williams, a farmer in the *ardal* of Bryn Crwn, related the history of the chapel and then his brother, Edmund, was on his feet informing the congregation that a Welsh artist called Kyffin Williams was among them and that he hoped they would all extend to him their hospitality. As he sat down I knew I had to reply. I stumbled through a few Welsh words but evidently I had not said enough, for I was invited onto the platform and from there, as I gazed at a hundred friendly faces, my Welsh began to fail me like a slow puncture. Perhaps they assumed that the Welsh language in Wales had changed since 1865, but it was down an aisle lined with smiling faces that I returned to my pew.

The vigour of the singing had so raised the temperature that cries for air from the front and cries of 'No, No' from the back mingled with the notes of 'Cwm Rhondda'. A window behind me was opened and a shaft of air generated in the Antarctic forced us to dive for shelter beneath the pews. Thereafter, there was a battle of wills until those who were half dead with cold triumphed over those who were gasping for air. The window was closed, and the dignity of the proceedings evaporated as Welsh men and women demanded the singing of their favourite hymns. Arguments broke out and the Roman senator tried vainly to bring some kind of order to the proceedings. Sunset broke over the valley, the wind howled, the people sang, the harmonium wheezed and Capel Bryn Crwn became as a boat on a wind-swept sea.

In Gaiman I found an inexplicable confidence that enabled me to lecture to groups drawn from every part of Dyffryn Camwy. I talked to Luned's pupils and encouraged them to make abstract mosaics from the millions of agates and cornelians that covered the desert behind the school. They listened with patience but with little understanding. I talked to the Salvation Army, for their Senior Officer, Major Edward Watkins, came from a farm in Pencaenewydd, near to the small town of Pwllheli. I had known his truculent father and therefore understood why the son had seen fit to remove himself to such distant parts. I even lectured to the Trelew branch of the University of Bahia Blanca. As most of the students were Spanish Argentinians, it was agreed that I should speak in English and that Senora Albina Jones de Zampini from Gaiman would provide immediate translation. I stood before the rows of sallow, dark-haired students and voiced my opinions on the state of the world of art. I spoke of my theory that abstract painting was doomed as it was an art form contained in a straight-jacket that prevented any true development, and as I talked freely and critically of the development of art today, I noticed that the students wrote down everything I said. Only later was I told that Argentinian students believed implicitly that every statement made by their lecturers was the truth, and that they were unused to anything controversial. The longer I lectured, the more disputable became my theories concerning Modern Art until, seeing no reaction on the impassive Latin faces, I deemed it wise to sit down. Their professor rose to his feet:

'I wish to thank Senor Williams,' he said. 'He has made many interesting observations. I agree with none of them, but it has been most enjoyable to have had a romantic amongst us.'

From Plas y Graig I moved to the Casa Britannica in the Avenida Miguel D. Jones. Albina Jones de Zampini was the sister of Mrs Valmai Jones who had organised my visit, and her husband Rubio was the local cultural director for the province. Albina was thin with a sensitive face. She said that she admired my skin and complained that hers was so hard and lined. 'It's the sun and the wind and the dust,' she moaned, but I didn't see that she had much to worry about. She laughed a lot and was good company. Rubio's mother was Welsh but he had the looks of an Italian. The Zampinis, in spite of their name, were pillars of the Welsh community. It was whilst I was staying in the Casa Britannica that I did most of my work in Dyffryn Camwy. I had drawn the farmers at Lle Cul but now I was on my way to the *ardal* of Drofa Dulog to draw Kenny Evans. He was a cheerful and cautious young man of Cardiganshire stock. He had a broad and honest face, and drove his ancient Pontiac along the dirt roads at nine miles an hour. His house, mud-built and straw-thatched, was minute. A yankee saddle almost filled the doorway, the walls were covered with books and in one corner of what appeared to be the only room, hung a reproduction of Cézanne's

'Mont St. Victoire'. As we walked along the river bank, I remarked on the peace and quiet of the place.

'Yes,' said Kenny, 'that is the difference between us and the Spanish. We love the silence and they love the noise.' He must have been correct for I have never met a Patagonian Welshman who appreciated the canned music that blared from amplifiers placed on the top of every telegraph pole in every village. When I settled down to draw Kenny, I found it an impossible task because he was unable to stop laughing.

I think I succeeded in portraying the enormous bulk of Winston Churchill Rees, a friendly man with a face like a large red cheese on which two small and wary eyes shone like buttons. His father, who had been born in the valley, had left to fight in the First World War in a battalion commanded by Winston Churchill. He had been so impressed by his commanding officer that he had decided to name his first born after him. Winston Churchill Rees' brother Iffi was a cheerful man who drove the two valley-buses that bore the names of Lewis Jones and Love Jones Parry.

It was in the Love Jones Parry bus that I ventured the 40 miles across the desert in order to visit Puerto Madryn where the original emigrants landed. The bus lurched along a track of deep troughs of dust and stones. I saw no sheep and only occasionally a guanaco. I had been advised to stay in a small hotel near the sea owned by a Senor Emilo Bezuanartea, a Basque who had married a Senorita Williams. She had given him three beautiful blonde daughters who demanded that I should teach them English. In a garden of roses and hollyhocks they gazed at me as if willing me to help them, but I knew that I could do no such thing in the space of two days. The town was clean and white, but marred by a pretentious piece of sculpture presented by the Republic of Argentina to commemorate the landing of the Welsh.

I slept in a newly-painted room adjacent to the hotel. All night mosquitoes, that had evaded the wire mesh which covered the window, made raids upon my face. Every few minutes I lept out of bed to swat them against the walls with a rolled copy of the *Jornada*. Dawn broke to reveal a battlefield of blood and dead mosquitoes on the previously pristine walls. In the morning I found Iffi Rees who told me that a Senora Williams from Anglesey wanted to see me. He told me where she lived and said he would drive 'Love Jones Parry' to pick me up in an hour's time. Over tea, and reminiscences of Llannerchymedd and Amlwch, I heard the sound of a horn and the Love Jones Parry bus drew up outside. There were farewells, and in an hour or two I was eating a steak with Sturdee Rogers in the Restaurante Patagoniocs. I drove with him in his pig-swill truck along the metal road from Trelew to Gaiman, past the signposts to Treorcki and Bethesda and on past the cemetery, to draw up, stinking under the heat of the sun, outside the Casa Britannica. My arrival coincided with one of the many skirmishes that I witnessed between Cola, the Zampini's sheep-dog, and one of the most repulsive dogs I have ever seen. It lived behind a house on the edge of the desert and appeared to be without an owner. It was brindled and hairy, with pink eyes that appeared to look in every direction at the same time. Every day his bark initiated a confrontation with Cola. From the security of their homes, they dashed into the *avenida* to stop nose to nose, legs quivering as they made sure that never at any time did they make contact. Backwards and forwards along the wall of the Casa Britannica they swayed. Stones shot from under their feet as they snapped and snarled, their teeth shining in the Patagonian sun, and every day they performed the same inconclusive ritual. The exciting smell of the pig-swill truck brought their skirmishes to

an abrupt end and Cola accompanied me into the coolness of the Zampini's living-room.

Albina filled the gap left by the loss of Glyn Ceiriog and it was with her that I continued my discovery of the valley. Her time was limited as Clydwyn Jones, a local boy who had become a Professor of Music in Buenos Aires University, had returned to the valley for a holiday and had agreed to conduct the Gaiman Choir, in which Albina was a leading soprano. The concert was to take place in Capel Bethel and for a whole week the community was in a state of excitement as rehearsal followed rehearsal and Clydwyn coaxed, encouraged, criticised and finally moulded them into a choir. On the night of the concert the people of Trelew, Dolavon and Rawson joined those of Gaiman as they streamed across the bridge over Afon Camwy and down the poplar-lined lane that led to the chapel. I sat in a pew next to an American who had arrived to record the concert. Rubio stood up and announced the programme. The concert commenced. Six village girls sang English songs. Albina's daughter Mary sang a duet in Welsh with her cousin Gloria. Then Valeria Pugh, another of Valmai Jones' sisters, sang the only solo. The American appeared to be impressed:

'Hell,' he whispered, inappropriately, 'they're goddam good.' Finally, when the whole Gaiman Choir stood on the stage and burst into song, he was in ecstacies. As I had been in the valley long enough to know most of the singers, I felt that I was able to share their triumph. One of the sopranos was Senora Irma Hughes de Jones, the editor of *Y Drafod*, the only paper in the valley written in Welsh, and after the concert Rubio and Albina drove her home to her farm in Treorcki. When we arrived it was already dark and Irma pointed out the Southern Cross and other constellations that shone in that huge Patagonian sky. She asked me if I would like to see her father's library. She led us through the poplars until, in a clearing, I saw a mud-built building. It was the library. Irma opened the door and by the light of her torch I could see shelf upon shelf of books from the great literatures of the world. There were books in Persian, Arabic and Hebrew, in Latin, in Greek and in all the languages of Europe. I saw the names of many of the great poets, of Shakespeare,

Dafydd ap Gwilym and of all the famous philosophers and historians. Here, in the midst of Treorcki in Welsh Patagonia, was a library of someone who had been obsessed with the beauty of the written word. Arthur Hughes, Irma's father, had been born in Wales but had emigrated to Patagonia in order to get away from the conventions of life. In Treorcki he had become a hermit, and allowed his hair to fall in curls over his shoulders. He may have died far away from Wales but in the dry air and soil of Patagonia his memorial library will survive.

Orlando Pugh, the director of all the water in the district, took me to Ceg y Ffos, mouth of the ditch, where lock gates diverted the waters of Afon Camwy down a broad channel from which it was taken to irrigate the farms in the valley. Ceg y Ffos was a place of great importance in the valley, and Evan John Pugh was its muscular guardian. I stayed in the village of Dolavon where water-wheels, with tobacco tins nailed to their paddles, dipped into the *ffos* to drop water into trenches. From above the *ffos* these trenches carried the water to the village. On a farm in the *ardal* of Bryn Gwyn I stayed with Henry and Eifiona Roberts who insisted on calling me Mr Kyffin. There we ate asparagus that grew wild on the banks of Afon Camwy, but because Henry and Eifiona Roberts were both devout Evangelical Christians they would not sell the wild crop. The *ffos* flowed silently near the house, and people were baptised in its soft green water. One day a thunderstorm broke over Bryn Gwyn. The sky became blue-black and the rain turned the ploughed land into a bog. In the evening we drove, sliding drunkenly over the greasy road, to attend a rehearsal of the Christmas Carol Service in Gaiman. In a small shed behind the Avenida Miguel D. Jones were several people grouped around a piano. A girl waved her arms and they sang '*Noche de paz, noche de amor*' and I joined in the singing of 'Silent Night' in Spanish. After a few days in Bryn Gwyn I returned to the Casa Britannica where the peace of Gaiman was rent once again by an encounter between Cola and his adversary.

After a month in Dyffryn Camwy I had made over 200 drawings, water-colours and gouaches. It was time that I left for Cwm Hyfryd and the Cordillera that lay four-hundred and fifty miles to the west. At a quarter past five one morning, Albina, Rubio and I stood in the main street of Gaiman. The sun had not yet risen, it was cold and the village was still sleeping. Suddenly, in the distance, I saw two lights and eventually an ancient Mercedes bus creaked to a standstill. Rubio put my bags and portfolios into the baggage compartments; then there were quiet goodbyes before the bus started on its journey over the dirt roads of the desert to the distant Andes.

9

At Ceg y Ffos I looked back over the valley, and a thin line of orange told me that the sun was rising. The Mercedes bus rattled and swayed along the dirt road. At Las Plumas a herd of guanaco fled in terror and a flock of Patagonian ostriches fluffed up their feathers and ran away into the desert. By the time we had reached Passo de Indios, the road was bordered by low hills and cliffs layered with different coloured rocks which, near Los Altares, had disintegrated either into fantastic isolated pillars or into cockscombs of pink and crumbling stone. I tried to draw but all I could achieve inside the shaking vehicle were notes from which I could work later. By midday the sun that had followed us was now blazing down from directly overhead. At a place called Languineo we drew up beside a *boliche*, a ramshackle shed that served as a bar in that desolate place. Six horses stood patiently outside with huge saddles of sheepskin piled on their backs. I went inside to find their Indian riders drinking and arguing, and I remembered that it was at this place,

more than a hundred years before, that a battle had taken place. The Araucano Indians had felt inferior to their lofty neighbours, the Tehuelche, so they decided that in order to improve their stature it was necessary to breed from the wives of the taller tribe. They mounted an expedition and, riding south, fell upon the unsuspecting Tehuelche and made away with their women. Lonely and disheartened, the larger Indians pondered on the tragedy of their situation. The Tehuelche were not noted for their mental agility, so it took time for them to realise that somewhere to the north were the discarded Araucano women. Eventually an expedition rode northwards and returned with the little wives, so that by today all the Indians in Patagonia are much the same height.

Near Languineo the distant hills were blue and flat-topped and rose above an arid desert. The Mercedes swayed on towards the sun that had passed overhead and was falling away towards the west. Down the valley of Nant y Pysgod it dived, and in a pool of water pink flamingos stood with their heads submerged in the shallows. It was into this narrow valley that two Americans had ridden towards the end of the last century. They broke into a store kept by one of the ap Iwan family and, after shooting him dead, made off with the money from the safe. I was told that the two murderers were Butch Cassidy and the Sundance Kid. Nant y Pysgod is a lonely place where anything might have happened, and even if it hadn't there would surely have been people who would have said that it had. I drew continuously until my head began to ache and my eyes became blurred, so that I was hardly able to see the sun when it began to disappear below the Cordillera.

The light was beginning to fade as the Mercedes bus drove triumphantly into the town of Esquel. I almost fell onto the road. A huge female taxi-driver picked up my bags and heaved them into her old Chevrolet. I gave her the address of Emrys Hughes. I remember driving through some streets but my eyes were shut, and I didn't really care where I went as long as I could be rid of the pain that wracked my head. The taxi stopped and voices took me into a house. I opened my eyes to see Emrys and his wife Lottie gazing down at me. They gave me some aspirins and took me down a path to a garden shed. They opened the door and showed me a bed. I fell into it and slept.

The next morning I awoke with a sense of unreality but no longer with the violent pain in my head. I pulled some strange absorbent paper from my portfolio. I had bought it in Trelew as I had used up all my sketchbooks. I cut it up into six pieces and began to paint in gouache from the notes I had made from the window of the Mercedes bus. Brightly-coloured pictures appeared on the paper and I realised that they were very different from anything I had ever done before. Pleased with what I had painted, I walked through the garden and joined Emrys and Lottie Hughes for breakfast.

Emrys Hughes became Don Ambrosio when he presided over his many interests in Welsh Patagonia. He was a banker, a sheep-farmer and a man of property who, as a boy, had travelled westwards from Dyffryn Camwy in a horse-drawn waggon. After breakfast he unlocked the door next to my garden bedroom, and I saw shelf upon shelf of the silver and gold trophies that he had won with his merino sheep. Don Ambrosio was a man of substance.

I wandered into the town. Its streets had been built along the insensitive grid-pattern of most South American towns and sat uncomfortably below large copper-coloured hills. The people in Dyffryn Camwy appeared to be related to everyone in Esquel and Cwm Hyfryd, so I had arrived with promises to introduce myself to several families. I called on Arthur Morgan and his daughter Ethel, who had visited Llansilin in Clwyd the previous year. Arthur Morgan was built in the same mould as Emrys Hughes. Both had succeeded and their waistlines and gold-watch chains recorded the fact. I visited the home of Senora Megan Rowlands and met a Senora Williams who had recollections of Bontnewydd, Brithdir, Llanfachreth and Dolgellau. As I walked through the town in search of lunch, a truck drew up beside me. At the wheel was a man who had crossed the desert with me in the Mercedes bus. He greeted me in a broad American accent.

'Hi, there. D'you want a bite of something? My name's Fernando.' I got into the truck and he drove furiously down the street to stop outside a restaurant. Amongst the many members of the Welsh community seated at small tables were a few of obviously different origins. There was a red-faced man with a clipped military moustache and a red handkerchief tied round his neck. His name was Jimmy Gough, a member of a distinguished Anglo-Irish family who had married into the powerful ap Iwan clan and consequently owned many sheep. I was introduced to Don Diego Neill, an Argentinian Scot, who had been born in the Province of Neuquen and was the Intendente of the Los Alerces National Park at Futalaufquen. He was short and stocky, with a powerful head and a short strong nose. He reminded me of a peregrine falcon. Fernando introduced him to me and Don Diego invited me to spend Christmas with him at his house in the Cordillera.

Fernando told me that he worked for the provincial government and had studied in Texas. He appeared to admire all things Welsh and had attended the eisteddfod recently held in Trelew. 'Oh, gee, those guys have culture,' he said as he put away a very large steak. After lunch he drove me erratically out of the town towards the Cordillera and Lago Futalaufquen. The truck lurched in the rutted road and almost hit a telegraph pole.

'Can't handle these goddam power brakes,' he yelled above the roar of the engine. He told me he had to visit some road-works on the shore of the lake, but I had a vague idea that the provincial government had asked him to check on me.

We climbed higher and higher until the lake lay in front of us. Huge wooded mountains surrounded it and the valley was rich and green.

'Hell,' cried Fernando, 'it's goddam Elysian.'

His language was awful and everything was prefixed by 'goddam'. He had learned more in Texas than his engineering skills.

The next day I walked over the hills to the west of Esquel. From above, the town looked even more unattractive. Indian houses seemed to have been built into the hillside, and lean dogs scavenged and snarled and snapped at the feet of the horses that seemed to be everywhere, for, unlike Dyffryn Camwy, this was the land of the rider. The horses were superb and stepped lightly along the dirt tracks as if on hot bricks, so high and so neatly did they lift their feet.

Their noses were convex, more like the Barb than the Arab, and their chests were broad under powerful shoulders. Their riders, balanced on a pile of saddlery and sheep-skin, rode arrogantly with one shoulder forward like Colleoni in Venice.

I drew the gauchos and their horses. I drew the bullock carts and the cur dogs. I also drew a yellow flower, like a lily, and later I heard that it was called a *Cennin Pedr*, the Welsh name for daffodils. Behind the town I saw a neat little black bird with a rich chestnut back. I asked Senora Williams Avenida Roca if she knew its name. She had never seen such a bird. Nobody in the neighbourhood of Esquel had either, and, yet, every day as I climbed the hill above the town I saw it flying away with its chestnut back bright in the sun. I consulted Ethel Morgan. 'Oh,' she said knowledgeably, 'this is what we call a *robin goch*.' I told her that I had seen the *robin goch*, or red robin, in Dyffryn Camwy and knew that it was a larger version of our robin at home. She said she would ask her sister. They discussed the matter in Spanish. 'My sister says it is a *pecco colorado*,' she informed me confidently, and I told her that I had been in Welsh Patagonia long enough to know that a *pecco colorado* was the Spanish for a *robin goch*. Later I was to learn that the Welsh called it a *siôl fach goch* and ornithologists referred to it as a rufus-backed negrito.

I asked a farmer the name of a little bird with a grey back and cream chest. 'Damn,' he replied, 'I don't think I have ever seen one of those.' I told him I had seen about three hundred in two days.

'Well, well,' he said, 'it must be a *chingolo*.' Of course, it wasn't and later I found it was called a *duica*.

One day, as I was sharing a cup of tea with Senora Williams Avenida Roca, there was a heavy knock on the door and into the room walked a red-faced man with a ginger moustache and watery eyes. He wore voluminous *bombaccias* over leather boots, a red scarf around his neck and a black Argentinian hat on his head. He was as taught as a piano string. He introduced himself in Welsh as Fred Green, stated that his mother wanted to see me, and led me out of the house into the Avenida Roca where, in a large car, sat a small woman with a face like a walnut. It was Senora Gwenonwy Berwyn de Jones. She told me that they were off to spend the weekend with the sheep up on the camp in the desert and that I should go to her house in Trevelin. She said that her Indian servant Nita would look after me. It was an order. Fred got into the car and it disappeared down the *avenida*.

Dennis Williams drove the bus down the ploughed field of a road that led out of Esquel. When the road turned to the right for Futalaufquen, he veered to the left, crossed the river and climbed a hill, at the top of which I saw a valley. It was Cwm Hyfryd. The fields were greener than any I had seen in Patagonia and through them flowed a fast-running river. To the west rose the Cordillera, snow-capped and protective, the highest summit of which was Gorsedd y Cwmwl, the Throne of Clouds. The bus passed four round cones of rock and away to the south I could see eight more on the high ground at the far end of the valley.

Dennis Williams drove his bus with discretion, as befitted an elder of Ebenezer Chapel. We passed several small farms surrounded by trees and after forty minutes of swaying and shaking entered the village of Trevelin. We drove between a forest of telegraph poles, and men were hard at work putting up many more. Most of the houses were hidden by small trees and in the middle of the village was a broad dirt street. Horses stood patiently outside the several bars and men in sheepskin chaps lounged against the walls, their large hats tipped over their noses. It might have been the setting for a Western.

The bus stopped at a gate that opened onto an untidy area of scrub-land. In the middle stood a small, box-like house. It was Tŷ Ni, the home of Senora Gwenonwy Berwyn de Jones. A pretty, dark Indian girl introduced herself as Nita. Holding on to her skirt was a beautiful little girl of about eight years of age. She had long black hair and huge eyes. It was Nita's daughter Norma. In the background I saw a sullen Indian boy with big teeth. He stood with his head on his chest. He had no shoes and tied to his belt was a huge knife. It was Paulino who had only recently left his father's shack in the desert to live with the kindly Senora in Tŷ Ni. He was the eldest of eight children living with their father and mother and the ten dogs that were introduced to generate some heat in that bleak and often bitter land. This method of heating depended on one dog being alloted to each person, so their miserable building of one room became elastic with the arrival of every child. Paulino, the eldest, had to sleep with part of his head exposed to the bitter Patagonian wind. Consequently, he was deaf in one ear. All three Indians spoke Welsh and when I greeted Paulino his face broke into a huge smile and his crooked teeth flashed in the sun. The household was completed by a small energetic dachshund called Nia. In the evening the Senora returned from camp.

The house was simple but not primitive. In the kitchen was a wood-burning stove, a table, where we had our meals, and a box by the sink on which Paulino sat to gnaw the raw sheeps' heads provided by the Senora. He was yet to graduate to a place at the table.

We only sat in the parlour on those evenings when the Senora lit a fire. The walls were covered by a strange arrangement of pictures that united Patagonia with Wales. There were Welsh calendars and a plaque with the words '*Cristo fue muerto por nostros pecados*'. There were ox horns and a puma skin, set below an elaborately framed picture of the Happy Valley in Llandudno. There were Welsh and Swiss dolls and an Indian carpet but, most important of all, were the photographs of the Senora's family and one of her father who had journeyed on the *Mimosa*. This photograph was looked upon with special reverence by Nita, Norma and Paulino. In front of the fire was a home-made screen plastered with photographs of the Royal Family. On either side of the wash-house were two bedrooms. I occupied the one in the front of the house and the three women shared the other. Paulino slept in the kitchen.

I looked out of my bedroom window when I awoke after my first night in Tŷ Ni to find a piebald horse tethered to a post nearby. At breakfast the Senora told me that her son had left it there for me to use for as long as I stayed in Cwm Hyfryd. She also asked me if I

would ride it up the valley to her son's farm in order to deliver a sack of onions. Paulino threw a saddle over the piebald's back, put a bridle on him and announced that the horse was ready. I trotted over the rough land and joined the track that led to the ford over the Rio Percy. Men were still busy putting up their telegraph poles as I rode through the village and into the fast-running river. I presumed that my horse was possessed with local knowledge and this proved to be correct, for with great confidence it crossed to the other side. The Senora had told me that Pennant, her son's farm, lay at the end of the valley under Gorsedd y Cwmwl, and it was to the mountain that I turned my horse's head. I need not have bothered as it evidently knew its way home and, breaking into a canter, we raced up the valley, eventually to pass under a huge wooden arch on which was cut the name 'Pennant'. I dismounted outside a fine wooden ranch-house, only to find a gaping hole in the sack tied to my saddle which told me all too clearly that the onions were strewn along the valley floor. I remounted, turned my horse towards Trevelin, and retraced my steps, stopping occasionally to pick up the onions that lay scattered over that rough land.

After lunch, Fred Green's younger son Iolo saddled a chestnut horse for me, jumped bare-back on to a dark bay, and galloped away to the foothills of Gorsedd y Cwmwl, followed by Gigo, a Welsh sheep-dog. I followed, clinging to the large Yankee saddle. Gigo chased hares while *chimangos* dived to chase Gigo. In the sky the *teru teru* wailed, and bravely attacked the small eagles that had disturbed them. My dislike for them in Dyffryn Camwy had turned to admiration in Cwm Hyfryd. Iolo picked his way through the trees to emerge at the top of a cliff above a torrent. He nosed his horse down an almost vertical slope and I followed, holding tight to my saddle and sketch-book. Iolo gave a freckled grin and I gathered that I had passed some sort of a test. Then up the cliff again, past the stumps of trees that had been snapped in the ferocious winds and into a field of large red thistles. Iolo lept from his horse and attacked them with fury. Back on his horse he told me that they were a plague which, he thought, had come from Russia. On we galloped across the foothills of the Cordillera to a corral where stallions fought over

the mares. Iolo told me to draw them but gave me no time, for he was away again chasing Gigo over the wild land that was his home.

Pennant must have been a paradise for a small boy and I wondered how he would have fared in the school in Dyfed where his brother and sister had been taught. Fred was an interesting man, who was curious about everything that was going on in the world and eager to bring new farming techniques to Cwm Hyfryd. I sensed that the more conservative Welshmen did not approve.

It was early summer, but in the Andes it was still bitterly cold and the loudspeakers on telegraph poles in Trevelin acknowledged the fact by broadcasting continually an American song called, 'Baby, it's cold outside'. Frozen, I wandered around the streets, looking at the addresses I had been given by Mrs Valmai Jones and by my friends in Dyffryn Camwy. I knocked on the doors of many houses and the owners seemed delighted to see me, offering me cups of tea which brought warmth to my body. 'Travel light,' had been the advice of Bryn Williams, the former Archdruid, who had lived in Patagonia, 'for it will be very hot out there.' Unfortunately, I had taken his advice and had few warm clothes, but luckily I had ignored his remarks that a sleeping-bag was unnecessary; without it I would hardly have survived.

Norma and Paulino played endless games around the house and Norma claimed that Paulino always lost. Sometimes Paulino won but Norma, dancing and laughing, always made him believe he had not. I sensed that Paulino knew that he was being fooled but all he did was give a huge generous smile and allow himself to be fooled once again. When Norma went to her music lesson, Paulino seemed to enjoy himself heading a large rubber ball against the side of the house. At meal times he sat at the sink while we sat around the table. I sat at one end and Nita, who did the cooking, at the other. Norma sat on my left and said grace in Welsh. She put her small hands together, her great eyes closed and temporarily she became serious. During the meal, however, she was tickling me under the table and calling me Senor Tigaretta. I felt flattered as that was the name of a delicate fork-tailed swallow that flew around the valley. I didn't know that she was referring to a revolting insect-like scorpion that lived under stones and had two claws which, in her mind, resembled my moustache. At meal times my companions consumed their food with vigour, seldom closing their mouths as they did so. I soon came to the conclusion that, loaded with a piece of Patagonian potato, the Welsh double 'l' assumed the proportions of a dangerous weapon. After every meal I went to the wash-house and looked at my face in the mirror. Invariably it resembled a picnic site. With resignation I decided that in life it is possible to get used to anything.

I had been in Trevelin for two weeks. The men were still putting up telegraph poles. Paulino was still heading his rubber ball; snow continued to fall in the mountains; and I was still frozen.

In spite of the cold I continued to draw. Every day I walked through the rose bushes that covered the hill behind the village and joined a road named Avenida John D. Evans, after one of the earliest settlers. His son, a flamboyant man who dressed like an Argentinian *estanciero*, told me how his father had been mistaken, by the Indians, for a Spanish soldier. He had avoided death by making his horse, El Malacara, leap an abyss in the desert. His escape, and his horse, passed into legend and the noble animal was eventually buried near Milton's House in Trevelin. At the end of the *avenida* lay the small hamlet of Pentre Sydyn and beyond it the ridge from which the Welsh first viewed Cwm Hyfryd. The land up there was good and there were many birds. Flocks of *bandurria* flew slowly in front of me and *chimango* wailed in the sky above, and occasionally I saw a little black bird with a yellow beak and white feathers on its wings. I was told it was a *gweddw fach*, or little widow. If the Welsh provided a name for a bird, invariably it related to human beings.

From the hills above Pentre Sydyn I often looked at the whole valley below me and thought of the border dispute between Chile and Argentina. The two countries had appealed to King Edward VII to settle their differences and the king had sent a Colonel Holditch to decide where the border should be. Logically, he decided that it should run along the tops of the mountain range and that the land in the valleys, through which the rivers flowed to the Pacific Ocean, should be given to Chile, and that the land bordering the rivers that flowed to the Atlantic should be part of Argentina. In making this decision he realised that the Rio Percy flowed through Cwm Hyfryd and emptied into the Pacific, so that, if his rule was to be adhered to, the Welsh community would be split in two. Consequently, he arranged a plebicite in which the Welsh voted almost unanimously to be part of Argentina. The Government of Argentina showed its gratitude by giving large areas of land to the British Crown. Above Pentre Sydyn I could see a part of Chile through a gap in the mountains through which the Rio Percy flowed, and the sea-gulls in the valley came from the Pacific.

As I was always enquiring about the names of the birds in Cwm Hyfryd, the word had been passed around that an expert ornithologist was staying in Trevelin. One day, Paulino burst into Tŷ Ni in great excitement to tell us that a very strange bird had been seen on a farm nearby and they wanted to know what it might be. Excitedly, he led the way through the bushes of wild roses to a small farm near Pentre Sydyn. The farmer said that he had caught the bird and, imploring me to be quiet, led us along a path towards a wire-netting enclosure.

The farmer pointed in the direction of what was to me a very common bird indeed. It looked at us with a fearless eye and only seemed to be mildly disturbed by our presence. It was an oyster-catcher, a bird so well-known in Wales that it probably has more local names than any other species.

A few days after my arrival at Trevelin, I was taken to a children's concert at Capel Ebenezer. The building was clean and polished and the pews were filled with people from as far away as Esquel. A large Christmas tree stood near the stage above which was written the words, '*Duw Cariad Yw*', reminding us that God is Love. Dennis Williams, the bus driver, addressed us in Spanish before the curtain parted to reveal half the children of Trevelin. Spanish children sang, the Welsh and Indian children sang. Paulino recited something, after which he bowed so low that he fell over onto his face. The audience cheered and when he gave an embarressed grin they cheered even louder. Norma followed him with a brief and almost inaudible song, before Paulino, with a crown of gold and silver paper on his head, bounced back again as one of the three kings in a nativity play. The climax of the evening came in the form of a chorus in which every child represented a particular nation. There was a Miss Wales, a Mr Argentina, a Miss Japan and a Mr Norway. The item ended with a boy *and* a girl representing England. So dolefully did they sing, I imagined that, in my absence, a disaster had decimated the land. Finally, a short and square Italian bounded onto the stage and put on a magnificent performance in Spanish. His voice, loud and mellow, might have been heard in La Scala, and when he raised one arm above his head in a gesture of triumph, I was so impressed that I could hardly refrain from clapping. Back in Tŷ Ni the Senora told me that he had been preaching a sermon.

Everywhere I went in Welsh Patagonia the people called me 'Mr Kyffin'. I presume that after a hundred years of comparative isolation, Victorian standards of behaviour survived to add greatly to the charm of Y Wladfa. Senora Gwenonwy was always very formal in the way she addressed me. One day, I insisted that she addressed me by my christian name. She appeared to be embarrassed and looked at me silently for a moment. Then, suddenly, she threw her arms around me, gave me a huge kiss and stood back:

'Well, how's that, Kyffin *bach*?' she said with a wicked glint in her eyes. I replied that it was much better, but it made no difference, for she continued to call me 'Mr Kyffin'.

I had become as fond of Trevelin as I was of Gaiman. I loved the horses. They were the result of breeding from the best of the descendants of those put ashore by the Spaniards in the sixteenth century. The Welsh had imported their cobs from Cardiganshire, and from the mixture of blood a fine strong animal had emerged. Nowhere could I see any Arab blood, for the ground was too hard for the feet of horses that had originated in the sandy areas of the Middle East. Horses with distinct markings were given special names. Soon I was able to tell a Pinto from a Picasso, and a Ballo from a Ballo Clarita. A horse with one white sock had a different name from one with four, and a spotted horse or a chestnut with a white blaze was spoken of as if it was a different breed. Horses were everywhere and I believe that they outnumber the humans in Patagonia.

I enjoyed the unfamiliar wildlife in Dyffryn Camwy but in the Andes the differences were even more marked. I saw many large and small eagles, and woodpeckers appropriately named *carpentero*. In Trevelin I could look up to Gorsedd y Cwmwl and the other peaks of the Cordillera, the home of puma and wild boar. Most of the trees were poplars and willows but there were some that I had never seen before. I loved the great rose bushes that grew everywhere, and the purple *malva*, some sort of mallow, that invaded the gardens of Trevelin. The *scawen* or elder reminded me of home as did the cow-parsley that grew to a greater height than I had ever seen before. The leaves of the sturdy evergreen *maiten* were used to feed the cattle in winter and the wood of the *chekay* to fuel the stoves, while the trunks of the *lenga*, or southern beech, were cut up and used as timber. Cwm Hyfryd was a tidy, self-supporting community.

Cwm Hyfryd, by virtue of its name, should have been a paradise but the longer I stayed in Trevelin the more I became aware that there was an unhappy division among the people. I remembered my own island of Anglesey where feuds divided families over generations, and such happenings are, I believe, natural in isolated communities where the people became confined and where mild disagreements become magnified into hostility. In Capel Ebenezer I noticed that Senora Gwenonwy did not speak to a large well-dressed lady seated in the pew in front of her, and Don Ambrosio poured scorn on the farming activities of Senora Gwenonwy's son, Fred. The trouble may have arisen from the division of land or even from which part of the world the settlers had come. The Senora's father had arrived on the *Mimosa*, whereas most of the land in Cwm Hyfryd was owned by a Welsh family that had moved south from the United States. I understood the situation so did not make further enquiries. Neverless I remained alert.

Before I left Wales I had been told that I could not return without recording the face of Brychan Evans, the most respected figure in Cwm Hyfryd. He was the most notable horseman in the whole of Y Wladfa and had been the first man to climb the mountains that looked down on the valley. He came through the garden of Fron Deg to meet me, a tall distinguished man with a finely modelled nose and a firm jaw. His body was spare, as one would expect of a man who had spent so much of his life in the saddle, and his legs seemed to bend as he walked. He was eighty-seven and had only recently ceased to work on his farm. When I said that I wanted to draw him, a slow smile started to crease his face until it burst into an explosion of uncomprehending humour. He sat for me by the window in his parlour as his eyes wandered over the valley that had been his home. He sat well but I drew badly and his daughter confirmed my self-criticism. Dispirited, I returned to Tŷ Ni and there, in the quiet of my small bedroom, I fought to record that magnificent face. It was a long battle but in the end I felt that I had done some sort of justice to Brychan Evans.

One day, the Senora and I were invited to a ceremony in the village school. There was a loud cheer as we entered a long low hall. Children clung to my coat and dragged me into a classroom begging me to draw on the blackboard. I looked at the eager faces. The Welsh were unmistakable with their red hair, soft skin and freckles, but were outnumbered by the dark Spanish and Indian children. I knew that I had to put on a performance, so I picked up a piece of chalk and drew a portrait of myself dressed as Father Christmas riding a reindeer. Screams of delight shook the classroom. I drew myself as a gaucho and the cries of appreciation were deafening. I began to think that they would cheer at anything. Finally, I did a drawing of myself being chased by the Hereford bull that grazed in the field behind the school. At the sight of this they clapped, they cheered, and banged the lids of their desks. It was with difficulty that I returned to the hall. Order was finally restored. The children sang songs in Welsh and Spanish, and gifts were presented for the poor of the village. A small boy vomited and, white-faced and shivering, he was led away. The Argentine National Anthem was sung and the celebration was over.

The next day, I found that wherever I went, the children followed me. As I passed through the field where the Hereford bull grazed, the children clung to the fence in silence, hoping, I sensed, that they might witness in reality that which they had seen on the blackboard.

Christmas was near and I felt that the Senora and her family would want to celebrate it together at the ranch-house down the valley, so when an invitation arrived to spend a week in the Los Alerces National Park as the guest of its Intendente, Don Diego Neill, I was happy to accept it.

Don Diego was an impressive man of about sixty-five years of age and obviously in love with the land he protected. When he stood at the window of his house built of wood and stone, and gazed across the lake to the forests and snow-capped mountains, he clearly gained strength from what he saw. I think it was because of his very genuine admiration of the Welsh that he invited me to Futalaufquen. He told me that he tried to employ as many as he could in the park because they were such excellent riders and skiers, but he added, with a smile, that no Welshman would ever make a first-class ranger because they lived their lives according to the Bible and therefore were incapable of ruthlessness. He recalled, without any criticism,

how one of his rangers called Eli Williams had reported that Chilean Indians had crossed the border and were squatting in his part of the park. Don Diego ordered him to throw them out, but Eli complained how his abhorrence of violence had persuaded him to leave the police and become a ranger; but now he was being asked to undertake a violent act. He looked at Don Diego and said that he would have to disobey his orders. His act of disobedience won the admiration of the Intendente for never before had any ranger disobeyed his orders.

When I arrived, Don Diego told me he had asked a ranger to catch a fish for our supper, and soon a man arrived with an enormous trout. Don Diego cooked it himself and, as he did so, he told me of his life in Patagonia, of his marriage, of his love of horses and the passion he had for the world around him. Even so I felt that he was not completely content for there was a sense of loneliness about him. He led me down a path to his offices and to a room where a bed had been prepared. I went to sleep that night thinking of the beautiful but different land of Futalaufquen.

I had my breakfast in a small tea-house owned by the Indian captain of Don Diego's official launch. I showed him my pass and he took me down to a smart white boat that was moored under the trees. About twenty people came aboard and the captain steered it into the middle of the lake. The view was superb, for on all sides the meadows and forests rose to meet the snow-clad mountains above. The lower slopes were covered with *chekay* and *maiten* trees and, in places, the rich pattern of green was broken by the bright red of the *notro* or Chilean fire tree, which covers the Andes much as the rhododendron covers parts of the Himalayas.

Occasionally I noticed clearings with blue lupins and sometimes a whiteness like a heavy frost seemed to lie over the lower hills. It was a strong bush much like our broom and known as the *retamo*.

At the far end of Lago Futalaufquen the Indian forced the launch through the shallow water of the Rio Arroyanos with its red-trunked *arrayan* trees growing from the bed of the river. Slowly and patiently the captain piloted the craft against the flowing water and the waving trees until we entered the beautiful Lago Verde, a lake of blue water surrounded by green meadows. It reminded me of

Austria. We were led over the long green grass to Lago Menendez, a lake surrounded by more fierce and more jagged mountain peaks, some of which were divided by the Ventisquero Torrecillas glacier. I tried to draw its crushing ice and imprisoned rocks, but on a small piece of paper I was unable to interpret its ferocity. Another launch set off towards the Chilean border and there, on the edge of a small bay, it stopped. Huge trees with shaggy trunks rose, as if to find some air, above that dark and unfrequented land. They were the *Fitzroya cupressoides*, ancient redwoods that were over 2,500 years old. It was a wild and sinister place. There was a weird silence and I could not even hear the sound of birds; indeed, the land appeared to be so lifeless that I do not believe there were any berries for the birds to eat. I climbed up the side of a waterfall and saw, in the distance, the silver water of Lago Cisne, bordered by the mountains of Chile. I was glad to return to the launch and reach the landing-stage on the far end of Lago Menendez. I walked alone through the trees and across the meadows to Lago Verde, and, as I did so, I became aware that for some reason I was falling into a state of ecstacy. The beauty of everything became exaggerated. The grass became greener and the sky bluer. A glorious happiness seemed to flow around me and I luxuriated in it. I don't know how long it lasted but it cannot have been more than a minute or two, for when the exhilaration ceased people walked beside me as if nothing had happened. It is possible that I had some sort of epileptic experience; perhaps the rhythms of the mountains and the hills and the sun on the lake acted as a trigger. I was still wondering about it as the launch was negotiating the shallows of the Rio Arroyanos and returning to the landing stage at Futalaufquen. I dined with Don Diego but didn't tell him of my experience.

The next day was Christmas Eve and I drew among the *maiten* trees as mosquitoes and large grey flies tormented me. In my attempts to kill them, the paint on my hands was transferred to my face so that I became as painted as my paper. A sheep-dog rolled on my dark glasses, smashing them beyond repair. He then upset a pot of water over my painting and, finally, shook his wet body over me. I threw sods at him but he thought it was a game. I aimed a kick at his belly but he seemed to laugh at me. Furious, I returned to the Intendencia where the more ruthless Don Diego hurled a large rock at him, knocking him over and sending him howling into the trees. Perhaps he was right when he said that the Welsh are not ruthless enough. After this experience I decided that, in order to escape from the flies, it was necessary to work above the shore of the lake. As I climbed up an orange-coloured track among the *maiten* trees and the bushes of *retamo*, I saw many different flowers and over the streams flew brightly-coloured kingfishers. The hillside was alive with small birds and covered with a wild sweet pea and wild strawberries, and on the *calafaté* bushes were succulent blue-black berries that resembled the bilberry. I saw strange basalt rocks that reminded me of the Giant's Causeway, and huge waterfalls fell over the gaps in the hills. High above this amazing hillside wheeled the distant shapes of the condor. Don Diego told me that, in order to catch one, they killed a calf and placed the body in a small corral. The voracious condor would then fly down to rip open the carcass and devour the body. When the men returned to the corral, the condor would be so weighed down that it would be unable to take off. Duly captured, it was then dispatched to the zoo in Buenos Aires.

It was a very beautiful land and I tried very hard to record features such as Cordon Situacion, a peak that dominated the landscape, the huge green forests and the great blue dome of the sky, but everything was so vast and it would have taken me more than a week to capture the scene. I could only look and let the sun thaw out the icicles that had formed inside me in Trevelin.

In the evening I dined once again with Don Diego. His Indian housekeeper cooked our meal and we talked of Scotland, of horses and the breeding of wire-coated fox terriers. After dinner, the housekeeper's daughter arrived with a young Welshman called Evan Williams to whom she was engaged. I looked at his face and it was unmistakably Welsh. I had seen that same face in Caernarfon and Llanberis, in Dolgellau and Bala; it could probably be seen in Brecon, in Merthyr and in any other part of Wales. I spoke to him in Welsh. He didn't reply but looked at me with an embarrassed smile. Suddenly he bent down to hold his hand about three feet off the ground. '*Bachgen*,' he murmured. The word for a small boy was the only Welsh he knew. We listened to the Chilean radio. Twelve o'clock struck. '*Feliz Navidad, Nadolig Llawen*,' we said to each other before finding our separate ways home under the starlit sky of a Christmas morning.

Don Diego had decided to celebrate the day with a lunch-time *essado* in his garden. Evan Williams had crucified some lambs and they were roasting under his expert care. The Intendente and I sat at a trestle-table and ate with knife, fork and fingers, but Evan, the housekeeper and her daughter stood beside the corpses, cutting away choice bits and eating them between two slices of bread. A slow drizzle drove us inside where we drank our coffee and I watched the lonely Scot as he stood at the window letting his eyes range over his domain. Perhaps he was thinking of Hamilton in Scotland where his father had been born, or of his wife whose portrait hung in his living-room. There was something good and something sad about Don Diego; a strong man who kept to himself.

Two days later a bus took me to Esquel. The Intendente had suggested that I visited Senor Nores Martinez who lived near the town and bred a hound called an Argentinian dogo. His father had perfected the breed by mixing the blood of Great Danes, boxers and Staffordshire bull terriers and he used them for hunting wild boar and puma. I opened a gate and saw a white house on the other side of a wood. As I was walking down a driveway, I saw a large puma coming towards me through the trees. I stood still as the animal approached, watching its measured tread and powerful body. As it reached me I heard a shout from the house:

'Have no fear, it thinks it is a dog.'

A tall man walked down the drive and told me that he had hand-reared the puma after its mother had been killed. It had been brought up with his pack of hounds and believed that it was one of them. As he spoke, two large white hounds ran towards me. They were shaped like Great Danes but were more stocky. Their heads owed much to the bull terrier. Followed by the two hounds, Senor Nores Martinez led me to some enclosures below his home. As we approached, two red pumas hurled themselves against the wire of their cage with a ferocity that I had never witnessed before in any animal. Using all four feet, they tore at the sides of their enclosure in a frustrated attempt to get at the two white hounds. In their eyes was a look of hatred and fear that, in turn, triggered their aggression. The hounds snarled with a terrible confidence. In another pen was a gigantic wild boar. Senor Martinez said that he had trained his puppies to attack it, but assured me that they did it no harm as its skin was so tough. I asked him how he killed the wild boar in the hills around Esquel and he told me that while his hounds held the animal by its ears he despatched it with a knife. When I suggested that this might be dangerous, he told me that a Senora Jones, who lived near Bariloche, killed wild boar with a pair of scissors. He added in broken English, 'That is not the sort of lady for whom I would very much care.'

Pondering the ferocity of hounds, puma, wild boar and Senora Jones, I boarded Dennis Williams' bus and returned to Trevelin.

'What did you eat on Christmas Day?' I asked Senora Gwenonwy. She thought for a moment. 'Well,' she replied slowly, 'I don't know what it is in English but I think they call it a sicking pug.'

With the New Year came the warmer weather, and Norma began to tease me unmercifully. 'Senor Tigaretta, Senor Tigaretta,' she cried as she danced around me, enticing me to chase her over the rough land around Tŷ Ni. Sometimes I drew her and then she

became quiet and sat well. Paulino did not like to be drawn for he knew that the Senora would want to brush his hair and tidy his clothes. On the occasions he did sit for me, he invariably looked uncomfortable and sullen, and as soon as I finished he would run away with his great toothy smile back on his face.

One evening, after a particularly hazardous meal, I retired to the wash-house and looked in the mirror. Potato and onion clung to my face. I knew I would never get used to it. I returned to the kitchen.

'I must be away tomorrow,' I said.

'Oh, Mr Kyffin. Where are you going?' enquired the Senora.

I had not made any plans but the name Tierra del Fuego came to my lips, and I knew immediately that I had to go to what is known as the uttermost part of the earth.

Two days later I bade farewell to the inhabitants of Tŷ Ni. I had been there for a month and had become very fond of them. I wondered what their future might be for I sensed that it did not have much in store for them. Solemnly they stood outside the house as Senora Gwenonwy presented me with a *maté*, a *bombilla* and a silver mounted puma claw. Dennis Williams' bus drew up outside the gate and Paulino heaved my bags and portfolios onto the front seat. I waved, they waved and I was on my way through the low trees and down the dirt roads of Trevelin, where men were still engrossed in the serious business of erecting telegraph poles.

A Mercedes bus took me back across the desert, and the next day I arrived at Casa Britannica where I began to make arrangements to fly to Ushuaia, the most southerly town in the world.

The plane flew south over the barren *meseta* and along the coast of the southern Atlantic. Occasionally, it landed on airfields on the outskirts of small towns that appeared to huddle, as if for security from the desert, at the mouths of the few rivers that carve through the plateau-land of Patagonia. Comodoro Rivadavia, Puerto Deseado, St. Julian, Santa Cruz and Rio Gallegos; in every name there was music. When the plane left St. Julian, I could see that the sky to the west was black and threatening. The plane banked sharply and returned to the airstrip. A violent storm broke over the runway

and torrential rain crashed against the shed that served as the waiting-room of the airport. It passed over almost as soon as it had arrived, and we flew on to Santa Cruz. A few silent passengers huddled around a stove in a shack beside the airfield at Rio Gallegos. A gale was blowing and it was bitterly cold, so I was glad that I had borrowed a warm coat in Gaiman. I broke the embarrassing silence to ask two shivering, ill-clad young men if they were on their way to Tierra del Fuego. I learned that they were American Fulbright scholars bound for Ushuaia.

The storm passed and someone told us that the plane was about to leave. Over a point called Dungeness, the Straits of Magellan disappeared westwards in a vivid sheen of silver and gold whilst to the south rose the fingering peaks of Tierra del Fuego. The land had been given its name by Spanish sailors who, as they sailed past its inhospitable shores, saw innumerable fires burning on cliffs, hills and islands. They did not know that they had been kindled by Yaghan and Ona Indians who, almost naked, huddled for warmth beside them with only a screen of guanaco skin to shield them from the perishing wind. There are no Yaghan or Ona left today for those who were not shot by the Spanish died from the chicken-pox introduced by the settlers. Tierra del Fuego is the land where the mighty Andes disintegrates into a disorderly coccyx of jagged peaks and islands finally to disappear into the terrible waters around Cape Horn. The peaks and broken ridges that seemed to claw at the plane had been the homeland of the Ona, although I could not believe that anyone would have wanted to live in such a place. The sun was setting and the snow-topped mountains were pink as they stretched far away to the west to vanish into a golden haze. I tried to draw but only succeeded in turning an immensity into a banality. The valleys below were blue and cold and sometimes became invisible as snow showers blew over them. Far below, a strip of water shone; it was the Beagle Channel. The plane landed on an airstrip beside the water. It was mid-summer but it was still snowing.

I went to collect my baggage and I was told that everyone's belongings had been removed. I searched through an inelegant pile of cases only to find that mine were not among them. I returned to the plane.

'Senor,' said a dark-haired man, 'there is nothing here. All is out.'

'Look again,' I shouted.

'Senor, there is nothing here. Nothing but the compartment for the day-old chicks.'

'Well, look among the day-old chicks,' I roared. He stretched out his arms in despair.

'But, Senor . . .' he started.

'For God's sake, search the bloody chicks.'

He turned and opened the doors of a small hatch. Inside were boxes of chicks and my baggage.

I hailed a car and was driven along an uneven track to the dirt road that led to the town of Ushuaia. I could just make out a jumble of wooden buildings and there was snow on the side of the road. I asked my driver to drop me at the only hotel. The Fullbright scholars were already there. They told me that it was full and that they were going to sleep in the street. I asked for the manager. An immensely tall and thin man appeared; he had a tiny head that created an impression of a billiard ball on top of a cue. He was very sorry but he had no bed. I believed him for he was obviously an honest man. I said I would sit in a chair until a bed became available. At midnight he motioned me to follow him. He led the way up two flights of stairs and stopped outside a door. He opened it slightly and with a long, thin hand switched on a light. He propelled me gently into a room. A nauseating smell met me.

'God bless you, Senor,' whispered the manager as he closed the door. Two beds were occupied by two large men who lay on their backs with their eyes closed, breaking wind from every possible orifice. Below a half-open window was a divan. It was covered in snow. I lay down on the floor and understood why God had been called upon to bless me.

When I awoke the men had gone. At breakfast I envied the women in their fur coats. I ventured into the unmade streets where huskies scavanged. I walked down a track and on either side were tidy wooden houses with stove pipes appearing above their corrugated-iron roofs. There was an ice-breaker in the harbour. I felt I was in Alaska.

All day I wandered around the town of Ushuaia and remembered a book I had read while staying at Futalaufquen. *The Uttermost Part of the Earth* had been written by Lucas Bridges whose father, Thomas Bridges, had, in the middle of the last century, set up a mission station on the shore of the Beagle Channel and had named it Ushuaia. Thomas Bridges was a remarkable man and it was sad that the only memorials in the town he had named and created were of Argentinian Commodores. This was the place that Captain Fitzroy and Charles Darwin had visited in 1832, and, or so I have been told, a distant relative of mine called Allen Gardener. He had been an officer in the navy, but resigned his commission in order to take the word of the Lord to the Indians of Tierra del Fuego. He was not, however, a very competent man for he not only felt it to be unnecessary to learn the Yaghan language but also landed on the shores of the Beagle Channel with a gun but no ammunition. His expedition was doomed and beside his decomposed body was found a piece of paper on which he had written, 'I am happy beyond words'.

Thomas Bridges, however, had learned the Yaghan language in the Falkland Islands and with a wife from Devon had brought up a family in a land fraught with danger. Not many people in Ushuaia know of Thomas Bridges but his descendants still live and farm on an *estancia* named after his wife's home in Devon.

I worked on the hilly slopes above the town. Behind them the *lenga* forests grew tall and green and, higher still, a glacier shone white against a black ridge. Presiding over the land and the sea was Monte Olivia, a lump of elephant-grey rock with a serrated crest. It was more like Wales than Patagonia. The grass was wet and green, and sparrows and handsome little birds like redstarts chased each other from rock to rock. The flowers that survived the constant wind were small and unusually yellow. Below me seagulls wailed from the corrugated-iron roofs of the buildings and terns dived in the harbour. I tried to draw but it was bitterly cold and I did nothing of any merit. After a frustrating day I returned, dirty and wet, to my hotel where the manager informed me that I would have to share my room with a man who had been landed by an Argentinian gun-boat. In my room I saw a tall fair man with a crew-cut. He grasped my hand. 'The name's Eklof,' he said, 'Call me Ek.'

Ek told me that while working on an Antarctic research vessel he had heard that his wife was ill in San Diego. He had been transferred to the Argentinian boat and wanted to know where the hell he was. That evening I learned that he had come from Cheyenne in Wyoming where he had worked as a cowboy. When the Vietnam war had started, he had been sent out east where he had been wounded. With his slow drawl and wicked glint of humour in his eyes, he enlightened me on certain aspects of life in the army:

'Gee, there sure was one right bastard of a lieutenant and they all hated his guts. A top sergeant told me that at Hue that guy had a bullet put through his backside by his own men. Yeah, straight through each cheek. Well, one reckons on the men putting a bullet through one cheek so this one must have been mighty bad to get it through both. They sent him home with a purple heart, and do you know, I met him later in San Diego and you couldn't have come across a nicer guy. It sure goes to prove what education will do.'

Ek was worried because the scientists on his boat had discovered that the mating habits of king crabs were changing:

'Yeah, and do you know that those old lady crabs will only take immature ones for husbands these days and something mighty funny is going on; those old boy crabs are getting a raw deal.' Ek seemed to think that the habits of the king crabs might be copied by the human race. There was no stopping him when he got involved in one of his stories:

'There was one old king crab that we had on our boat and he sure had personality, if crabs can have such a thing. We all got mighty fond of the old boy and called him Clyde. He used to walk about the deck and always managed to appear at the chop-house door at about chop time. Some scientist said he was going to cut him up so we said: "No surr, not Clyde." The guy said he had never taken no from a crewman, so we just said, "Well, you are taking 'no' from three crewmen right now".'

"Hell," said the scientist, "he'll be opened up tomorrow morning and that's for sure."

'Next morning, there was no Clyde to be opened up 'cos we had caught him, stuck a damn great name plate on his shell with "Clyde" printed on it and heaved him overboard with a couple of girl friends to keep him company.'

Ek was a kindly soul, but with doubts; perhaps the war in Vietnam had shaken his American confidence.

The next morning I tied my camera and paints to my back and, carrying my portfolio, set out to climb up to the glacier. Near the sea there were bushes of *calafaté* and the *lenga* grew tall and straight. The floor of the forest was a bog and often my boots disappeared into the clammy mud. I noticed that the higher I climbed, the shorter and more bent were the trunks of *lenga*, so that when I reached the tree-line they rose vertically for a few feet and then, as if to avoid the wind, grew horizontally. In some moss that grew in the stony moraine that accumulated below the glacier, I saw a delicate pink flower with grey-green leaves. It looked like a Fuegian *edelweiss*. I took a photograph of it that later appeared in an atlas of wildlife. Its name was *Lucenia hanii*. I saw many other unusual plants in that cold glacial valley that opened out to the Antarctic. I climbed up the moraine and looked down over the forest. The Beagle Channel stretched far below me and beyond it lay Navarin Island where the Chileans had built Puerto Williams, a settlement that they hoped would replace Ushuaia as the most southerly town in the world. It seems that the people of Chile had no desire to live in such a place, for today it serves only as an air station. Further to the south I could see great cliffs and islands and I was sure that one of them was Cape Horn. As I drew under the green wall of ice, an Indian boy appeared over the ridge. He climbed down and sat beside me as I worked. When I had finished, he started to tell me the names of the places far below me. He spoke in Spanish but the names were English and incongruous.

'Slogget Bay,' he shouted into the wind, and his finger pointed somewhere to the south. 'Resolution Island, Picton Island, Woolaston Island,' excitedly he pointed to many of the islands below. Finally, he indicated a place to the east of Ushuaia. 'Harberton,' he yelled, and far below in some trees on the edge of the Beagle Channel I saw the land that Thomas Bridges had claimed for his family. Suddenly, he lept on to the snowy slope and, using his backside as a toboggan, descended to the tree-line far below. It looked easy, so after I had packed my paints and drawings, I sat on my portfolio and followed him. The speed of my descent exhilarated me but I had no idea how I could stop before I made contact with the trunks of the trees. I dug my feet and arms into the snow and performed a somersault. My paints, camera and portfolio flew into the air as, spreadeagled, I reached the bottom of the slope. Dark patches on the snow above me indicated the location of my scattered paraphernalia. I retrieved them and, after splashing through the boggy *lenga* forest, returned to the hotel. Ek greeted me with the news that, because of the weather, no planes could fly out of Ushuaia.

The next day I drew on the shore of Lago Fagnano, the most

southerly lake in the world. An albatross skimmed across the surface of the lake, and at its far end I could see the Chilean mountains. Waves broke at my feet, bringing more driftwood to add to the piles already on the shore. That evening Ek and I were told that a plane might take us away early next morning. At a quarter past four we were woken and taken down to the landing-strip. A plane flew low over the channel and landed beside the hut in which we were sheltering. We got on board and soon we were flying eastwards below the cloud-covered mountains and out over the Atlantic. We landed at Rio Gallegos where Ek found a large plane about to depart for California. It disappeared into low cloud while I waited in a cold shed; it would have been boastful to have called it an airport lounge. The air-bus landed and once more I flew from one small town to another along the Patagonian coast. In the evening I was back in the comfort of the Casa Britannica in Gaiman, where I was told that a carnival had been held in the village whilst I was away and that the first prize for fancy dress had been won by a boy who had masqueraded as the artist Kyffin Williams.

I had accumulated about seven-hundred drawings. Some pleased me but the majority were very rough and sometimes bad, for they were often done in difficult conditions. Their quality, however, did not worry me as I intended to use them for information when I was painting my oils. I had also taken seven-hundred photographs but had little confidence in my ability with a camera. I had found that the exposure meter was too much for my unscientific brain and in

Tierra del Fuego it broke down altogether. It is possible that it had suffered in my fall above Ushuaia. I knew that my photographs would be awaiting my return, but I was faced with the problem of carrying my drawings back to London. The problem was solved, however, when I discovered a carpenter in Gaiman who constructed for me a light wooden box. Carefully, I filled it with my record of Welsh Patagonia. Before I left Gaiman I was presented with gifts from several people. My delight was lessened by the fact that, as the Welsh had not been creative during their hundred years of colonisation, what I received were invariably Indian arrowheads.

I flew over the desert to Esquel and saw, the strange land I had passed through in the Mercedes bus. From the air it appeared to have been blasted by shell-fire. Red, pink, yellow-ochre and pale brown were the colours that made up that strange desert land and I was reminded of the multi-coloured chasms of the Parys Copper Mine in Anglesey. At Esquel, I boarded a bus for Bariloche in the northerly Patagonian province of Rio Negro. Two English girls, who lived in Paraguay, sat beside me.

'We have just visited a little village called Gaiman,' one of them said. 'It is full of Welsh people and they speak Spanish with such funny sing-song voices.' I felt homesick.

The bus rattled through the foothills of the Andes. Once, I saw a puma beneath a cliff. Gardens of tiger lilies covered the lower slopes, and the further north we went the more exotic became the foliage. The bus visited isolated communities and in the village of El Bolson I was reminded of Bavaria, for there were men in *lederhosen* smoking *meerschaum* pipes. I had lunch in an insalubrious café where, I feel sure, I consumed more flies than meat. It was a fascinating but uncomfortable journey and I was glad when the bus stopped in a town beside a beautiful lake. The church and the buildings were Tyrolean, and dachshunds roamed the streets. It was Bariloche.

I had been given the address of a Senora Fricke, a large lady who lived with her son Hans. Much to my surprise, I found that I could speak more German than they could. I had a silent supper but a noisy night, as I was woken continually by cuckoo clocks and the barking of their dachshund.

At eleven o'clock the following evening my plane landed at the airport in the middle of Buenos Aires. The temperature was 95 degrees. I took a taxi to the hotel in which I had stayed the previous year. I was dishevelled and weighed down with bags, boxes and portfolios. The manager looked at me in amazement. Then, with a smile he said, 'Ah, Senor, we always welcome explorers.'

At Heathrow, the luggage from the plane that had flown me from Buenos Aires, passed before me on a moving belt. After my fellow-passengers claimed their cases, I found that I was alone and no more baggages appeared. I enquired of an official when the rest of the luggage would be unloaded, only to be told that it had all been delivered to their owners. On being informed that I had not had mine, he shrugged his shoulders and said that the cargo hold was empty. I asked him to look again. He wandered away only to return and confirm his previous statement. He tried to be helpful and said he would check to see if my baggage had been off-loaded either at Orly or Rio de Janeiro. I waited. A small man tugged my sleeve and said that the airport bus was about to leave. I was aggressively rude to him. The official returned in the company of another and I was told that nothing had been unloaded either at Orly or Rio. When asked if I was certain I had taken my baggage to the airport, I told them what I thought of their suggestion. I shouted at them to search the plane again. They shrugged their shoulders.

'Senor,' one of them said, but I cut him short and uttered many things I should not have said. Obviously surprised at my explosion of rage, they turned and disappeared. I sat down weak with anger and fear that I would never see my seven-hundred drawings again. I waited for what seemed to be an age until suddenly I heard a voice:

'Senor,' it asked, 'could these be yours?' I looked up and saw that officials were holding my portfolio, my box of drawings and my bags.

They explained that my baggage had been put among the aeroplane's spare parts. My fear and anger evaporated. I apologised for my unedifying language and caught another bus to take me to my studio off the Fulham Road.

When I left Buenos Aires the temperature had been 100 degrees; in London there was snow on the streets. It was dark and I was still shaken by my experience in Heathrow. I opened the door of my studio to find it in chaos. The canvases I had prepared before I left were lying on the floor daubed with paint. Cups and saucers were broken in the kitchen and the bathroom was a shambles. I had lent my studio, for a period of my absence, to an old pupil who was studying at Hornsey School of Art. I could hardly believe that he could have done the damage. When he returned the next day to hand over his key, I asked him the reason for the chaos. He replied that it was nothing to do with him as he had lent my accommodation to some friends.

During the following week I tried to bring some order to my studio. I looked through my drawings and selected those from which I felt I could paint in oil. I started to work, and images appeared on my canvases that were very different from any I had painted previously. I painted the road across Dyffryn Camwy, the irrigation ditches, and the bright cream cliffs at Lle Cul. I painted Ceri Ellis harvesting his alfalfa below the waving poplars. As I worked I relived the time that I spent in Dyffryn Camwy and Cwm Hyfryd. I painted Gorsedd y Cwmwl and the mountains that bordered Chile, and so I continued until, one day, I drew onto a canvas an old wooden barn that stood beside the Avenida John D. Evans. I started to paint and as I did so the colours became grey and dull. It was my forty-fifth canvas and I knew the spell was broken. I never painted another picture of Patagonia.

I shall never forget the land and the Welsh people who still live there. I remember the two valleys and their people, the *ffos*, Dilys Owen de Jones, Capel Bryn Crwn, the weeping willows, Gorsedd y Cwmwl, the high-stepping horses of Cwm Hyfryd, and the children of Tŷ Ni. It had been a wonderful experience. Having completed my visual record, I then had to fulfil my other commitment to the Winston Churchill Trust, namely to deliver lectures to people throughout England and Wales.

I had taken seven hundred photographs while I was away and had sent the films back to London to be developed. The excellent quality of the colour transparencies I saw on my return convinced me that I should give away my camera for fear that I might be seduced into taking photographs in my search for pictorial information, instead of creating working drawings. The colour transparencies, however, were to prove invaluable for my lectures.

I addressed gatherings in lecture halls, village halls, in schools and in colleges, and in many of these places I had to suffer the eccentricities of local organisation, for seldom did I find an efficient projector, a screen that was large enough or a blackout that was complete. However, despite the unpredictable conditions, I enjoyed these occasions, for they never failed to rekindle memories of my visit to that far-away land, recollections that are today almost as vivid as when I left Patagonia over twenty years ago. It had been a remarkable experience and there are not many people who are able to say, 'When last I was in Tierra del Fuego . . .'

10

I had been living in artistic frustration in the confining accommodation afforded by a semi-detached house in Woodside Park in north London. The ground floor was occupied by two unmarried mothers who had been placed there by the local authorities. Access to my upstairs flat was through a door at the bottom of a flight of stairs that rose abruptly from a small entrance hall. Despite the fact that it was difficult to work in the poorly-lit accommodation, I did manage to paint a few portraits as well as my usual Welsh landscapes.

I saw little of my ground-floor neighbours but occasionally infantile screams did break the silence of the suburban backwater. One evening, on leaving the house to indulge in an energetic game of badminton with the Sergeant-Major of the Highgate School Cadet Force, I heard piercing cries from the room occupied by a dark and swarthy girl, inappropriately called Sandy. I knocked on the door but all I heard was the deafening noise of a desperate child. On opening the door, a puppy jumped towards me, dragging behind it an electric fire. A red glow told me that it was alight. On the floor, behind the fire, was the baby lying in a jumbled heap of clothing. After greeting me, the puppy ran across the room, the fire still entangled in its lead, and proceeded to lick the terrified baby. I found the power point and turned off the switch. I am not particularly skilled at soothing babies and all my efforts to do so were of no avail. I decided to turn to Mrs Birnbloom who, with her husband, a kosher butcher, lived in half the house next door. I explained the situation to her.

'The little monkey,' she declared indignantly, 'going off dancing and leaving that poor little thing all alone. I'll give her something to get on with.' Mrs Birnbloom stirred herself into such a state that I almost felt sorry for the wayward Sandy. She followed me into the bedroom, picked up the baby, which immediately ceased to howl, and returned to her house uttering the confident words:

'Leave everything to me, Mr Williams.' I was happy to do so.

I stored all my paintings in an attic to which access was afforded by a ladder. It was a shambles that was made the more so whenever I stored yet another picture from my easel. There must have been about five-hundred paintings in that confined space, so in the circumstances I could have been excused for not counting them before I retired to bed at night.

A few years after I had left Woodside Park and was living in my new studio, a man telephoned to say that he had just bought fifteen of my paintings in a sale-room in Broxbourne. I replied that they could not be mine. He informed me that fifteen more had been sold the previous day, and was sorry he had failed to buy them as well. I told him that his story was ridiculous, but he was certain that all the paintings were by me and asked if he could bring them to my studio so that I could give them their correct titles. I acceded to his request but warned him that he would be wasting his time. But when he showed me his purchases I was able to confirm that they were, indeed, my paintings. As I pondered how I could possibly have lost thirty pictures, I began to suspect that Sandy might have got into the habit of visiting my flat when I was teaching. Since Broxbourne was not too far from Woodside Park, it would have been easy for her to take a few pictures at a time and sell them for a pound apiece in a junk shop at Tally-Ho corner, from where they could have been removed to the sale-room with considerable profit. I reckoned that she might have found a ready source of income. Although I provided the young dealer with the titles, I told him that I had certain rights over the paintings. I suggested that I took all the pictures which I believed to be so bad that they would do me little good if sold to the public, and told him that he could keep the rest. He considered my proposal and finally agreed to it. I think I retained about eight paintings, which I subsequently destroyed, and he departed happily with the rest. Quite a time passed before some of the other fifteen reappeared. One day, I was in a north Wales gallery when a man entered and tried to sell one of them. When I informed him that he was trying to sell stolen property he departed hurriedly, leaving the picture behind. At about the same time, the Professor of Philosophy at Swansea University wrote to say that he had bought one of my paintings in Hay on Wye and wondered if I would sign it. He enclosed a colour photograph of the work. I informed him that he had purchased a stolen picture but I added that, as I liked the painting, I would certainly sign it if he cared to bring it to my studio.

My flat in Woodside Park was a useful sanctuary when I had nowhere else to live, but I was determined to find a more suitable place to work and persuaded all my friends and ex-pupils to embark upon a search on my behalf. Many addresses were produced and I visited countless unsatisfactory dwellings, until word came that Michael Salaman, a distinguished painter, wanted to reassign the lease of his studio. I visited him and realised that my search was over.

The Bolton Studios resembled an architectural warren. A long, dark, unhealthy tunnel, reeking with dry rot and other unpleasant odours, gave access to about twenty-five studios of character. Few were occupied by artists. One entrance to the whole extraordinary complex was at the end of a short passage that led from Gilston Road to join the main corridor, and the other, after negotiating the dustbins, gave access to Redcliffe Road. An atmosphere of undistinguished decay hung over the place and people were frightened to enter after dark. When they had been built in the early years of the century, a red carpet covered the passageway and a resident staff cooked meals for the artists. In 1966, when I moved into number twenty-two, there was no carpet and the floor was covered with paper, beer cans and pools of water. However sinister the passageway may have been, my studio, once the door had been closed, gave such a feeling of peace that I knew instinctively that I could work in it. The studio lay beyond a small hall and it was everything an artist could have desired, for there was space, height and a large window facing north. A narrow staircase led to the floor above, where there was a minute bedroom; a living-room above the studio; and a bathroom and kitchen; and all the rooms were embellished with curiously carved woodwork that had been used in the construction of the Great Exhibition of 1851. The whole accommodation was gloriously eccentric. However, my only worry was a lime tree that grew in the garden of a house in Gilston Road and pressed against the glass of my studio window, plunging it into semi-darkness. I visited the owner of the garden. His name was Paul Martel, a French journalist. I asked if I could cut some of the branches but my request was met with a polite but firm refusal. Back in my studio, I considered how I might destroy the tree. I bought a quantity of poison particularly dangerous to limes and pondered my nefarious scheme. It would have been unwise to have climbed down into the garden as two huge dogs lived there and barked ferociously if anyone entered their domain. I devised a cautious, if cowardly scheme, which involved dangling a cupful of poison from the end of my fishing rod and pouring the potion into a hollow formed where branches had grown away from the trunk. My other worry was that some of the poison might also fall to the ground and destroy the dogs. I was about to put my plan into action when the Vicar of Highgate asked me to paint his portrait. I liked the Reverend Harry Edwards and his letter made me feel guilty at the fearful deed that I was about to perform. I decided on a last appeal to Paul Martel.

'Are you a Welshman?' he asked. I assured him that I was.

'And you play rugby?' he continued.

I informed him that I had played for the London Welsh but did not explain that my experience amounted to one very undistinguished game for one of their lowly fifteens.

'Ah,' he slapped me on the back, 'and I play rugby, too, in Aberystwyth in the First War. Find me a good story about Wales so that I can broadcast it to France and maybe, if it is good enough,' he said holding his forefinger up to his head, 'maybe I will let you trim the tree.'

That night I decided to tell him the story of Maria Stella. Back in his library I told how, in 1770, the Duke and Duchess of Orleans, travelling under the names of the Count and Countess de Joinville, had stopped in the small village of Modigliana in Tuscany. The Duchess was about to give birth to a child and did not want to travel further until after the event. Her husband was concerned that the child should be a boy in order to retain an inheritance in the family, and also because he might eventually succeed to the throne of France. He learned that Lorenzo Chiappini, the village constable, had a wife who was also about to give birth. A meeting took place that must have been financially rewarding to Lorenzo, for when the Duchess produced a daughter and the signora a son, an exchange took place and the royal couple returned to France with an infant Chiappini. In 1830 he succeeded to the throne of France, as Louis Philippe, but because his features lacked any distinction, he was often known as the bourgeois monarch.

The Orleans baby was christened Maria Stella, and at the age of thirteen was acting in Florence. Lord Newborough, a peer from north Wales, became so entranced by her beauty, that he followed her to her home in Modigliana and brought her back to Wales as his bride. Maria Stella consistently maintained that she was, in truth, a Bourbon and that Louis Philippe was an imposter, but her battle was in vain and she died in poverty in Paris in 1843.

As I related the story I realised that Paul Martel was becoming increasingly excited and when I ended, he shouted:

'*C'est incroyable*, but can it be true?'

I suggested that he consulted the Encyclopedia Britannica in his bookcase. I watched his face as he read from the heavy book. His eyebrows lept upwards. His mouth opened.

'*Ma foi, ma foi, c'est vrai.* And what a wonderful story. What romance, what . . .'

'What about the tree?' I asked.

'What tree? Oh, that one. Oh, cut the bloody thing down.'

With a saw and a long pair of clippers I trimmed the tree from the safety of my living-room, for in spite of my new friendship with the journalist, I did not trust his dogs.

As I needed to store my canvases, I asked a little Irish carpenter to make some racks for me in the studio. He worked efficiently and cheerfully and when he had finished, he looked at me with foreboding.

'And ye'll be in dreadful trouble come the mating season,' he said. I was fascinated and asked him what might happen.

'Ah,' he went on knowledgeably, 'come the mating season them little woodworms will be starting to fly and I can't be sure that ye'll not be through the floor.'

The floor boards were riddled with thousands of small holes but I decided that my paint would asphyxiate any woodworms that might be breeding there. I lived and worked there for ten years in safety, and it was only after I had sold my lease to a girl about half my weight that the planks collapsed and she disappeared through the floor.

It was appropriate that such an unusual studio should attract such eccentric occupants. We were an amazing cross-section of society: Welsh, Irish and Europeans of almost every nationality; Philippinos who worked for the landlord; Americans; refugees; journalists; girl friends of the wealthy, and even a few artists—we all lived in unsociable proximity. There were two studios near the entrance to Gilston Road. From one of them 'pop' music blared continuously both night and day, and although I never saw anyone emerge I presumed that it was occupied by hippies. Opposite lived a quiet, respectable lady by the name of Mrs Peachey. I was to learn that her well-fed appearance was due to the fact that she was the mistress of a Clapham pork butcher. Sometimes I saw him sneaking into the studio *boudoir* of his beloved, laden with sausages and chops.

Most of the studios, occupied by the permanent tenants, lay on the north side of the sinister passage. In the first of these lived Honorine Catto, the doyenne of our community, and a born fighter who must have been in her late fifties when I arrived on the scene. At one time she had been a talented actress, but her life had been shattered by an unhappy love affair. Honorine, a French Canadian by birth, was short, thin, asthmatic, and gravel-voiced. Her hair was curious for she annointed it with a black dye in an attempt to retain her youth, but her efforts only produced the mottled colouring of a badger. Under this unruly thatch blazed two piercing eyes, made all the more menacing by the dark black lines she painted around them. Her rouged cheeks were sunken, coming together at a small, richly-painted mouth, opened all too frequently to utter the spiciest language that I have ever heard from any female. Under a dirty, blue

sailor's sweater lurked her asthmatic pigeon chest that was wracked by a terrible cough caused by the cigarettes that always hung from her mouth. Dried paint stained her trousers that fell limply above her sandals. I liked Honorine for there was something magnificent in the way she wanted to take on the world if she sensed a lack of justice. Her most intense battle was with a fat, monoglot Spaniard who was employed by the landlord to clean the passage and empty the bins. In spite of being incurably lazy, he was a genial lout, but he had obviously never met anyone like Honorine before, for, whenever he saw her, he burst in paroxysms of uncontrollable laughter.

This infuriated her and far away at the other end of the corridor I could hear her deep and husky voice bellowing:

'Go back to Spain, you stupid sod.' And later she would tell me how, 'The stupid bastard has swept all the leaves off the roof to block my gutters. I told the bloody bastard to piss off,' she roared, 'but all he bloody did was to stick two of his fucking fingers in the air. Blast his guts.' Honorine and the Spaniard reminded me of Cola and the cur-dog in far away Patagonia.

Outwardly Honorine appeared to quiver with aggression but behind her shield of invective she was immensely kind, and it was she who fed the pigeons in Gilston Road and looked after the stray cats and dogs which congregated in the tiny garden at the entrance to the studios. Her sympathy with sick animals made her use her studio as some sort of a veterinary clinic and she seemed to be unaware of the nauseating odours that emanated from it. One day, she asked me to read a letter she had received from the landlord, and unwisely I entered her domain. Cats leaped from chairs, dived under cupboards and even tried to climb the curtains in order to reach the window. Oblivious to the reactions of her animals, she picked up two small flowers.

'Kevin, darling'—she could never pronounce my name—'don't they smell delicious?' I presumed she had become so inoculated against the overpowering smells in her small home, that in a miracle of acclimatisation she was able to sense the delicate fragrance of the stocks. I could smell nothing but the odour of cats and dogs.

Honorine enjoyed ambushing people as they passed her studio door and when she had backed them against the wall, she related her latest encounter with the Spaniard. I was an easy victim as she knew my heavy tread. One day, after returning from an arduous day of teaching, I took off my shoes at the entrance and was silently passing her studio when a roar of hoarse laughter came from the furthest end of the corridor. I turned to see Honorine bent double with laughter at my attempt to avoid meeting her.

A few days after my arrival, Honorine obtained a small West Highland terrier. It accompanied her everywhere, even into food shops that displayed notices which read 'No Dogs Allowed'.

Nobody gave orders to Honorine and into the shops she went, dragging the little dog with her, and ready to tell anyone who might challenge her to 'piss off'. Occasionally I felt she went into some shops with the intention of having a battle, but the people in the Fulham Road knew her well and denied her the luxury of conflict.

A state of cold war existed between Honorine and an elderly Hungarian refugee, who lived with his wife, an air hostess, and their small son in number twenty. He was a distinguished looking man who employed himself in some artistic enterprise about which he was remarkably secretive. I came to the wicked conclusion that he forged Old Masters. Apart from the air hostess, the great joy of his

life was his beagle bitch Babette. Due to lack of exercise, her stomach had grown so enormous that it almost grazed the floor as she swayed along the corridor in the company of her doting master. In Gilston Road she staggered to her master's car and, once inside, he drove her around Kensington. This daily ritual was her only exercise. A dark stain on the floor of the corridor made me suspect that Babette was being encouraged to relieve herself there and not in the road outside. My suspicions were confirmed when one evening, as I left my studio, I saw some newspaper being placed on the floor outside number twenty. Out of the studio swayed Babette and, on the paper, she relieved herself to the satisfaction of her master. Unobserved in the darkness of the corridor, I watched with horror. Finally, I could no longer contain my rage. I shouted at him and accused him of being insanitary, thoughtless, lazy and anti-social—all these accusations I hurled at the surprised and alarmed Hungarian. Soon, however, a dignified composure asserted itself as he turned two limpid eyes on me:

'Do you know, Mr Williams,' he said quietly, 'every time Babette looks at you she want to do pee-pee.'

Two days later he appeared at my door:

'Mr Williams, please we are friends, no?'

I replied that it was conditional on Babette performing her bodily functions outside the studios.

'It is a very, very long walk down the corridor in the evening,' he pleaded, but I was adamant. Finally, he agreed to my demand. A change came over his face, which became creased with middle European charm.

'Please to call me Olly?' he invited. I nodded.

'Good, good, very good,' he went on, 'now what do I call you?'

I said that my name was Kyffin.

'Ah, very good. You Cuffy, me Olly. We are friends, yes?'

Peace had broken out but I was not sure that he would abide by his part of the bargain.

One of the few professional painters in the Bolton Studios was Alex Portner, an Austrian of whom I was rather jealous, for beautiful girls often passed me in the corridor, invariably to go no further than his studio door. I felt sure that they were debutantes who recommended him to each other as much for his middle European charm as for the excellence of his work. Little wonder that Alex always seemed to be happy. However, he proved to be a good friend and looked after my more valuable objects when I was in Patagonia.

The only sculptor was the Czechoslovakian Peter Lamda. One day, I saw in his studio a very fine head of Aneurin Bevan. I got in touch with the National Museum of Wales and it is now in its permanent collection.

Of all my neighbours, the one I knew best was my next door neighbour, David Collins. He was a brilliant designer who was able to undertake any project, from typography and lay-out to the making of record players and the designing of books. It was unfortunate that David was a perfectionist for every project he undertook demanded the maximum amount of research, concentration and application, with the result that he was unable to charge enough to cover the time and labour he took over any enterprise. Unlike my studio, that was in a permanent state of disorder, David's was immaculate with beautifully painted woodwork and stained floors. Everything worked—the locks, the shining bolts, the stoves and the machinery that filled his studio workshop. He could have become a wealthy man, so great was his ability, but all he appeared to want was the pleasure gained from the pursuit of perfection. He was serious, scrupulously honest and conscientious, and must have been an inspiration to the students in the art schools where he taught. Life for me, in our eccentric community, was made much easier by the knowledge that the capable and kindly David Collins lived next door.

The other studios at our end of the corridor were occupied by tenants who came and went with amazing regularity. One, for a brief period, was used as a brothel. One evening I heard loud and angry voices, and, on opening my door, I saw my landlord locked in vociferous battle with half a dozen screaming girls in different stages of undress. I had never seen any of them before and could only assume that our hours of work did not coincide.

The inhabitants of the studio lived their own lives and appeared to have little in common even though a few of them were artists. One thing united them, however, and that was a mutual dislike of the landlord. This, in my opinion, was unwarranted because having invested in a derelict property with a view to developing it, he found that the local council was continually thwarting his schemes. However, panic began to spread among the residents when we were informed that plans had been drawn up to erect on the site about thirty bijou residences masquarading under the name of 'studios'.

It was decided that a meeting should take place in my studio to discuss the matter and to prepare a plan of action. One evening, many of the tenants appeared dragging chairs behind them to form a disconsolate circle amidst my piles of canvases. Somebody proposed that I should be the chairman. The proposition was confirmed by a show of hands. Honorine objected. David was elected vice-chairman. Honorine objected again, and after Olly's girlfriend agreed to be our secretary she staggered to her feet like some enraged houri and poured upon us her entire vocabulary of invective. She demanded to know why she, who for years had fought the 'bloody bastard of a landlord', was not allowed to lead the campaign. She turned on me, her eyes blazing:

'And you, Kevin, you are too fucking machiavellian. Have your bloody little committee and to hell with the lot of you.' Dragging her small dog with her, she swept out of my studio with the dignity of a deposed queen. Slightly shaken, we started to discuss our plan of campaign. The telephone rang and I picked up the receiver.

'Bloody bastards,' came a gravelly voice at the other end of the line. I put down the receiver and we resumed our deliberations. The telephone rang yet again. This time the invective was qualified:

'Stupid bloody bastards,' growled the same gravelly voice. I left the receiver off and peace returned to the committee.

For the purpose of an official complaint, I had to find out the professions of all our members, and soon I had on my list a surveyor, an accountant, a journalist, as well as a designer, a painter and a sculptor. Only Olly had failed to say how he earned his living. I asked him what I should put after his name.

'I study Art at the Academy of Budapest,' he stated with gravity. I asked if he could be more specific.

'I study in Berlin, in Paris, in London. I study Old Masters in Florence, in Venice, in Madrid.'

It was very impressive but, once again, I begged him to state his precise occupation; and, yet again, he seemed determined not to inform me.

'I love great art. I study great art; I study modern masters. I study all art everywhere. I know much art.'

'Yes, Olly, I'm sure you know all about art, but what do you do?' I persisted. Olly's head dropped onto his chest and his large wet eyes searched the worm-holes in the floor as if he wanted to escape down one of them. A great sigh came from him as, turning towards me with a look of dignity and infinite sadness, he whispered:

'I design waistcoats.'

We were all shaken and I felt unbearably guilty. I said a few words and the members of the committee shuffled away to their various studios. I replaced the telephone receiver and climbed upstairs to my bedroom. As soon as I was in bed, the telephone rang. I dashed downstairs and lifted the receiver.

'Machia-bloody-velli,' croaked an inebriated voice. I left the receiver off for the rest of the night. The next day, David Collins told me that he had been woken by the telephone and had suffered a rich flow of French-Canadian invective.

After these skirmishes, Honorine formed her own committee of one and took the battle to the council offices of Kensington and Chelsea. I believe that their rejection of the plans was not due to our committee or Honorine, but to pressure brought to bear by the powerful Boltons Association who complained that a proposed underground car-park would have a detrimental effect on the roots of the splendid trees that grew in the gardens of Gilston Road.

Now, for the first time, I had a studio in which I was able to paint portraits. I have never enjoyed working on commissions as the stress involved was considerable. Months before the sitting I began to worry, and apprehension built-up as the day drew nearer; I prayed for anything to prevent the arrival of the sitter. Nevertheless, I have always believed that an artist, if he claimed to be a professional, should undertake to paint anything, and so forced myself to conquer my apprehension. Once I started work, the worry seemed to slip away as my concentration grew, and I found that I was able to finish a full-length life-size portrait in a single day.

I painted many worthy Welshmen. Dr. Huw T. Edwards, who had been President of the Transport and General Workers Union and Chairman of the Wales Tourist Board, arrived in an impressive car outside the studios. There was a knock on the door and on opening it I was confronted by a huge chauffeur with a cockade on his cap. From behind him emerged a small man in a coat so long that, as he entered, it swept the dust off my floor.

'I will not be painted side-view,' he ordered. I fully understood why he made this imperious demand, for his lower lip protruded aggressively.

'And you must put a twinkle in my eye.' I felt I had to obey.

As I painted, he recalled his boyhood above the Conwy valley and how he used to accompany his father on the mountains to see *y bobl bach* or 'the little people' who inhabit a different world from ours. He told me that nothing in his long and interesting life had ever made him cease to believe in them. I looked at him and sensed that perhaps he was one of them. On one occasion, a doctor told me that if ever he went to a confinement in that part of the Conwy valley, the husband was never at home, but was always to be found on the mountain asking for the blessing of *y bobl bach*.

The British Broadcasting Corporation asked me to paint their Controller in Wales. All six-foot-six of Alun Oldfield Davies arrived and I placed him in a low chair so that his huge limbs crossed in front of him. I thought it was rather good but the BBC, on seeing a photograph of it, pronounced it to be 'repellant'. I suggested that another artist from Wales should paint him but the Controller appeared to be determined that I should try again. In order to discourage him, I told him that he would have to stand for his second portrait which would be full-length and life-size. He replied that he was prepared to suffer for the cause of art. He arrived at my studio at half-past eight one morning, and all day I attacked my canvas. I painted with it on my easel and also on the floor. I sweated and cursed until at about five o'clock in the evening, his vast figure emerged as a likeness, if not a particularly attractive one. This time it was not considered to be repellant and hangs today in the headquarters of the BBC in Llandaf.

Apparently, word had been passed around the Principality that I was prepared to undertake commissions. One day I was asked by the Justices of the Peace of a north Wales county to paint the portrait of a military squire in order to record, for posterity, the fact that he had survived the numbing experience of sitting on the local bench for fifty years. The Colonel arrived at my studio, a magnificent sight in his Lord-Lieutenant's uniform suitably covered in medals, and he sat with a discipline that I would have expected from a soldier who had been awarded the Military Cross. When I put down my palette, he told me that I had made his medals too big, an expression of modesty which demanded that I reduce their size while he waited. After I had completed the minor operation, he asked me when I wanted him to return the next day. When I said that I had finished, he looked surprised and bewildered.

The justices asked me to send a photograph of my painting. On seeing it, they replied that they were delighted and asked me to get it framed and to arrange for it to be dispatched to the county town where it was to be presented. The day of the ceremony arrived. The portrait rested on an easel, invisible behind a blanket. Speeches were made and finally the blanket was swept away to reveal the Colonel gazing fiercely at the assembled company. There was an audible gasp and the Colonel's wife was on her feet:

'I can't have that,' she declared, 'I can't have people saying that I have co-habited with Himmler for fifty years.' And she swept out of the hall, followed by her husband. Interviewed by the *Sunday Express*, she stated that some people might have liked it but she would have preferred to have some garden ornaments. The Colonel merely remarked that he thought he was going to be given an ordinary portrait but had, instead, been presented with an extraordinary one. After being bought by a local judge, the portrait eventually came into the possession of the Colonel's son, who had liked it from the outset but had kept his opinions to himself out of loyalty to the family.

The publicity aroused by my controversial likeness did not deter the justices of yet another county from commissioning me to paint the portrait of the distinguished figure of Lord Morris of Borth-y-gest, a Lord Justice of Appeal in Ordinary. This much-loved man came from a Porthmadog family and was known far and wide as 'John Willy'. He was well-known for his excessive good manners. When he met people, he lowered his mighty frame, charm and perspiration exuding from every pore, and indulged in pleasantries that warmed the hearts of the ladies of north Wales. He appeared to be the most gentle of souls and was constantly referred to as 'dear Lord Morris', but his outward charm camouflaged a brilliant legal mind that obeyed not the spirit but the letter of the law. I never heard anyone contend that he was unfair but he was known for the severe sentences that he meted out.

The magistrates of Caernarfon asked me to paint him full-length and life-size in his peer's robes. This I undertook to do on my usual 'take-it-or-leave-it' condition. As he stood in my studio, his face, so well-known for its warmth and geniality, almost disappeared beneath a black ridge of brows which burnt with intensity. This transformation from the John Willy that I knew so well bewildered me. I liked him, yet in front of me was a man whom I had never met before. I began to realise that I could only paint what I saw before me, and after I had finished I did not like what I had done. I had enjoyed painting his robes in an exuberance of Cadmium Red but I had never, at any time, been happy with my interpretation of his character. Perhaps I had not been ruthless enough. The portrait was placed before the magistrates who turned it down by thirty-three votes to one. I think they were probably right.

Lord Morris then wrote to tell me that he wished to buy the picture. I felt certain that he did not like it, and I came to the conclusion that he was only offering to purchase it in order to help me recover the cost of painting him, for I believe that, during the sitting, I had told him the price of Cadmium Red. Although I informed him that the painting was not for sale, he insisted that I should take the portrait to his house near Porthmadog so that he could see what it looked like on his walls. I laid the vast canvas on the floor of my van and drove from Anglesey to his cheerless home. He welcomed me by asking me how much I wanted for the portrait but, once again, I told him that it was not for sale. He asked me to see if it might hang in the drawing-room, the hall, the dining-room, and on the landing at the top of the stairs. I staggered around the house placing it against innumerable walls and after leaving each possible position, he asked me what was my price; and on each occasion I told him I did not want to sell the portrait. As I was about to leave, with his recumbent figure once more in the back of my van, he asked a surprising question:

'Kyffin, I would like to know why you gave me a beard?'

'I didn't,' I replied.

'Oh, yes, you did,' he said pointing to a thick piece of impasto. 'There, it's just like my uncle's beard.'

In order to help me, he was attempting to buy a portrait of himself with a beard that he did not possess. I knew then that behind his complicated personality he was, at heart, a kind and decent man.

Autumn had come and I had to return to London. When my builder arrived to make some alterations to my Anglesey studio, I told him that he could remove anything he wanted from the room while he worked as long as he put it back when he had finished. I returned home in mid December, and outside my house I saw a large board leaning against a tree. It was my canvas of Lord Morris. It had been standing there in all weathers and was covered in green, brown and orange mould. I found a rag and wiped it off. Two eyes blazed at me as if in reproach, but the picture of Lord Morris of Borth-y-gest was undamaged. But I was never happy with the picture, so one day I scraped down the canvas, turned it on its side, and over the recumbent form of Lord Morris of Borth-y-gest I painted a storm above Nant Peris.

I have never been very good at negotiating the price of a portrait, mainly because I have looked upon the whole operation as an unusual situation in which I was being paid by my model. So when the Chairman of the Board of Governors of a well-known public school offered me £250 to paint a full-length, life-size portrait of his retiring headmaster, I was happy to accept this meagre offer. He was a tall, distinguished city man who wore an expensive suit and an Old Etonian tie. Having struck a bargain, he must have decided that he could chance his arm once more.

'Actually,' he remarked, 'we want two portraits; one for the school and the other for the headmaster. If you do two, perhaps you could come down a bit on the second.'

As I never expect that anyone might try to cheat me, I am normally very slow to react verbally when they do. So I was most surprised when I heard myself telling the governor that I would only reduce my price if he ordered a dozen. A slow smile of capitulation crossed his face. I later heard from a master at the school that the portrait, when it arrived, was received with horror, one senior member of staff remarking that it was a 'damned insult to the memory of a great gentleman'. It was duly wrapped up and confined to the darker recesses of the carpenter's shop. A few months later a local bishop arrived at the school and asked if he could see the portrait. It was extracted from among the planks and chair legs, and placed to lean against the wall in the Common Room. The bishop expressed his episcopal delight and insisted that it should be hung among the portraits of the other headmasters. Today, I'm told that it is the most popular portrait of all.

Ivor Roberts-Jones, a fellow member of the Royal Academy, had been invited to submit preliminary studies for a competition organised by the House of Commons. The winner would receive the commission to make a statue of Sir Winston Churchill which was to be placed in Parliament Square. I believe that eight sculptors were selected to provide maquettes. The judges decided that the one submitted by Ivor was the best and announced that he would carry out the commission. Unfortunately, they had underrated the determination of Lady Churchill to ensure that her own candidate, Oscar Nemon, should carry out the work. The fact that his maquette had already been rejected by the judges was of little importance, and she insisted that Nemon was the only man who could possibly immortalise her husband. To pacify her, the embarrassed committee decided to have yet another competition, this time between the already rejected Nemon and the winner Roberts-Jones. Once again, Ivor won and yet again Lady Churchill objected. Resolutely she insisted:

'Over my dead body will the Welshman make a statue of my husband.'

It has never been discovered why she objected so much to my fellow-countrymen. Maybe she had disapproved of her husband's friendship with Lloyd George, but whatever her objections might have been there was now an impasse of embarrassing proportions. Finally, it was decided that she should see Ivor's many studies for the statue, and it was arranged that she should view them in my studio for it was felt that she would be unable to negotiate the stairs that led to Ivor's room.

One day, while Ivor waited in my studio, I stood in Gilston Road to receive Lady Churchill. She was extricated from a large car and, accompanied by a genial Lord Chandos, disappeared into the corridor that led to number twenty-two. She looked distinctly unhappy and made disparaging, if accurate, remarks about the cleanliness of the building. I felt that Ivor was in for a rough time. After introducing her and Lord Chandos to Ivor, I went upstairs from where I listened to her critical remarks.

'My husband never had a crooked mouth,' was one that surprised me. I wondered if she was the only person who did not know that he had. Lord Chandos' voice occasionally interrupted her list of complaints.

'I think they are very good, Clemmie,' I heard him say in the kindliest of voices, but nothing of praise came from Lady Churchill.

The time came for them to depart. Ivor escorted her down the corridor while I followed in the company of Lord Chandos. He enquired if I had heard what Sir Winston had replied when asked, by members of the family, what he thought of Graham Sutherland's portrait. The old man had looked very aggressive, and growled:

'Just wait until I get a chance to paint him.'

Lord Chandos roared with laughter as we passed Honorine's studio, but I feared that she might open the door to tell us to 'piss off' and not make such a 'goddam bloody noise'.

An unsmiling Lady Churchill departed and I feared the cause was lost; but Ivor appeared to be confident. The committee, however, was left in little doubt that the work did not meet with her approval. Believing that justice was not being done, I visited the House of Commons to see my local Member of Parliament. Cledwyn Hughes was sympathetic and took me to see Jim Callaghan, who said that a matter of such delicacy could only be handled by a Welshman and that there was nobody better equipped than Cledwyn. I felt that Big Jim had passed the buck with a subtlety he must have acquired after many years as a Member of Parliament representing a Welsh constituency. Months went by until, one day, Ivor was told that he could begin the statue on the understanding that it might never be put up. No objection came from Lady Churchill. She had fought tenaciously in defence of her husband's immortality and had decided that she had done enough. Eventually, the statue was unveiled by the Queen in the forgiving presence of Lady Churchill and a generous letter of congratulation was received by Ivor from Oscar Nemon, his vanquished opponent.

Even if I might have been jealous of the ability of Alex Portner to entice so many beautiful girls into his studio, I too had a source of willing models as many of my friends employed attractive German *au pair* girls. But whenever I asked them to pose for me there was another reason behind my request. When they saw the squalor in which I lived, I knew that their Teutonic obsession with hygiene would be so outraged that they would immediately offer to clean not only my studio but also my living quarters. Invariably my mild protestations were swept aside as the girls, with bucket, mop and duster in hand, threw themselves into their voluntary task of making my habitation respectable.

My best model was Karla Ludewig, the daughter of the captain of a Rhine river steamer. Something about her face was so attractive, that every time I exhibited her portrait it was sold immediately. I showed two at the Royal Academy and both were sold on the day of the private view. A potential purchaser of one such painting appeared to be unwilling to pay me, and towards the end of the exhibition I received a pathetic letter to say that his wife was a very jealous woman and had refused to allow the portrait of so pretty a girl to enter her house. I put it up for sale for the second time and it was bought by the Royal Academy.

I have always been apprehensive about asking people to sit for their portrait, and seldom did they offer their services, but one day the telephone rang in my studio and I heard the heavily accented voice of a German woman:

'My name is Gertrude Stöckl. Do you vant me?'

As it was such an ambiguous question, I asked her to elaborate.

'I am a model. I verk for the Herr Professor Coldstream. I verk for the Herr Professor Darwin. I verk for der Schlade School and I verk for der Royal College. Do you vant me?'

Since the voice sounded so aggressive, I replied by saying that I was busy painting landscapes.

'Ah,' she continued eagerly, 'The Herr Professor Coldstream he say that I stand like an oak tree.' The thought of a female oak tree did not attract me so I declined the generous offer of Gertrude Stöckl.

While studying at the Slade I had painted so many nudes that, when I left, I felt released from this, the most exacting of pictorial exercises. Nevertheless, as I was now the occupier of a most excellent studio, I felt once again the excitement and challenge of painting from life. The daughter of an old friend offered to pose and I could not have wished for a better model. I painted several nudes and exhibited one of them in the Royal Academy Summer Exhibition. It was bought on the opening day by a Californian and he telephoned to ask if he could bring his wife to see me. One afternoon, there was a knock on my door and I opened it to be confronted by a large military lady who could have been a 'daughter of the revolution'. Behind her stood a little man wearing a bow tie.

'Mr Williams,' she barked, 'I want to make it quite clear that my husband Hiram did not buy your picture because it was a nude but because he is genuinely interested in works of art.' Hiram gave an embarrassed twitch and straightened his tie as his forceful lady entered my studio. She wanted to buy a picture for herself and settled on one of some stone buildings and cottages.

'And where might that be?' she asked.

'California,' I replied.

She seemed surprised but it was, in truth, a picture of a public house in the middle of Anglesey known as the 'California'!

My delight in exhibiting nudes evaporated when I began to receive letters asking me for the telephone number of my model. One day, my telephone rang and a middle European voice asked me if I had any more nudes of 'the same leetle girl'. Unwisely, I said that I had.

'Gut,' said the caller with evident excitement. 'I vill come to see her.'

A few days later a large, fleshy man entered my studio accompanied by a small, bespectacled and bird-like wife.

'And vere iss my leetle girl?' he enquired. I placed the nude on my easel.

'Ah, but she iss lovely,' he exclaimed, 'I vill have her.'

He asked me to get the picture framed and to deliver it to his home in Purley. The house, with its curved corners and veneer of white tiles made it resemble some sort of an architectural maggot. The door was opened by the same bird-like lady and I was led into their drawing-room.

'Ah,' said the fleshy man as I entered, 'and haf you got my leetle girl?'

I unpacked my large parcel to reveal the nude.

'But she is so beautiful, so beautiful,' he exclaimed as he placed the picture on a silken sofa, stood back to look at it with obvious enchantment and suggested that I should see all his 'leetle girls'. He led me into his dining-room and pointed to a fish-like nude.

'That iss Margaretta,' he said proudly. We went upstairs and in every room there were at least two nudes of unsurpassing vulgarity. He told me their names as his little wife stood beside him beaming with pleasure.

'Und vat iss the name of your leetle girl?' he asked.

'Natalia,' I replied, and felt guilty that I had allowed my painting of her to enter that brothel of a house.

'Gut, gut,' said my client. 'I have Margaretta, I have Camilla, I have Maria, I have Claudia, I have Sophie, I have Madalena'—these and many more names fell easily and proprietorially from his guttural tongue—'and now I have Natalia.' He appeared to be a happy man, much happier than I was as I made my way to Purley railway station.

I had enjoyed painting Natalia but my experiences after exhibiting my nudes were so distressing that I never painted another.

My home, the Bolton Studios, was of vital importance to me and a haven from the world outside. Once I had closed the door of number twenty-two, the only sounds I could hear were the mellow tones of wood pigeon and the strident screech of a jay. Occasionally, a low-flying aircraft on its way to Heathrow shattered my peace, but so infrequently it was tolerable. Pigeons, blackbirds, thrushes, chaffinches and sparrows inhabited Paul Martel's tree, so I was glad that I had not attacked it too ruthlessly. Once, I saw a flock of long-tailed tits flying around the large window of my living-room and on summer mornings the dawn chorus became almost deafening as it rose and then died away around the back gardens of Gilston Road. In peace and solitude, I was able to recreate from my drawings the landscape of my native Gwynedd. In the middle of London I painted large canvases of the land around Snowdon and

Cader Idris, and the sea that surrounds my native island of Anglesey. If I felt lonely, I only had to walk down to Fulham Road, for there a friend had a shop that made clothes and dresses from Welsh fabrics and other materials. Jane Richards had been born near Trawsfynydd, a village lying in the wild area of land between Bala and Harlech. Wild the land might be, but there was nothing rough or agricultural about Jane who appeared to be possessed of a natural, if sometimes eccentric, good taste. I don't think I have ever met anyone so truly Welsh, for she was emotional, hospitable, warm-hearted and with an amazing ability to involve herself with other people's tragedies. This was all the more remarkable as she had suffered so many herself. In the accommodation above the shop I was allowed to make myself at home, and her two daughters, together with the girls who worked for her, made me endless cups of tea and sometimes acted as most willing models. When first I moved into my studio, it was Jane Richards who arrived with her family to clean and repair the premises. Afterwards, I knew that if ever I needed anything I would only have to ask them and they would do their best to provide it for me.

I had also joined the Chelsea Arts Club, located less than a mile away from my studio, and, almost every day I walked there to have my lunch. A number of Royal Academicians also ate there. Sir Charles Wheeler, alert and bow-tied, had been the Sculptor President and he was often joined by Sir Edward Maufe, an architect who wore a false ear modelled by Jacob Epstein. Vivian Pitchforth brought immediate cheer to the sedate dining-table as he related hilarious artistic stories in his broad, Yorkshire accent, and involved everyone present by passing his writing-pad to members so that they could write down their replies to his questions. More often than not, people shelter behind their deafness; Pitch stood unconquerably in control of his handicap.

As I had only taught in a secondary school, I had not come across many of the artists who taught in our art schools but there, in the club, I met them. It was mainly in the evening that they came to prop-up the bar, to play snooker and to rollick like schoolboys. A life-long abstainer, I stood aside and watched.

It was in my studio that I first met John Ormond, who had come to discuss a film that he wished to make for the BBC in Wales. I had seldom met a man who seemed to be more alert to everything around him. His head was round and appeared to shine, and behind two intense and emotional eyes I sensed a hatred of hypocrisy and injustice. His mouth always seemed to be about to open in a burst of devastating wit or observation. Slightly hunched, his body appeared to lean forward as if to anticipate a reply, and once, in a public house in Cardiff, I watched him using words like tennis balls. He served, and a piece of Southwalian wit sliced through the men at the bar, one of whom hit it back with a challenging reply; and so the game continued involving others and encouraging newcomers. This was the real south Wales where a wit has developed from the danger of the mines. John Ormond was born in Dunvant, near Swansea, and grew up in the village where his cousin, Sir Granville Beynon, a nuclear physicist, and Ceri Richards, one of Wales' most distinguished artists, were born. John had gone to an art school but had left in order to study philosophy in the University of Wales, Aberystwyth. After he left, he joined the staff of the new *Picture Post* and embarked on a career in journalism, including television. He not only continued to put before the public the tragedies that confronted our national and international communities with devastating honesty, but also, at the same time, created poems of great beauty and understanding that show a love of mankind that is total. He ranked as one of Wales' most distinguished poets. John Ormond was to make two films about my work. As I had complete confidence in his judgement, I allowed him to use me much as a model allows a painter the freedom to interpret in whatever way he or she desires. I only wish I could have made a film about him and his contribution to our understanding of the world around us.

I had moved into the Bolton Studios at a most important moment in my life as an artist. In basements, bed-sitters and attics I had learnt my trade. My new accommodation allowed me to develop that which I had learnt and enabled me to paint some of my best pictures. When, in 1970, I was elected to the Royal Academy, I decided that it was time for me to give up teaching and return to

Wales, for I believed that my newly acquired qualification might encourage people to buy my work. My studio had served me well and in many ways I regretted having to dispose of it, but at home in Gwynedd I had at my disposal a larger and more beautiful studio: the open air, the mountains and the sea. However, I stayed for three more years at Highgate School and enjoyed one more uncommitted year in the Bolton Studios before returning to my native Anglesey in May 1974.

At home in Wales I have often remembered London with affection. I had enjoyed the charm of Highgate village and Kenwood. I had wandered over the Heath and had been happy in its loneliness on a winter evening. I had been excited by the exotic world of Soho and the bustle of the City. I had always loved the winding river and its bridges, but never more so than in the autumn when the mists made more gentle the buildings that lined its banks and more mysterious the lights that glowed from within them. For thirty years I had been able to visit the many art galleries and had learned to love some of the greatest paintings in the world. I had met many painters and sculptors and it was in London that my artistic appreciation had been formed. In many ways it is essential for an ordinary painter to be close to one of the great centres of the art world, for it is only the extraordinary artist who can live and work in isolation in the early years of his professional life. Although great art never made me imitative, it was necessary for me to see it, so that its beauty and splendour could recharge my aesthetic batteries and stimulate the creation of my work that had its source in the land of Gwynedd.

11

After living in south Caernarfonshire for nearly thirty years, my mother returned to Llansadwrn, the parish in which she had been born and where her father had been the Rector.

Cefn Gadlys, the small house she bought, was two fields away from Tre-ffos, the old home of my father's family, and about a quarter of a mile from the Rectory. When she died she left the house to my brother and he allowed me to use it when I was not teaching in London. As I had nowhere to paint, except in a poorly lit garage, he allowed me to build a studio in the garden. Unfortunately, however, it had to be built so close to the house that, in order to gain the maximum amount of light, the window had to reach to the floor, and the light created such a glare on my canvases that I was unable to see what I had painted. My predicament depressed me so much that I could hardly contemplate any work at all. I sought advice from several architects. One suggested blinds, another a screen outside the window, and yet another a screen inside that moved up and down. The fact that they could not agree on a solution increased my depression, and when I had lunch one day at Plas Newydd with Lord and Lady Anglesey, I was in a state verging on the suicidal. After I had related to them the whole sad story, they told me that they had some empty property on the estate and wondered if one of their buildings might be of use to me.

Lady Anglesey drove me down a long and muddy lane that ended in a farmyard. The empty house appeared to be in good order but the buildings were sited in such a way that I knew I would have yet another problem with the light if I tried to work there. We returned to the main road and turned down a rough track towards the Menai Strait. After about a quarter of a mile it turned sharply, and from a bridge over the river Braint I could see some buildings beside a harbour. It was Pwllfanogl. The car stopped at the water's edge in front of a house with broken windows. Inside, the floor hardly

existed, and there was no kitchen and no bathroom. A door in the living-room opened into some dark, damp and sinister vaults, a reminder that the building had been a public house before the First World War. One small room had been used as a kitchen and another as an extension of the bar. The house had been empty for six years. It was an ideal situation: outside the front door lay the Menai Strait, and beyond woods that grew to the water's edge, rose the mountains of Caernarfonshire. I felt I would be lucky to live in such a place.

However suitable the house, I knew it would be of little use if there was nowhere for me to paint. At one corner of the harbour there was a building that had been used for storing beer. Because the window had been blocked up, I knew that the darkened room would make an excellent store for my paintings. Outside, a flight of steps led to the first floor, and on the door, beside the track down which we had driven, I saw the crudely written words 'Mrs Martin is a bitch'. I felt sorry for her but later I was to learn that the implied criticism of the previous occupier of the house was justified. Inside, I found a long room with a window at the far end facing south-east. The roof was low and I thought that if a window was cut into it, it was possible that the light might be suitable. I was told that I could decide whether to take the house when the problem of the light was solved. The situation was perfect so I asked a builder to work on the roof. One day I put a canvas on an easel and started to paint. The light from the new window was perfect. I decided immediately that Pwllfanogl would be my future home.

Builders moved in. A bulldozer demolished the vaults, and a bathroom and kitchen were built. The whole house was restored and within a single week in May 1974 furniture vans arrived with the contents of Cefn Gadlys and 22 Bolton Studios and there, by the Menai Strait, on the island where I was born, I entered upon one of the most satisfactory periods of my life as the tenant of Henry Paget, seventh Marquess of Anglesey.

His ancestors had lived in Plas Newydd for centuries and were descended from the Griffiths of Penrhyn, one of the most powerful families in north Wales. The mixture of French, Irish and English blood had produced many adventurous, passionate and cultured people, the most famous of whom was the first Marquess who lost a leg while acting as second in command to the Duke of Wellington at Waterloo. Lord Anglesey appeared to possess all these qualities, together with an ability to pass on to others his own habitual cheerfulness, an attitude that concealed his dedication to preserving our national heritage and his professional life as a distinguished military historian. Both he and his wife worked unceasingly. She was the daughter of two remarkable novelists, Charles Morgan and Hilda Vaughan, but her own talents lay in public service, and at different times she had presided over the fortunes of the Women's Institute, the Welsh Arts Council and many other important committees in England and Wales, ranging from broadcasting to the pollution of the environment. In between times she raised a family of two sons and three daughters. Plas Newydd, their home, has always been a happy house, and my new home at Pwllfanogl was only about a mile away along the Strait.

The Menai Strait is one of the most beautiful stretches of water to be found anywhere around the coast of Britain. Sheltered between wooded shores, it winds from Penmon, on the easternmost tip of the island, to Abermenai, a few miles to the west of Caernarfon. Small tankers pass Pwllfanogl at full tide and fishing boats, with seagulls screaming around them, make their way past the house to their home port near Bangor. In summer, both small yachts and larger ones with brightly-coloured spinnakers tack into the wind and weave their way among the variable currents.

When I first came to live on the edge of the Strait I saw dolphins and shoals of mackerel shimmering as the sunlight caught their backs. Bass, pollock, plaice and wrasse were caught in front of my house, and nearer Plas Newydd very large lobsters lived in the deeper water. Pollution has ruined the fishing and in 1980 there were fewer mullet in the harbour than when I arrived.

The house at Pwllfanogl was built about two-hundred years ago and at that time it was the home of a sea captain. He often journeyed to Bristol to take command of a larger boat bound for the west coast of Africa, where the vessel was loaded with slaves. In the Caribbean they were exchanged for molasses, and with his new cargo he sailed back to Bristol and from there he returned to Pwllfanogl. I don't know when Pwllfanogl became a public house but as the Pilot Boat Inn it was one of many nautical hostelries on the shores of the Menai Strait. It catered not only for the needs of sailors but also local people, for at Pwllfanogl there was, at one time, a thriving community. In a large shed on the site, slate that came from Llanberis was cut up and in a warehouse, near my studio, the pieces were placed in wooden frames and despatched to schools. Later, bacon was cured in the same building. Reeds from Newborough were made into mats; chicory was burnt in a shed near the harbour; and a slaughter house stood near to where my back door is today. The public house ceased to sell liquor at the time of the First World War, and after it had closed several different people occupied the house—the last being Mrs Martin. She was disliked locally because she tried to prevent the people of the nearby village of Llanfair Pwllgwyngyll from gaining access to the shore. War was declared on her and eventually she departed, leaving behind her a legacy of ill-will. This rebounded on me when I arrived, as certain of the locals believed that I too was going to deny them their right to launch their boats. For six months there was a period of tension until they realised that I did not share the provocative attitude of Mrs Martin.

The harbour was used by small trading vessels and also for loading stone from a nearby quarry. Later, it silted up but trawlers have continued to tie up alongside. The fishermen did not use the harbour but left their boats on the grass in front of my house, while the larger boats were tied to moorings. One evening, as a strong wind blew from the south-west, I saw that one boat had broken adrift. I tied a rope to a scythe and threw it in the hope that it might, somehow, attach itself to the boat. By good fortune, the blade dug into a wooden seat so that I was able to pull the boat ashore. The owner, a farmer from Penmynydd, was so grateful that he said that he would repay me for saving his property. A few days later I went up to London for a week, and on my return I opened the front door to find something wedged in the letter-box and a nauseating smell of fish in

my living-room. He had indeed shown his gratitude, and for a whole week in mid summer I was made only too aware of it.

Not long after I moved into the house, I visited Maggie Williams at the alms-houses in Penmynydd. She was strong and humorous and had helped my mother in her home in Llansadwrn. After I informed her that I was living in Pwllfanogl, a wicked look came into her eyes:

'Well,' she said, 'now that you are living in Pwllfanogl, you'll have to get yourself a woman.'

I agreed that it was a good idea but added that it would be sad if I didn't get on with her. She looked even more wicked.

'If you don't get on with her,' she said, 'damn, it's a grand place to drown the bugger.'

I went to see her again after the alms-houses had been rebuilt.

'Well, well,' she informed me with pride, 'we had a ceremony and the Marquess and Marchioness of Anglesey came with the Archbishop, and the Marquess he stood there.'

With reverence her finger pointed to a flagstone in her parlour. She looked indecisive.

'No, not there but there,' and her finger moved at least a foot away to indicate another hallowed spot.

Close to Pwllfanogl, but on the other side of the track, stood another building. It went by the name of Cambrian Terrace, which elevated it to an unwarranted status as it only consisted of two houses. The first was occupied by the Cadwaladers. Mr Cadwalader was a large and jovial man, greatly addicted to telling pointless and endless stories. Indeed, the yarns caused him so much mirth that they became incomprehensible to the listener. He had worked for the local council and was a handyman. When I arrived, I found that it was necessary to raise the height of the ground in front of the house in order to repel a tide that was expected to be the highest for 300 years. As I worked, so inevitably, Mr Cadwalader appeared.

'Mr Williams,' he began, 'I tell Mrs Cadwalader, "Mr Williams is working and I must help him"—that's right, Mr Williams, isn't it? I like working for you, Mr Williams. I says to Mrs Cadwalader, I says, "Mr Williams is hard at work. I must give him a hand." That's right, Mr Williams, isn't it?' And so he went on. I knew that no work would be done, so I leaned on my spade and listened:

'Did I ever tell you when I was in Liverpool during the blitz?' He had done so a dozen times or more but there was nothing I could do but hear about the bombs and Mr Cadwalader saving Liverpool.

One day, he knocked on my door to ask if I had any gramophone records. I found some very old ones that I had put under the stairs. I allowed him to borrow them and a week later he arrived holding a television set. He asked me where he could put it and, as I thought he wanted to throw it away, I suggested my dustbin. He looked aggrieved and said that he had made it in order to give it to me as a present. He put the set on the floor of my kitchen, opened a little trapdoor on the top and asked me to choose a record. To my surprise he had made a gramophone inside the old television set. I chose 'Whispering' and he placed it delicately on the turntable. He inserted a needle in a rudimentary arm, flicked on a switch, and 'Whispering' groaned out of the depth of the gramophone.

'What do you think about that, Mr Williams? I says to Mrs Cadwalader, I says, "I want to make Mr Williams a present," I says. So what do you think of it, Mr Williams?' I couldn't tell him.

Mrs Cadwalader was a kindly soul who had trouble with her eyes, and sometimes this appeared to affect her balance. One day, as I was driving up to the main road, I saw a figure with one arm raised lying across the track. It was Mrs Cadwalader.

'Hello, Mr Williams,' she said. 'Well, well, what a proper to-do.' I picked her up and laid her on the floor of my van. I turned it around and drove her back to the house. Mr Cadwalader came out.

'Well, well,' said Mr Cadwalader with a chuckle as he gazed at his wife, 'and what are you doing there? Well, well, what a to-do.' Although I felt he was not taking things very seriously, he picked her up and, still chuckling, carried her into their house. I got on very well with the Cadwaladers.

In the other house lived the Houldings who, like the Cadwaladers, had come from Shropshire. George Houlding was a keeper on the Plas Newydd estate and could not have been mistaken for anything else. I always thought of him as the soldier who had served in every army from the beginning of time. Short and wiry, humorous and resourceful, he was the sort of man I would have enjoyed having with me in a difficult situation. On summer evenings we used to walk around the harbour together as he told me stories about Pwllfanogl in the years before I took up residence. On those evenings we plotted to catch the wiley mullet as George laid a net across the Braint at its narrowest point, then threw a stone under the bridge where the fish were warming themselves. The idea was to catch them as they dashed for the harbour, but they always saw the net, and leaped over it and were away. Mrs Houlding was also very kind and made me excellent apple tarts.

In mid summer the sun rises above the spire of the village church. Throughout the year I watch it as it appears as a flash above the Carneddau until, at mid winter, it creeps from behind the western side of Elidir Fawr. I enjoy the seasons. The mists of autumn often cover the water so that the Faenol Woods melt into the Strait and in winter the mountains are often white with snow.

Pwllfanogl is a wonderful place to live for anyone who is interested in wildlife, and during the course of fifteen years I have recorded eighty-nine different breeds of bird. In the walled garden, behind the house, live all the common species and occasionally I have seen a treecreeper, nuthatch, goldfinch, the long-tailed tit and the handsome bullfinch; while in the summer the chiff-chaff and whitethroat add their voices to the chorus. The river Braint flows into the harbour and there I have been able to watch the mallard throughout the year. I must have seen over two-hundred ducklings but only one has survived the attacks of the carrion crows, the seagulls and the rats that used to grow fat on the food that Mrs Houlding fed to her hens. In the harbour I have observed eider, teal, wigeon, tufted duck, golden eye and, occasionally, a great crested grebe, while at low tide I watch curlews, redshanks and oyster-catchers as they wander across the mud-banks. Once, I saw a green-shank, and a strange little bird that was being mobbed by a pied wagtail. On closer examination I discovered that it was the rare shore-lark. Sometimes I see kingfishers. They sit on a rock or on the end of a boat and dive diagonally to spear their fish. I have seen terns behaving in the same way when perched on the top of a spiked pole marking the entrance to the harbour. When I first came to Pwllfanogl I was able to watch the families of swans that brought some ornithological distinction to the place. There were many battles as young males tried to join a particular family. With wings raised like sails, the resident cob charged through the water like a galleon and defied his challenger to enter the harbour. Today there are fewer swans and only occasionally in early spring do I see a pair: but, sadly, they never stay for more than a few days. Shell-duck and the red-breasted merganser are also to be seen in early spring, but the birds that I like the most are the swifts that arrive in early May and nest under the eaves of the old warehouse. On warm summer evenings I listen to their piping as they chase each other high above the house and harbour, and then, throughout the long winter months, I wait for their return.

Out on the Strait I watch the terns diving like small gannets and the cormorants fishing off the end of the broken jetty. One day, as the house was being restored, I saw a cormorant sitting on the harbour wall. As I approached the bird, it did not move. It looked at me as I came closer but did not appear to be frightened, and even as I sat beside it there was no fear in its eye.

Sometimes I have seen white-fronted geese and great northern divers but these are rare visitors. Always on the shore or in the harbour I am able to watch the herons, for they nest across the water in Faenol Woods. They invariably appear to be solitary and unhappy and are often attacked by crows, gulls and even smaller birds. I will always remember that the first bird I ever shot was a heron. A gamekeeper was instructing me on how to use my first small shotgun when, from behind a rock on the river bank, rose a huge bird.

'Shoot it, shoot it,' roared the keeper, and dutifully I fired. The beautiful grey and white bird disintegrated into a mess of legs, beak and feathers as it fell into the water and was carried silently away. I have never forgotten the horror of my act so that today I always feel protective towards the herons and enjoy watching as patiently they fish for eels around my house.

Sometimes seals come into the harbour, and in the trees nearby live many red squirrels. Only once have I seen a grey one. In the parkland surrounding Plas Newydd I hear the raucous cries of the jay, the magpie and the green-woodpecker, and on one occasion I saw a peregrine emerging in an attempt to take a mallard duckling.

If I was unable to identify a bird, I would drive along the coast to Malltraeth where Charles Tunnicliffe, a fellow member of the Royal Academy, would give me the benefit of his store of ornithological knowledge. I was happy to make any excuse to visit him, for I would always be able to gaze with wonder at his remarkable measured drawings of the birds of Britain, and learn from his many sketch-books.

I have found that herbs grow well in Pwllfanogl. Lemon balm, apple and eau-de-cologne mint grow around the house, while common mint seems to thrive in the long grass above the shore. Rosemary also does well in my garden and, in July, an avenue of fennel reaches a height of seven feet between my house and the garage. The soil is poor but good enough for the common fuchsia, hydrangea, clematis and buddleia, while a pink-flowering weed, with the painful name of hemp agrimony, flourishes and grows to the height of four feet in mid summer. When I first took up residence at Pwllfanogl my studio was covered in ivy and after I cut it down a lovely honeysuckle grew in its place, so that today the unattractive smell of turpentine inside is ameliorated by the sweetness without.

I found it difficult to discipline myself to work, for the whole atmosphere of Pwllfanogl is not conducive to labour of any sort. I have often gazed across to the mountains to see if the light was good enough for me to paint in one or other of the valleys. I have done most of my mountain paintings in the vicinity of Nant Ffrancon and Nant Peris and know from experience where to go in order to be sheltered from the different winds. If the clouds have hung too

heavily I have gone either to Aberffraw, on the south coast of the island; to the cliffs at the South Stack in the north; or to Llanddona in the east where groups of cottages and farms huddle above Traeth Coch. There has always been somewhere to paint, so that I have never thought it necessary to travel abroad too often.

Even when I was quite young I had become fascinated by the mountains of Gwynedd. I had walked over them in all weathers when out hunting foxes and knew what lay on the other side of the hill. The geology of the ridges and valleys was also of great interest to me, as my great uncle Andrew Ramsay had scrambled over the same land a hundred years before me as he attempted to unravel its complexity on behalf of the Geological Survey of Great Britain. In 1849 he discovered the existence of Pre-Cambrian rock and in 1863 became the President of the Survey. I have always loved the rocks, and have marvelled at the primaeval contortions that moulded the ancient strata.

For thousands of years the mountains have remained largely unchanged but in the eighteenth century man began to attack them, blasting them and loading waste upon them; some summits were destroyed and new man-made hills of spoil began to grow in the valleys. I understand why in Welsh the names of mountains are prefixed by the definite article, as in 'Yr Wyddfa', for as they rise above a valley or lake they achieve dominant personalities. I have always known these mountains and have praised them and cursed them as if they could hear me. I have hunted the fox over the ridges and in the wooded valleys of scrub oak and birch, and sometimes in the dark softwood forests. I have seen the mountain hare in winter and followed the footprints of the rare pine marten in the snow. High above the valleys I have watched the ringed ouzel and the wheatear, the peregrine and the buzzard. One day, high above Nant Ffrancon, I saw a wandering golden eagle.

Strangely enough, however, I have never wanted to paint the birds, wild animals or the flowers: perhaps they are too particular in such a majestic land. The farms have filled many of my canvases and, dwarfed by the immensity of rock, they become almost as much part of the land as the mountains on which they were built. I have always known the hill farmers in their old coats, with a sack, fastened by a horseshoe nail, thrown over their shoulders; I have known their nailed boots and their hazel sticks, and have painted them with their sheep-dogs, their invariable companions in the Gwynedd landscape. The hill farmers would never have been able to work their mountains without the help of these dogs. The black-and-white border collie has been preferred to the slower Welsh brindle dog, but sometimes I have seen both breeds working together.

I have always enjoyed a gathering. Over a wide area of mountainside the sheep run and bunch together. Men and dogs appear over the ridges and in front of them the sheep come together in a fluid mass, one minute spread wide over the breast of a hill and then narrowing into a gulley like the sand in an hour-glass. The farmers control, while their dogs range the flanks, darting, driving and threatening their charges until they are safely gathered in the small fields around the farm.

I have always loved the valleys of Cwm Bychan and Cwm Nantcol that lie inland of Harlech. They are so close to each other and yet so different. Cwm Bychan is gently wooded while Cwm Nantcol ends at the old farm of Maes-y-Garnedd, the home of Colonel John Jones who signed the death warrant of Charles I. Beyond each valley are steps leading away from the land of Ardudwy. I have tried to paint in Cwm Bychan but no painting I have done there has proved satisfactory. Perhaps it is too charming. In Cwm Nantcol I have painted many pictures of the old farm of Hendre Waelod and its buildings made of huge stones. I went there for the first time before the war, while working on an arbitration case, and the farm had appealed to me long before I began to paint. It has been the home of a whole family of poets known as Phylipiaid Ardudwy, of whom Siôn Phylip was the most famous. I believe that I have paintings of Hendre Waelod in the United States and in Iceland.

Many of the people I had met in Patagonia have come to visit me at Pwllfanogl, and often they have remarked that the potholed track that leads to my house reminds them of their homeland in South America.

At the age of ninety-three, Lias Garmon Owens returned to Wales to live with a niece in Llanuwchllyn. When he died a year later, I went to his funeral at Capel Garmon, the village where he was born and after which he had been christened. It was a cold December day and the rain was falling above the Conwy valley. The chapel was full and the funeral clothes of the congregation seemed to be in visual harmony with the unimaginative colour-scheme that decorated the uninspiring building. As the ministers crept into their seats like men who were about to officiate at an auction, I thought of Lias in Patagonia, of his hospitality and of the sun above Dyffryn Camwy. I wondered at the nostalgia that brought him home.

The service began and the voices of the ministers brought life to a congregation that had appeared to be as inanimate as the man they had come together to remember. With the singing of the first hymn, the chapel was transformed as voices harmonised into a glorious choir that created sounds of beauty which contrasted so strongly with the tasteless surroundings. The hymn ended, but an old lady who was sitting beside me was not satisfied. Once more, she started to sing: the harmonium and the congregation were only too happy to follow her example, and again those lovely voices echoed around the walls of the chapel. A tall man with rimless glasses then rose to tell of the life of Lias Garmon and every word of praise was followed by cries of *'Ie'n wir, yn wir'*, as men and women voiced their agreement. During the entire service I heard not a word that was not in the Welsh language. I sensed that the chapel and its congregation represented a Wales that was unknown to the English, a Wales that had survived, and a Wales that is so important to preserve. The coffin was placed on a trolley and pushed through the only street in the village of Capel Garmon. As the rain fell we buried the little Patagonian Welshman in a graveyard above the valley.

Back at Pwllfanogl I looked at my South American drawings and wondered what I should do with them. As I had journeyed so far to record the people of the Welsh community and the land in which they lived, it seemed wrong to sell that record; so I gave sixty drawings of Cwm Hyfryd and Dyffryn Camwy to the National

Library of Wales, where they now form part of its permanent collection.

My painting took me all over Anglesey. It had been necessary for the first twenty years to paint outside because I knew I had to learn about the colour of my landscape. These early paintings were factual and done without any attempt to interpret. Gradually, I began to realise that I was able to create a more powerful image if I was enclosed in my studio where, surrounded by my drawings and water-colours, I could pick and choose and, in the process, evolve in my own mind the essence of the land around me. I continued to make drawings of the coast, the farms, the cottages and the people who lived in them. After working, I often visited the old people who remembered my grandfather as well as my father. My grandfather was obviously a great character and many were the humorous stories I heard about him. He was a person who seldom abided by the rules and was the more loved because of it. One day, I visited Mrs Rowlands of Cefn-du Mawr, a farm in the parish of Llanrhuddlad. As I entered the kitchen, the old lady got to her feet and threw herself into my arms. She was in her late eighties, dressed in black with a lace covering on her head. I wondered why I was the recipient of such affection, and later I was to learn that she had mistaken me for my uncle who had meant much to her in the past. I told her that I wanted to know about a battle that had taken place on her land long ago between the locals and the Roman legions who, under the command of Suetonius Paulinus, had landed in the bay nearby. I was also interested to find where the bodies had been buried. She was very reluctant to tell me but as I was so insistent, she confided that they were under the dung heap. Mrs Rowlands also informed me that a man had once tried to dig them up, but on hearing a terrible rattling of chains he had been too terrified to continue the task. Surreptitiously, I did a drawing of the old lady and from it painted a portrait that is now in Los Angeles.

I was more hopeful in my search when I went to a farm called Rhyd-y-beddau, which means 'the ford of the graves'. The farmer said that from time to time he had unearthed a few old skulls but he had never enquired as to how they had got there. He asked me if I knew of the four prophecies of Tŷ Wion, a neighbouring farm. When I said that I had never heard of them, he sat deep in his chair and began to tell the tale:

'A very long time ago they found a very old bottle in the chimney of Tŷ Wion. In it was a very, very old piece of paper and on it were written the four prophecies: the first was that there would be a day when men would be able to go up into the air and fly like birds. That's true, isn't it?' I agreed. 'And the second prophecy was that men would go down to the bottom of the sea and swim like fish; and that's true.' 'Yes, indeed,' I replied. 'And the third prophecy was that there would come a time when people in one continent would be able to speak to people in another continent. True, isn't it?' 'Indeed,' I replied, once again. He leaned forward in his chair. His voice was grave and he spoke more slowly. 'And the fourth prophecy was the date of the end of the world.' 'My God,' I said, 'when is that?' There was a long silence, finally ... 'Damn!' he said 'I've forgotten.'

Another Mrs Rowlands, of Penyrorsedd, had looked after my grandfather when he was over ninety. It was obvious that she had been devoted to him. She told me that when my uncle, the Reverend Kyffin Williams, had died the family had not told the old man. On the day of the funeral, Annie Rowlands, at the age of fifteen, had been called in to sit with him while the rest of the family had gone to the service. Suddenly, my grandfather had asked her to open the door as my Uncle Kyffin was waiting to be let in. She went to the door but nobody was there. She returned to her seat. The old man then said that my uncle was knocking at the window, and was upset that nobody had answered. It was to be a very long wait for Annie Rowlands before the family returned.

She also told me how my grandfather could tell when my aunt was returning in the pony trap. He would lie down in the middle of the road outside the Rectory and place his ear to the ground for, because of a geological fault, he could hear the pony's hooves when they were over two miles away.

One day, in the company of a local farmer, I walked along a narrow road in the north-west of the island. Ahead of us was the slight figure of an elderly man. 'Look,' said Tom Jones, 'there's Richard Evans. He's not one of us.' Two-hundred and fifty years previously, a little boy, who could not speak Welsh or English, had been rescued from a raft. When he was still a child he was found putting the broken leg of a chicken into a splint. Later he became a gifted bone-setter and nearly all his descendants inherited his gift; but one of them, Richard Evans, was still regarded as a stranger in that part of the island.

My studio could hardly have been better. Gradually, I got into a rhythm of work, and painted larger pictures than ever before. I also hoped that they were better paintings. At all times, I received help and hospitality from Plas Newydd, and seldom did a week or two go by without an invitation to dine with them. Meals with the family were stimulating, as all five children were encouraged to air their opinions. Being Pagets, their views, which embraced both left- and right-wing doctrines, were often expounded with passion. Christmas dinner in the Rex Whistler room was unforgettable. A long table stretched in front of the magnificent mural that looked even more mysterious by the light of candles. If ever I was ill, I knew I could find sanctuary at Plas Newydd. Lady Anglesey told me that on one occasion I had been so depressed that she insisted that I left my house to stay with them. I suppose I must have been very depressed indeed as I have no recollection of my visit.

I also enjoyed my games of tennis with my landlord, as we were fairly well matched. Although he had been taught to play and I had not, I hit the ball very much harder and my forehand, on occasions, was unplayable. I particularly enjoyed serving and my serve looked impressive, but, in truth, I could never tell where the ball was going, and it seldom landed in the desired section of the court. When it did, my immediate joy was so great that I was totally unprepared for the return. Unfortunately, however, our rivalry on the tennis court was terminated after my opponent broke his leg very badly in an accident in London.

As I lived nearby, I was often invited to dinner when Lord and Lady Anglesey were entertaining their guests. Writers, soldiers, politicians, philosophers and scientists, and many others, I have met around the dining-table at Plas Newydd, as Mr Morris, the butler, quietly placed our dishes in front of us. He was an unusual butler for in the past he had been a quarryman, and after being ferried across the Strait at Moel-y-Don he would walk to his work above Llanberis. He was very much part of the family and when the Plas Newydd children got married, he related a poem he had composed for the occasion. He ran the local sheep-dog trial and every year he came to see me to collect my subscription. I always enjoyed his visits for we were both Anglesey men.

My brother Dick often came to stay with me at weekends. He had retired from his work as a solicitor in Chester to live in lodgings about eight miles away in the village of Llangoed.

His life had been a tragic one. At the age of two he threw his nurse's knitting from a first-floor window and, knowing that he had done something wrong, he decided to retrieve it. He jumped onto the roof of the porch from which his fat little body bounced onto the gravel below. Dick was unhurt but my mother blamed herself and always insisted that he had never got over his fall. In truth, it was she who had not got over the accident, and from that moment she devoted her life to protecting him. The best chair in the drawing-room was reserved for him. It was he who had to be dried after bathing in case he caught a chill. He was never allowed to lay the table, lift the potatoes or skin a rabbit, for these jobs had to be done by me. I accepted, without question, his superiority in work as well as in play, and I suppose the reason I did not become jealous was because of his invariable kindness towards me. As a scholar, he helped me patiently as I stumbled through my schooldays. I was later to realise that I was the luckier son for, even though my mother was concerned with providing me with the necessities of life, she did not worry about me as much as she did about my brother. Consequently, I was allowed greater freedom and learnt how to look after myself. When the day came for him to take up a scholarship to Shrewsbury School, my mother realised that protection of her elder son had been justified. In truth, however, I was the more delicate child and even when I developed epilepsy she continued to show more anxiety about my brother, even though he was physically fit.

Gradually, her continual worry and apprehension over his well-being affected him, so that by the time he entered Shrewsbury School he had become over-sensitive and self-conscious. One day, a prefect called him 'funny-face' and this chance remark destroyed his life. It is possible that another remark might have had a similar result but from the moment of its utterance he looked on himself as some sort of pariah unfit for any social contact, even though he was a good-looking boy. We had never been able to discuss things within the family, so the idea that he was repulsive was allowed to fester and grow out of all proportion until he believed that people crossed the road to avoid his dreadful face, rather than simply to visit a shop. All this he told me at the age of forty-five and it was the first time he had mentioned it to anybody. I was told by a psychiatrist that he could be treated by drug therapy but, unfortunately, he turned down the appointment I had made for him. Perhaps he had made a safe world for himself and was too frightened to emerge into the rough and tumble of human relations.

Dick could have won a scholarship to Oxford but refused to sit the examination. At Jesus College he devoted his life to playing games, as it had become important for him to prove that he was physically superior to others, even if he was socially unacceptable. He scrambled a third-class degree and became articled to a firm of solicitors in Pwllheli. When war broke out he was commissioned into the Royal Welch Fusiliers. One day, I met his commanding officer who asked me what was wrong with my brother as he never went out of an evening to enjoy himself with the other young officers. At that time I did not know of his secret obsession and hence I could give no answer. After he lost a foot in an accident at a battle school, he must have been even more certain that he was physically undesirable. Had my brother been an unpleasant person his obsession might have made him socially destructive, but he was a truly kind and gentle person without an enemy in the world and quite incapable of hurting people. His kindness was an asset to the many people he defended in court. In front of the magistrates he became fearless for he took on the being of those for whom he was acting and was no longer himself. He was extremely well read and able to quote at length from any author whom he felt might appeal to the local bench. In Ellesmere Court he always chose Surtees for most of the magistrates rode to hounds.

Dick was popular in his office, but after work he preferred to hide himself in the public house where he lodged and it was there that he began to become an incurable alcoholic. Sometime after leaving the army he had asked me to sign a paper that would allow him to draw on what he was to inherit on the death of our mother. I did not know of the damage I was to do to him by signing, for, at that time, I was unaware that he had started to drink heavily and had become a compulsive gambler. One day, when he came home to Anglesey for his summer holiday, I asked him why he never went abroad. My question seemed to annoy my mother for she asked me to explain how he could possibly travel alone. I replied that I did but, apparently, I was different. I offered to accompany him to Ireland the following year. Whilst at Kinsale we received a telegram to say that our mother had broken her arm and it was necessary for us to return. We cut short our holiday to find there was little wrong with her apart from a desire to see her elder son.

The next year we set off for Scotland and stayed in houses offering bed and breakfast. The further north we went the more worried Dick became about the possibility of not finding a room for the night and finally, in Ullapool, he collapsed and begged me to take him home. It was a difficult journey back to Anglesey for I sensed that, beside his other ills, he had also developed agrophobia. Apart from visiting our mother, I do not believe he ever set out on another holiday.

Life must have become increasingly difficult for him and on several occasions he told me that every night, before going to sleep, he prayed that he would never wake up. On two occasions he took an overdose of the drugs that had been prescribed to alleviate his chronic emphysema, but I was not certain if he had tried to kill himself or had merely become confused whilst in a state of inebriation. It was obvious that his health was deteriorating, and a minor car accident after he had been drinking meant that he had to appear in the court where he worked as a police prosecutor. He avoided this indignity by entering a hospital for treatment, and as he knew that he would have to give up driving he decided the time had also come for him to cease practising as a solicitor. I was established at Pwllfanogl and he told me he wanted to return to Anglesey so that he could see me from time to time. He was unable to look for rooms himself because he would have interpreted any rebuff as an intimation that nobody so physically unattractive as he could possibly be allowed in the house. All my efforts to find him a home came to nothing since I had to admit that my brother was an alcoholic who had possibly tried to kill himself. In desperation I appealed to my doctor in Beaumaris and it was he who found adequate accommodation in the village of Llangoed. It was necessarily near to a bus stop, for his artificial leg and chronic emphysema made it difficult for him to walk anything but the shortest of distances. Every morning he went into the small town of Beaumaris to change his library books and sit at the bar of the Bulkeley Arms where the headwaiter co-operated in his daily gamble on the horses. When he came to stay with me he was always eager to see on television the horses on which he had risked his money, and was upset when I selected a winner on looks alone and not on the form and knowledge of racing that he had acquired over the years.

Occasionally, his lungs collapsed and, secreting a bottle of whisky in the hollow of his artificial leg, he would be taken to hospital at Bangor or Caernarfon. He never complained for I knew he was hoping that death would come sooner rather than later.

One Christmas he came to stay with me over the holiday. As usual he went to bed early and I knew that once in his room he would seek consolation by drinking himself to sleep. The next morning he could hardly move and an ambulance arrived to take him to the hospital at Bangor. I don't believe he knew it was Christmas Day and if he did I doubt if it meant much to him. After a week he was moved to a convalescent home in Caernarfon and it was from there that I picked him up to take him back to Llangoed. He said he was feeling very cold and as I left he said goodbye in a strange and unusually definite manner. The next day his landlady telephoned to say that she had found him dead in his chair.

Although I knew he wanted to die I had hoped desperately that he would stay alive, for I always believed in the possibility that some circumstance might arise in which he could find happiness. His death ended all such hopes and, selfishly, I was wounded by it.

However tragic my brother's life may have been, it had an almost unique epitaph, for I do not believe he had ever done anything that could possibly have hurt anybody. He was over-sensitive but his sensitivity towards others was as great as that which destroyed him.

In my studio at Pwllfanogl I painted the portraits of several worthy Welshmen but nevertheless continued to dislike the idea of a commission. There was one which I was happy to accept. The Colonel of the 3rd Battalion of the Royal Welch Fusiliers wanted to know how much I would charge to paint their Goat Major in his full-dress uniform, together with the Regimental Goat. I replied that I would not charge anything as long as I could use him as a model. I added that in no way would I include the goat, but that I would not mind doing a separate drawing of it. We decided that I would paint two portraits, one for the regiment and one for myself, and one day Norman Pritchard arrived with all his regimental paraphernalia. As he laboriously attached belts and medals to his scarlet uniform, he told me that his twin brother had also been the Goat Major before him. Eventually he took up his pose at about eleven in the morning. I looked at the proud figure in front of me and chose a canvas that was four-feet square. I drew him onto it and started to paint, without even correcting the drawing as he appeared to fit naturally within the confines of the canvas I had chosen. At half past twelve we went down to the house for lunch. Perhaps it was a mistake, for when he took up his pose again his eyes shut and his head dropped onto his chest. I woke him and once more he sat solidly and unflinchingly; but the beer and cheese seemed to have anaesthetised him. I knew I had to work quickly, and soon, I realised I could do no more. I had completed the picture in three hours of painting time. Corporal Norman Pritchard looked at his image:

'Damn,' he said, 'it is the dead spit of my twin brother.'

He made the same remark when he saw the second portrait. I decided to keep the larger picture in order to send it to the Royal Academy; the other was collected by the Colonel who took it to their mess in Wrexham. Later he told me that he had hung it in an ante-room, and one evening, after dinner, he took his officers to see it for the first time.

'Do you know, sir,' said a young officer, 'it's the dead spit of his twin brother.'

I went to the barracks at Caernarfon to draw 'Billy', the regimental goat. He was young and wild, and Norman Pritchard found it difficult to keep him still. Norman was proud of his charge and appeared to despise the goats of the Royal Regiment of Wales for, unlike those of the Royal Welch, they were always castrated. As I found it almost impossible to draw the energetic goat, I decided to turn my attention to Welsh Black cattle.

Most of my reverend ancestors were rectors of country parishes in Anglesey and one of them was responsible for introducing the swede, another the first steel plough, while my great great grandfather was very much concerned with the improvement of the island's livestock. I have two drawings from the early years of the last century by James Ward who was a member of the Royal Academy; one is of an Anglesey bull, the other of a steer. I believe that both were owned by my family. As we were closely associated with agriculture, it is not surprising that I have always taken an interest in Welsh Black cattle. Against the green of a Welsh hillside their colour creates a magnificent intensity. I have painted them many times and I suppose I will continue to do so.

One day I went to Bryn Coch, a farm owned by Evan Pritchard, a well-known breeder of Welsh Black cattle, in order to make some drawings of his famous Welsh Black bull, 'Bryn Coch Tomos'. Evan and his two stockmen, Ifor and Gwilym, met me in the yard. They told me that Tomos was in a field nearby and asked me to help them drive him down to the farm. We got into a landrover and made our way up a lane to where a gate led into the field. I was asked to get out and prevent Tomos from wandering up to the main road. They drove off into the field and soon, in the distance, I heard the

strangulated bellow of a bull, a noise that became increasingly terrifying as it got nearer. Suddenly Tomos appeared in the gateway. He was a gigantic animal and looked at me with regal indifference as, with his huge belly swaying, he made his way to the yard below. We followed him from the safety of the landrover. Ifor and Gwilym, each armed with a gate, approached him with discretion, hemmed him against a stone building and tied him to an iron ring that hung from the wall. Tomos first looked bewildered and then indignant as he expressed his displeasure by uttering a ferocious squeal of rage.

I sat on the ground and looked at my model while Evan Pritchard, Ifor and Gwilym stood behind to watch me recording the champion Welsh Black bull. It would have been ill-mannered to ask them to leave me alone, so I took a large piece of paper from my portfolio and started to draw. I found that the proximity of my audience inhibited me and my work became indecisive. Soon the knowledgeable criticism began, as I heard Gwilym whisper,

'Well damn it, he hasn't given old Tomos a very straight back, has he?'

Evan Pritchard grunted as I tried to correct my drawing.

'*Duw*,' said Ifor in a louder voice, 'old Tomos has got a better head than that.'

'And look at that belly he's given him,' exclaimed Gwilym, 'old Tomos wouldn't win many prizes with a belly like that, would he, Mr Pritchard?'

Evan Pritchard gave another disapproving grunt as I tried to create some semblance of the magnificent Welsh Black bull.

'And look at the bag he's given him,' shouted Ifor, 'old Tomos wouldn't be any use to us with a bag like that, would he, Mr Pritchard?'

Desperately I tried to master the noble proportions of old Tomos but all I could see in front of me was something that resembled a Labrador retriever. His owner sensed my disappointment and frustration and offered to help by lending me photographs of Tomos that had been taken by some visiting Americans. Burdened by my failure I declined his offer and, turning my back on Evan Pritchard, Ifor, Gwilym and Bryn Coch Tomos, I wandered into a field where, unobserved, I drew a very ordinary Charolais ox.

When my father was a young man, the social life of Anglesey was restricted to the town of Beaumaris but as it was too far for him to reach on horseback in a day, he stayed at home to enjoy the company of the farmers in his father's parish and grew up with a warmth of feeling towards them and their families. I too have always felt at home in their company and ever since I started painting have wanted to record their weatherbeaten faces.

Some farmers came to my studio to be painted. Hugh Rowlands from Llanddona had a fine face but work in the fields prevented him sitting for long. He told me that his farm had been in the family for a long time but his only son was studying engineering, in Loughborough, and would not be likely to follow him on the land. I tried to paint Eddie Pierce of Pont Ronwy but there was always a smile at the corner of his mouth and I could do nothing with his mobile face.

Occasionally I visited Ysgol Parc y Bont, a primary school in the nearby parish of Llanddaniel-fab. The children came from both Welsh and English families but no English was ever spoken. It was a happy school and the reason for it being so was the presence of Nan Hughes, the headmistress. Cheerfully and efficiently she organised the small boys and girls into an alert and hard-working unit.

Whenever I arrived I was asked to select the child I wanted to draw. But it was not easy to choose. Inevitably, some small child desperately wanted to act as a model, but the willing volunteer was not always suitable for me. Consequently, I found that I had to try to draw a selection of those I wanted and those I did not. They all sat very seriously. I made a large drawing of a little girl called Colleen and from it I painted her portrait in my studio. I sensed she was shy so I placed her as a small figure on a large canvas. I exhibited the portrait in London and it was bought by someone in Hong Kong. I suppose I shall never see it again.

When I paint, the thought of a purchaser is far from my mind for I work in order to satisfy some creative necessity. Nevertheless, a full studio tends to dampen creativity and, from time to time, it becomes important to disperse the paintings and drawings. I would prefer to give them to my friends but this would be impracticable because even an idealist has to earn a living: consequently, I have had to find sympathetic dealers to sell my work for me.

One day, in 1969, I received a letter from Priscilla Anderson inviting me to show in a gallery she had recently opened in Kensington. I was flattered as such an invitation had never come my way before. As I was already connected with two galleries in the West End, I replied that I did not wish to leave them and asked her if I could keep open her invitation. I was fortunate that I did for almost immediately one of them closed down and the other ceased to show contemporary art. I wrote to her and became one of her Thackeray Gallery artists. It was a piece of good fortune, for every other year I have been able to show the paintings and drawings I have produced in my studio at Pwllfanogl and in other parts of Wales. Incongruously, the walls of the Kensington Gallery have been hung with paintings of Cwm Idwal, Arddu, Cnicht and Snowdon. I have exhibited pictures of the sea around Anglesey and the coast of Pembroke, and at the private views people from all over Wales have rubbed shoulders with those from many other parts of Britain. I have been able to live at Pwllfanogl with a sense of security for I have always known that in London my affairs were in the capable hands of Priscilla Anderson.

It has always been my belief that an artist should live a lonely life, dedicated entirely to the creation of his work. Nevertheless, I also felt it was very important that I should make myself a part of any community in which I have lived. I suppose such a feeling is due to the fact that so many of my forebears have been clergymen who devoted their lives to the welfare of their parishioners. My Uncle Kyffin had been the Rector of Llangwyllog. My two grandfathers held the livings of Llanrhuddlad and Llanfaethlu and my four great grandfathers were the Rectors of Llanfair-yng-Nghornwy, Pentraeth, and Rhoscolyn in Anglesey, and Llanystumdwy across the Strait in Caernarfonshire. My great great grandfather, John Williams, lived in Llansadwrn and was the Rector of Llanddeusant and Llanfair-yng-Nghornwy for fifty years, to be followed in the latter parish by James, my great grandfather who stayed in the rectory he built for fifty one years. It was my great grandfather and great grandmother who stationed the first lifeboat in Anglesey near their rectory. She was an artist who painted pictures and sold them in order to buy the lifeboat, while he acted as the reverend coxwain as did his son, my grandfather, Owen Lloyd Williams.

In 1978 it was decided to celebrate the 150th anniversary of the placing of the first lifeboat at Cemlyn, a sheltered bay near the rectory at Llanfair-yng-Nghornwy. A young man and a girl were to ride on horseback along the cliffs re-enacting the moment when my great grandfather and great grandmother watched helplessly as a ship sank with the loss of all on board, a tragedy that incited them to form the Anglesey Society for the Preservation of Life from Shipwreck. Cledwyn Hughes, the Member of Parliament for Anglesey, was to make a speech and unveil a memorial on the grass above the bay. This was to be followed by services in the churches of Llanfair-yng-Nghornwy and Llanrhuddlad.

On the day of the celebration, the wind blew a gale from the south-west, driving the rain before it much as it would have done when local men rowed out into the storm in the previous century. The young man and girl, dressed in period costume, sheltered behind their horses but did not dare to venture towards the cliffs, and those attending the ceremony stood bravely as they were lashed by wind and rain. Cledwyn Hughes must have made the shortest speech of his distinguished career before removing a tarpaulin from the commemorative stone, initiating a rush for the sanctuary of the church where the Archbishop of Wales took the service and dedicated a slate memorial to my family. The church was crowded and I was so deeply moved that I was unable to join in the singing of the hymns. Afterwards, I admitted to the Archbishop that tears had filled my eyes.

'Of course,' he said, 'we are Welsh and we can't help it.'

Later, at the service in my grandfather's church of Llanrhuddlad, Dick Evans, who had been awarded two gold medals as coxswain of the Moelfre Lifeboat, read the first lesson and I managed to control myself enough to read the second.

The following day a reporter from the BBC came to interview me. He asked me to lean on a boat in front of my house as a television camera hovered above me.

'Tell me,' he asked, 'what did it feel like to go out in a lifeboat 150 years ago?' He was a pleasant young man and I realised he had a dreadful cold in his head. I think I replied that a hundred and fifty years ago was a very long time and that my memory was not as good as it had been in the past.

I have always loved the mountains and, however cruel they might be at times, I hope I have always painted them with affection; but, as a man of Anglesey, the sea, which can be seen from every parish on the island, has always been part of my life. Towards the south, it appears in the distance like a far-away strip of silver and gold as the sun shines on it, but nearby it exerts a more dominant influence and its presence can never be ignored. I often walk along the cliffs and across the many sandy bays. At Fedw Fawr I watch the black guillemot and enjoy the carpets of wild orchids that grow on the heathland above the sea. At Cemlyn I walk over the shingle banks to see the terns, and in the west I often visit the South Stack to watch the sea-birds and wonder at the primaeval convulsions that created the distorted bands of rock. The geology of Anglesey is even more fascinating than its natural history. I am always conscious of the battle between the sea and the land as the waves continually beat against the rocks as if determined to destroy them. The conflict never ceases. The storms exhilarate me and I love to interpret their violence and the terrifying noise of crashing waves; but I am also soothed by the beauty of a still evening when a warm sun rests gently on the placid water.

During the many years I spent in London, my mind was never far from the island and the shining water that surrounds it. In some strange way the strength of the land, as it stands resolute against the fury of the elements, has always given me a sense of security.

One summer evening, not long after I arrived at Pwllfanogl, a friend came to visit me with his small son aged five. As we stood at the water's edge, with gentle waves breaking at our feet, the little boy looked up at me:

'What will happen to you here when you die?' he asked with a look of concern on his face. I knew I had to answer with a confidence I did not possess.

KW.